Surviving the Bible

Surviving the Bible series:

Surviving the Bible:
A Devotional for the Church Year 2018

Surviving the Bible:
A Devotional for the Church Year 2019

Surviving the Bible:
A Devotional for the Church Year 2020

Christian Piatt

Surviving the Bible

A Devotional for the Church Year

2020

SURVIVING THE BIBLE
A Devotional for the Church Year 2020

Cover design: Brad Norr
Design and Typesetting: PerfecType, Nashville, TN

Print ISBN: 978-1-5064-2063-9
eBook ISBN: 978-1-5064-2064-6

The paper used in this publication meets the minimum requirements of American National Standard for Information Sciences—Permanence of Paper for Printed Library Materials, ANSI Z329.48-1984.

Manufactured in the U.S.A.

Contents

Series Introduction

The Bible clearly says . . .

We've all heard this phrase, usually in the middle of some ideological combat about "values." And yet, it seems like we tend to use the Bible to reinforce whatever we already believe. But when we see what we want to see in Scripture, it mutates from being a light and path to being a sword and shield.

As Anne Lamott says, "You can safely assume you've created God in your own image when it turns out that God hates all the same people you do."

That, or the Bible feels too big, complicated, beyond our reach. So many people understand it better than we do. At the same time, we have this need to connect, to find wisdom in its pages. We feel a pull back to it, over and again. And in a time of "alternative facts," when we long for something true, something real to offer us some deeper wisdom, we wonder what Scripture really says about climate change, war, sexuality, gender roles, and money. We would welcome its guidance, if we only knew how to get at it.

I have tried, more than once, to read the Bible from start to finish. Maybe you have too. I can't count how many times I've started with Genesis and by the time I get to the labyrinth of laws in Numbers (if not before), I give up. That's why I'm writing this three-book series called Surviving the Bible.

The Bible is the best-selling printed volume in world history. It was the very first thing printed after the printing press was created, and it's sold over 2.5 billion copies since. Over 100 million copies are sold or given away every year, or more than 190 every single minute. The entire Bible has been translated into more than 650 languages; the New Testament has been translated into more than 1,400. It's consistently at the top of the list of favorite books in America when people are surveyed.

And yet I'd argue it's also the most misunderstood text in our culture, partly because most of us have never read the whole thing. In fact, only about 9 percent of folks asked claim to have read it all.

My kids love what I call my "dad jokes," or at least I tell myself they love them so I have an excuse to keep telling them. And of course I can't resist sneaking some lessons in there when I can. One of my favorites is "How do you eat an elephant? One bite at a time." Yeah, they roll their eyes, but I know they're laughing hysterically inside.

The point is that we don't have to read the Bible all at once. It's not a book written from start to finish, meant to be read like a novel either. It's a collection of laws, stories, history, poems, and predictions written by dozens of different people from multiple cultures and in several languages over thousands of years. It was written for different people with different needs at different times. But the reason we still consider it important today is because so much of its wisdom, sometimes buried mysteriously like treasure, still rings true.

But who goes looking for treasure without a map? It would be a waste of time. The problem is that so many so-called maps to the wisdom in Scripture are more like instruction manuals, telling us what to think and how to believe. Maps, on the other hand, offer a way to find something without telling us what you have to do with it when we get there.

We crave meaning, grounding. We long to separate fact from opinion, to grab hold of something bigger than ourselves. We want to broaden our vision in a time when everyone seems so utterly blinded by the immediate reality, right in front of them. We want answers, but more than that, we want peace. We want to separate fact from opinion and to discern truths that transcend immediate facts, wisdom that has resonated across cultures and generations since we started asking questions as a species about why we're here and what our purpose is.

Fred Craddock was right when he claimed that the Bible can be used to make any point we want. But it's too important a resource to depend on others to tell us what it means. We can think for ourselves; all we need is a guide.

This book is set up like a weekly meditation, breaking down the Bible "elephant" into bite-sized pieces. It follows the church calendar in case you're a part of a church that observes it, but you don't have to be. In fact, you don't have to go to church at all to use this. You don't have to know what you believe either. You don't even have to be a Christian. Use it as a weekly study, or browse the glossary for themes you're curious about. It's an ideal resource to use with a friend or small group, but it's set up to be accessed by anyone who has enough curiosity, openness, and a desire to grow.

Start anywhere. Set it down and come back to it, over and over. There's no "wrong way" to use *Surviving the Bible*. Just open it up, grab a Bible, and take a bite.

Christian Piatt

Come Together, Right Now

Lectionary Texts For

December 1, 2019 (First Sunday in Advent)

Texts in Brief

My dog ate my Bible!

First Reading

Isaiah 2:1–5

Isaiah's vision in this segment comes just after he describes bloodletting and rebelliousness of ungodly scope within the people of Judah and Jerusalem. Now, the prophet offers a hopeful image of warfare and violence replaced with peace in the near future.

Psalm

Psalm 122

The psalmist describes a "return home" of the twelve tribes of Israel to Jerusalem to seek reunification with

God. In this great reunion, the author envisions peace, prosperity, and safety.

Second Reading
Romans 13:11–14
Paul encourages the early church in Rome to set aside their old ways of doing things, taking up instead what he calls a divine "armor of light" in preparation for salvation of the world at God's hand.

Gospel
Matthew 24:36–44
Jesus's followers want to know when to be ready for God's return to earth, and his answer is "always!" He doesn't know, nor does anyone else, when that time will be exactly, but he reminds them of the excessive living of those consumed by the great flood. Basically, Jesus says to expect God's return when you expect it least, and that when it happens, a lot of people will be taken by surprise.

Bible, Decoded
Breaking down Scripture in plain language

Amoz—The main significance of Isaiah's father being named here is that this was usually done to indicate that both father and son were prophets. So the prophetic apple didn't fall far from the tree.

Plowshares/Pruning Hooks—Basic farming gear. The image is that tools used to bring about death would instead be converted to those used to yield new life.

Judah—This kingdom was just south of Israel, which existed about one thousand years before the birth of Jesus. It was a mostly rural region that lacked the military fortifications that somewhere like Jerusalem would have had.

Armor of Light—Paul is intentionally making a reference back to the images evoked in the Isaiah text, calling on people to stop concentrating on the stuff of war and death, opting instead to focus on life-giving things.

Points to Ponder

First Thoughts

Like the Psalmist, Isaiah believes that the city of Jerusalem is a particularly holy place, one where God effectively resides on earth. He believes God will issue judgment over the conflicts among all of the twelve tribes and that only then will people finally recognize the futility of their war games. Some translations actually say that the text says people will no longer "play war" anymore, which seems to point to the ridiculousness of it all.

It's hard to know for sure what the psalmist in Psalm 122 is saying in their prayer for peace, but it could be argued that they are asking for a more personal, internal peace for those who seek and follow God, and not for the reign of the city itself. It certainly changes our perspective on whether they're praying for particular worldly outcomes or personal and collective transformation.

In Paul's letter, war isn't so much the problem but rather internal fighting, most likely within the church itself. But of course that never happens . . . right?

The Gospel text can present a challenge for those who understand Jesus to be fully divine and who believe God is all-knowing. Doesn't it seem like Jesus is professing not to know the answer to their question about the timing of God's coming? That, or maybe it's a brush-off in a vernacular figure of speech, suggesting that their question is pretty dumb to begin with.

Digging Deeper
Mining for what really matters . . . and gold

On the one hand, in Paul's letter to the Roman church, he seems to be complimenting them for rising above the less-than-savory ways of the Roman populous around them. But then he's also cautioning them about what most likely are signs of division and possibly succumbing to the immediate appeal of partying it up with their fellow citizens. If I was to guess, I'd wager that one of the splits bubbling up within the fledgling church was around what was acceptable and what wasn't. From there, it's not a stretch to imagine conflicts about who was a better Jesus-follower and who was worthier to represent the new faith to Rome.

If there's one unifying theme throughout the four passages this week, it's that of unification. It's the division among the tribes, communities, and churches that seems to be inhibiting the coming of God's imagined kingdom on earth for all people.

And here's where it gets sticky, especially for those of us who prefer to identify our faith as somehow particular and exclusive. Yes, there is much to celebrate and share about our religious identity, values, history, and stories. But once we become intent on somehow possessing it, controlling it, or otherwise arbitrating who gets access and who doesn't, God's desired here-and-now kingdom is pushed back to the margins.

If there's one call in every text, it's for us to come together. And it doesn't say that the aim is to make everyone like us; instead, we're to seek unity for the sake of itself. As for the timeline when this should take place, there's undeniably no time like right now.

Heads-Up

Connecting the text to our world

Remarkably, I just heard a radio interview today about how much we human beings hate waiting, just before I sat down to work on this set of Scriptures. Go figure! But it's so true, isn't it? And the more technology and the more the rest of the world seems to accommodate our longing for instant fulfillment, the more we seem to adjust our expectations to remain just out of reach of what is possible.

Just two nights ago, I tried to watch a TV show (in ultra-high definition, mind you) with my wife, Amy, while my kids were in their rooms doing their own You-Tube browsing, when we got the dreaded "pinwheel of death." You know what I mean: that damn spinning circle that is telling you to be patient while the system you're using tries to fulfill your request. After a minia-ture rant, it dawned on me that we were sitting in our house, which is well outside of city limits, trying to watch three different streaming videos all at once on one semi-country internet connection.

Right about then, my indignation for not being instantly satisfied seemed pretty ridiculous.

We were kind of set up to ask the question "But when?" if we consider the future visions the psalmist and Isaiah cast out there, weren't we? I mean, who wouldn't ask that after someone tells them this amazing thing will happen soon. We want to know!

The problem with us is that once we actually have a deadline, we tend to take it as permission to slack off until more or less the last minute. So it's not so much that Jesus is holding out on us in Matthew to be obnoxious; it's more like he knows our nature.

If the point were just to straighten up and do the right thing to avoid consequences, it would stand to reason that knowing the deadline would be really helpful. But it's not. The call to right thinking and acting is simply for the sake of righteousness itself. I'm guessing it's not unlike when I remind my son that there will be consequences if he makes bad choices, only to have him ask me specifics on what those consequences will be. Clearly, when he asks that, he hasn't internalized a sense of right and wrong yet.

I have to wonder if Jesus has a permanent palm print on his forehead like I do, from smacking myself in frustration every time I hear that question. Just do the right thing because it's right, for crying out loud!

Prayer for the Week

It's always in my nature to act out of self-interest and self-preservation. So instead of asking for the results I want this week, help me focus on the internal, personal transformation to find the desire to do the right thing, rather than focusing on what will happen if I don't.

Popping Off

Art/music/video and other cool stuff that relate to the text

"One," by U2 (song, 1991)

"Come Together," by The Beatles (song, 1969)

The Universal Christ: How a Forgotten Reality Can Change Everything We See, Hope For, and Believe, by Richard Rohr (book, 2019)

Welcoming the Fire

Lectionary Texts For
December 9, 2019 (Second Sunday in Advent)

Texts in Brief
My dog ate my Bible!

First Reading
Isaiah 11:1–10

The prophet's foretelling of the family line (the shoot) that will come from Jesse and eventually lead to the birth of the savior (the branch) of the people of the world. His vision, wisdom, and understanding will far exceed that which is limited by human senses, and with his coming, there will be peace and reconciliation among even the most natural of enemies throughout creation.

Psalm
Psalm 72:1–7, 18–19

A song or poem written about King David, asking God to endow him with many of the same attributes as a leader that the prophet Isaiah says the Messiah will possess. The psalmist asks for long life for David and that he will rule over a peaceful and prosperous people.

Second Reading
Romans 15:4–13

In a long greeting, Paul assures his readers that Jesus is the one that the ancient Scriptures told about and that this means that God is a God of kept promises. He goes on to remind them that, also as it is commanded in the ancient texts, they are to go out among those who are not Jewish (a.k.a., the uncircumcised) and preach the gospel that Jesus left with them.

Gospel
Matthew 3:1–12

While John the Baptist is baptizing people in the Jordan river and warning listeners of the coming kingdom of God, he also condemns the arrogance of the Pharisees and Sadducees. He warns that just being from the lineage of Abraham (same lineage as Jesse), from which the Israelites came, isn't enough to merit God's grace. He tells them they have to repent of their shortcomings and begin to bear different spiritual fruit.

Bible, Decoded
Breaking down Scripture in plain language

Stump of Jesse—This could sound either pretty gross or a little bit naughty, depending on how you take it. But it's actually a reference to a lineage of people from which the Messiah is to come. The most beautiful thing about the image of this lineage being like a tree is even as part—or even much—of it is killed off or dies, life will still persist and emerge from it. Put another way, the coming of the Anointed one (Jesus) can't be stopped, no matter how people may try.

Holy Mountain—The reference God makes (through Isaiah) to "my holy mountain" could be understood as referring to the "city on a hill," which is how the holy city of Jerusalem was described. Considered more broadly, it could be taken as a reference to all the earth, which is also God's.

Gentiles—A term used among the Jewish people to describe anyone who was a non-Jew.

Pharisees and Sadducees—These were two sects within Judaism at the time of Jesus. They differed in some of their beliefs, like on whether there was life after death (Pharisees believed in it; Sadducees didn't) and how strictly the Torah was to be interpreted (Sadducees were literalists, while Pharisees were open to debate about the meaning, or meanings, of texts).

Points to Ponder

First Thoughts

We should keep in mind that the image of such pervasive peace and reconciliation is especially appealing to the tribes of Israel, who have been embattled with each other and outside tribal factions for a really long time. But it may also be seen as a challenge to have to coexist with those who they perceive as an imminent threat.

In the Psalm, it seems to me that this author is definitely getting paid by the king to write flattering stuff about him. His own personal motivation aside, it's not an accident that the features David clearly wants to inherit directly mirror those that the prophets predict the future Messiah will have. Whether he seeks such attributes in order to be a ruler more in favor with God or because he may have a Messiah complex is unclear.

As for the members of the early church in Rome, I can only imagine the angst they must have felt about having to go out among the people of the very city at the heart of the occupying empire to preach about a different faith. My guess is that without Paul's urging, they'd be just as happy to stay safely tucked away in the privacy of their gathering places. But Paul, the zealot that he is, isn't having it.

Finally, we have John the Baptist, who is always quite the charmer. Unlike the early Christians in Rome, he's not afraid at all to call out the powers that be, promising all sorts of gross, terrible stuff in their future if they don't turn from their present course. He, like the psalmist and Paul, is referring back to the ancient prophets as his authority for his convictions.

Digging Deeper

Mining for what really matters . . . and gold

Though Isaiah is referenced by John the Baptist in the Gospel, Paul's referral back to a prophetic text is actually from Samuel, who some consider to be more of a "minor" prophet. Status in the hierarchy of prophets aside, we could think of both Paul and John the Baptist as prophets as well, though they're not a part of the ancient prophetic texts found in the Hebrew Bible (a.k.a., the Old Testament). And though the psalmist seems to be endeavoring to place David in similar standing, calling King David a prophet would be more of a stretch.

So what defines a prophet? A lot of times, we think of prophets being almost like fortune-tellers, gazing into the future and painting vivid, often terrifying, images of what was to come. And while looking ahead into the days to come was part of the gig, it's not the only attribute that tends to be identified with prophets.

First, we should consider the source of this future-vision capability they seem to have. Often, it seems that they have visions come to them in dreams, but sometimes it seems that it's a particular clarity of understanding of the present that helps them look ahead toward what would likely transpire if things stayed on their current course. It definitely helps that they are able to examine the current culture more critically and objectively than those who are so immersed in it that it all just seems natural and, therefore, right. This might help explain why so many prophets are kind of weird; they have to have some degree of removal from the typical buy-in of the status quo in order to look at it with fresh eyes.

They also speak openly and publicly of what they understand has been given to them by God to share. Often, they're fully aware that speaking about such things will likely cost them, maybe dearly. But their passion for imparting the things they believe God has given to them tends to override their own innate desire for self-preservation or social approval.

Finally, even though they may seem like they hate the people to whom they are preaching, the impetus for their teaching comes from a divinely inspired love for their people. Just like with parents, there is such a thing as occasional "tough love," but it's from a place of concern for their people's overall well-being and salvation.

When you break down the roles of a prophet like this, it makes it seem a lot less mysterious. Yes, it doesn't make their work any easier, but it does show us how we can access our own prophetic voice as followers of the way of Jesus (the greatest of all prophets in the Christian tradition and considered a prophet by other faiths as well).

We're not all called to be prophetic in the same way. Sometimes it may be more as an overseer of the safety and future of those in your care. Other times it may be to share your own experience with the stories of faith from the Bible or beyond. And still other times it may be necessary to speak out some difficult truths, even when those around us don't particularly want to hear them.

Probably no one hopes for "prophet" to come up as a recommended calling when taking their career-inventory survey. But if we really mean what we say when we claim to embrace the gospel and all it stands for, there's bound to be a prophetic challenge for each of us along the way.

Heads-Up

Connecting the text to our world

The end of 2018 witnessed the largest fire in the history of the state of California. Hundreds were missing and scores died as a result of the so-called Camp Fire. Millions, if not billions, of dollars in property were lost, and the landscape of what had been considered by many to be one of the most desirable places in the nation to live has been altered for generations to come.

In general when we look at something like this, we consider it to be a tragedy by all accounts. Everywhere we look is loss and destruction. But while the destruction certainly is heartbreaking, there's also life and hope hidden at the heart of it all if we look closely.

There are some families of trees that produce cones or fruit in which the seeds for new saplings are entirely sealed within a casing of tree resin. This means that the trees can't reproduce unless they are subjected to extreme conditions—like a fire—that will melt the resin, releasing the seeds into the soil. So for those trees, their long-term survival depends on occasional fires to sweep through and free their full potential to propagate.

Sometimes prophets like Isaiah and Jeremiah have messages that are hard for people to hear. Even Paul and Jesus hit people between the eyes sometimes with their prophetic teaching. They call for a cutting back or a clearing out of the old ways and values we have gotten used to clinging to. Letting go of those things can feel like a small death, if not at least an unbearable loss. But it can take a hard truth to help us release our grip on old ways that have kept us in death-spirals so that we can embrace something new that allows for an entirely different kind of living we couldn't even see from our old perspective. Like the gospel according to the Rolling Stones says, you can't always get what you want, but if you try, sometimes you might find you get what you need.

Prayer for the Week

I know I can get stuck, trapped inside my own thinking about how things should be and what I really need. Help me loosen my grip and make room for new life that I may not even be able to imagine.

Popping Off

Art/music/video and other cool stuff that relate to the text

"How Trees Survive and Thrive after a Forest Fire," from *Your National Forests* (article, Fall 2017)

"The Prophets Song," by Queen (song, 1975)

Work in Progress

Lectionary Texts For
December 15, 2019 (Third Sunday in Advent)

Texts in Brief
My dog ate my Bible!

First Reading
Isaiah 35:1–10

Isaiah offers a beautifully poetic picture of hope for the future for the exiled people of Judea. They've lost everything and, while wandering without a sense of place or future, he assures them that, looking ahead, God will come to their rescue and no more harm will come to them. They will have everything they need and won't know want anymore.

Psalm
Psalm 146:5–10

This is another poem of hope for the Israelites (also plenty familiar with exile and suffering), assuring them that they worship a God of provision and protection, particularly for the marginalized. Their future is secure.

SECOND READING
James 5:7–10

James calls on Jesus's adherents to be patient, like a farmer is patient with his crops, trusting that they will come again. He offers them the example of the prophets, who spoke of amazing things not yet realized, but who waited in faithful steadfastness for these visions to be fulfilled. Finally, he offers them a gentle warning not to get cranky as they wait, taking out their impatience on each other.

GOSPEL
Matthew 11:2–11

John the Baptist hears about Jesus and his ministry from prison. He sends word to ask if Jesus is the Messiah John has been speaking of who was coming. Jesus questions people who come to see him to determine if he is who they hear he is. He says that the evidence of his works should be all they need. Then he tells those around him that John is not just a prophet but is himself a fulfillment of the ancient prophecy about the coming of a "way-maker" for the Anointed One.

Bible, Decoded
Breaking down Scripture in plain language

Lebanon—A territory that stretches along the Mediterranean coast, known especially for its mountains. In particular, Mount Lebanon was considered to be a particularly holy place. It was also a region known for its cedar trees, which were perfect material for ship building and other construction.

Zion—Zion is considered to be a sort of geographic and spiritual center for the tribes of Israel. Specifically, the city of David was located on Mount Zion.

Carmel—This can usually be translated as "the park." It was a hilly (some might say mountainous) region in what we now call central Palestine. Mount Carmel was the highest peak in this region, which stretched to the sea.

Sharon—Contrasted with the other elevated regions described above, Sharon was a valley lush with vegetation, often prized as valuable grazing area for livestock.

Points to Ponder
First Thoughts

It's frequent that the visions and promises of hope described in the Bible are cast out sometime in the indefinite future. In particular, these usually are intended for those currently suffering or marginalized. Most of the warnings are more immediate and are reserved largely for people of comfort and privilege.

In the James text, there is something strangely comforting in knowing that, even way back then, people were getting snappy with each other because they hated to wait. And in a time when immediacy is the currency of the culture, our snappiness tends to border on a nervous breakdown. Imagine how we would respond now to such vague, indefinite timelines!

It's particularly notable, given all of these words of comfort and assurance, that John the Baptist—who is in prison and likely facing his death—isn't focused at all on his own situation. Rather, his sole focus is knowing whether the things he has been talking about are coming to be for everyone else. He knows his fate will likely be execution, but like a true prophet, his heart is with his people, rough as he may be around the edges.

Digging Deeper

Mining for what really matters . . . and gold

If this text seems at all familiar, it might be because some of it appears in Handel's *Messiah*. That familiarity aside, there are lots of words and phrases that are straight-up confusing if you're not a Bible history nerd. Honestly, I don't think you have to get too deep in the weeds in order to get what the author is trying to convey.

One of the best things about many of the prophets, as well as a lot of the psalms, is that they're written in lyrical or poetic form. This means that we're not just supposed to focus on what the words help us know; we should also take time to reflect on what they help us see. A more contemporary approach in postmodern theological thought calls this nonliteral, nondidactic approach to the Bible *theopoetics*. When we engage things theopoetically, we're supposed to get out of our "right-brained" thinking and allow the images and other senses the text evokes wash over us.

One benefit of this sort of engagement is that it is more inductive rather than deductive. By this I mean that we're not taking big ideas and distilling them down to one or two straightforward points. On the contrary, it's an opening up of the text, allowing each person to connect with it on their own terms.

Some contemporary preachers and teachers hedge at this approach because it requires them to let go of a lot of control of what people walk away with. But if the authors are comfortable with conveying their messages in this nonliteral, nonlinear way, it stands to reason that we should consider teaching this way too. Even in the Gospel, when John's messengers ask him if he's the Messiah, he doesn't answer directly, but rather in this more inductive way. If it's good enough for Jesus . . .

Usually I spend time in this section teasing out what the texts mean, but this week, I suggest that we put more emphasis on how we read and experience them. And if you preach or lead a class, see if you can resist the urge to tell people what to think. You might be amazed by what you all find together.

Heads-Up

Connecting the text to our world

As many times as I've spoken publicly about the complications around praying for particular outcomes, I've prayed for said outcomes myself just as often. It's in our nature to throw a line out there into the universe, just in case, if nothing else. Can't hurt, right?

While it may not be directly damaging, I think it's a problem of misplaced desire and intention. We have a natural inclination to assume that if we can organize the world around us just so, we will finally be content and at peace.

To quote one of my former counselors, much as it pains me to do so: How's that working out for you?

We think we want answers. We think we want results. We believe on some level that we can make a deal with God so that we will feel good about things, whether it's about certainty in making a tough decision, solving a problem, or just checking off a personal wish list.

But our divine selves know better. The peace and wholeness we are yearning for is an inborn part of our being, and there is no amount of stuff, absence of suffering, or answered questions that will help us feel we have it all sorted and we're finally, completely content and complete.

That's not to say that we just have to find answers within ourselves. After all, this isn't some fluffy self-help book. The irony is that we find wholeness in coming to terms with the utter incompleteness of everything, including ourselves. Philosopher Peter Rollins calls this coming to terms with "the gap." Like the fingers of Adam and God on the ceiling of the Sistine Chapel that nearly connect but don't quite make it, there's a sensed distance between what is and what might be that just doesn't go away.

But that doesn't have to be cause for despair. On the contrary, if it was all sorted, fulfilled, and answered, what would be the point of life?

There is curious hope to be found in the already-but-not-yet tension in creation. We're creatures of both dark and light, suffering and healing, joy and sorrow. The goal isn't necessarily to extinguish the less-palatable option entirely but to find hope in the basic, simple, elemental stuff of daily living. It's only in such deep, patient presence that the rush of really living—and not just being alive—comes breaking in.

It's a never-ending work in progress.

Prayer for the Week

I want it all fixed; help me sit with the brokenness. I want to feel better; help me make peace with the pain. I want to know; help me find hope in the dimness of ignorance.

Popping Off

Art/music/video and other cool stuff that relate to the text

Just This: Prompts and Practices for Contemplation, by Richard Rohr (book, 2018)

Awaiting the Already: An Advent Journey through the Gospels, by Magrey R. DeVega (book, 2018)

Who Is Keyser Söze?

Lectionary Texts For
December 22, 2019 (Fourth Sunday in Advent)

Texts in Brief
My dog ate my Bible!

First Reading
Isaiah 7:10–16

Unsolicited, God offers to fulfill any request Ahaz wants, but Ahaz demurs. This annoys God, who was attempting to provide evidence of God's presence with Ahaz and his people. God pronounces that a baby will soon be born from a young woman, who will name her baby Immanuel. This baby will save Ahaz's kingdom from his enemies before he is even old enough to walk.

Psalm

Psalm 80:1–7, 17–19

This psalm starts by acknowledging the sovereignty of God over the Israelites and basically pointing to the history they have together. Then it begs plaintively for the end of the people's suffering, asking that God would restore things back to the way they were. Finally, there's a kind of reminder toward the end that the Israelites had been God's chosen people, and it asks for such favor again.

Second Reading

Romans 1:1–7

This text is effectively a long introduction to the message coming after it, but it's still important. It's referring to Paul in the third person, aiming to lend credence to his calling as a messenger of the gospel. It's also laying out the most important specifics of what the gospel is about, and since it's written to non-Jews, or gentiles, it's explicit in stating that Jesus and his message were for them, and that he loved them and not just the people of Israel.

Gospel

Matthew 1:18–25

When Joseph discovered his fiancée, Mary, was pregnant, he wasn't so sure he bought the "I was impregnated by the Holy Spirit" thing, so he was going to break it off quietly. But then an angel spoke to him, confirming that this was what was going on and that this was part of the fulfillment of prophecy, which meant this baby was kind of a big deal.

Bible, Decoded

Breaking down Scripture in plain language

Ahaz—The king of Judah who is under threat from the kingdoms of Syria and Israel to the north, who are plotting to join forces to crush him and his people.

Immanuel—This name means "God is with us," which is one of the names used in reference to Jesus as well.

Cherubim—Of course we think of fat little winged babies when we hear the word *cherub* (singular of *cherubim*), but they actually have a job aside from being cute. They are believed to be attendants of God, serving at God's pleasure, and they are some of the most revered angels, second only to archangels.

Ephraim/Benjamin/Manasseh—The tribes headed by Ephraim and Manasseh are two of the original tribes of the Israelites who stand in resistance against the siege by Judah and Syria on David's kingdom. The Benjamin reference is a little hazier, since he isn't a descendant of Joseph like the other two, but it likely refers to a faction within Syria that also opposes the invasion.

Points to Ponder

First Thoughts

"Immanuel," the name God uses to refer to the coming baby, directs attention to the real point of the miracle God announces in Isaiah. Though the birth of the baby may, indeed, be miraculous, the miracle to which God is pointing is that God is with Ahaz and the people of Judah, even when they feel alone and are wracked with worry about their own demise.

The proclamation of the miracle to come in the child's birth is an imminent event, while also referring indirectly to the miracle of Jesus's birth to come, as stated nearly word for word in the Gospel according to Matthew. Remember which Gospel we have this week? Got to love those biblical Easter eggs. Exegesis, baby!

In the psalm, it's not uncommon for us to see these sorts of "transactional" prayers, where the psalmist (in this case, David) is trying to strike a deal with God. Basically, he wants all of the conflict and related suffering that is besieging his kingdom to stop, and in exchange, the Israelites will stay faithful.

Digging Deeper

Mining for what really matters . . . and gold

In the psalm this week, David could use some good news. The onslaught on his territory by Judah and Syria is in full swing, and the discontentment among his people is probably leading them to question his leadership. So while the request he is making on behalf of the Israelites could be seen as magnanimous to some degree, it's also a desperate act of political survival.

David has screwed up before—way more than once. He's the first to admit he's anything but perfect. And yes, as part of the special bloodline starting with Abraham, God continues to bail him and his people out, regardless of whether they've earned it. David can definitely share in the gratitude I've expressed before that

God is not a God intent on giving us exactly what we deserve. And David is not one to hold back on trying to tap into that abundant outpouring of unearned grace, over and again.

Ahaz is another example of this unexpected divine abundance, even though he doesn't seek it. But Ahaz is still missing the one thing that David gets (at least sort of) right, which annoys God. While David seeks God's mercy and grace as the mouthpiece of God's chosen people, Ahaz still thinks God's offer to fulfill a request is about him, personally. Rather, it's about two other things: affirming the chosenness of his people and expressing that God is a God of loving generosity.

Then in the Gospel, we see Joseph learning of his role in the birth of the prophesied Messiah. For him, though, it's a little bit messier than it is with Ahaz. Since he's not married to Mary yet, this will give rise to all kinds of scandalous rumors about her and, by association, him. And I'm sure there's no small amount of doubt in his mind about her moral integrity too. After all, if my fourteen-year-old daughter came to me with news of being impregnated by God, I know what I'd think.

But again, the whole situation isn't about Joseph. Or Mary, frankly. It's about God's irrepressible desire to be known for what—or who—God truly is. Being good Jewish citizens, Mary and Joseph knew about the foretelling of this event. But like anyone else, they probably didn't see themselves as part of that unfolding.

While it is an incredible gift to be called to be a part of such a big in-breaking into the world, that doesn't mean it's clean, tidy, and easy. Maybe Ahaz doesn't want another kid; it's not like God asked. David is probably losing plenty of sleep, wondering if the next morning will see the end of his kingdom. And neither Mary nor Joseph signed up for all of the complexity and drama that will follow.

None of them could be blamed for calling out, "Why me?" in a moment of crisis over being a part of this story. But the author in Romans reminds us that it's not just about them. In fact, it's not just about the Israelites either. It's about the forging of a bond between God and all of creation in which God-given love and grace cause all human-made labels and boundaries to crumble.

Paul gets it later on in Galatians 3 when he says that labels like "Jew" and "gentile" no longer apply to all who fall within the big, beautiful tent under which all are welcome. Even Paul, the emissary who made a living slaughtering those who David had called God's chosen. Even the citizens of Rome, who are part of the very machinery that destroys the very gift alluded to in Matthew.

All of the "Why me?" talk can actually be addressed in one word. Actually, it's in the name referred to in Isaiah and Matthew: Immanuel. God with us. It's not about me, or you, or "those people." It never was. It was, is, and always will be about all of us, all within God's unconditional embrace.

Heads-Up

Connecting the text to our world

If you haven't seen the movie *The Usual Suspects* but plan to at some point, you might not want to read the rest of this section (SPOILER ALERT).

One of my favorite films of all times is *The Usual Suspects*, which is a twisting, turning psychological crime thriller that surprised nearly everyone with the final reveal. But if we had really been paying closer attention—that and brushed up on our Turkish before watching it—we might have seen it all coming.

Kevin Spacey plays Verbal Kint, a meek, mobility-limited associate of some suspects the police have rounded up for possible involvement in a recent crime. When they get to Verbal, they get a story that seems airtight as an alibi, and just based on the richness of details and his explanation for every single question and accusation they hurl at him, they finally let him go.

Little do they know at the time that he master-minded the whole thing.

Verbal spins a tale about a crime boss named Key-ser Söze behind the whole scheme, peppering in details he pulls from words and images around the very office in which they interrogate him. What the cops don't know is that the name he gives them is a sort of puzzle. It turns out that the name "Söze" comes from the Turk-ish slang *söze boğmak*, which basically means *bullshit artist*. More specifically, it refers to casting a blizzard of words so copious and confounding that they leave the audience scratching their heads.

And Keyser, as you can probably guess, is remark-ably similar to *qaysar*, the title for an Ottoman ruler, pronounced much like *Kaiser* in German, which means *king*. So in giving up his supposed associate, Verbal is basically confessing that he is the king of obfuscation. It is right there in front of the cops, and yet it is invisible. It isn't until it's too late that they realize Verbal (another connection to the root meaning of "Söze") is, in fact, Keyser Söze. By then he is gone, never to be seen again.

If you're like me, sometimes you have these moments when something is so obvious and so palpably close, and yet you miss it. It's enough to make us smack our foreheads flat on a nearby table. Fortunately God knows this about us. It's not like it hasn't played out before throughout history.

It's enough to make me wonder how many of those moments, just today, I've missed. Maybe someday I'll start paying closer attention.

Prayer for the Week

Just because I don't see or feel you nearby doesn't mean you're not there. Help me remember the message of Immanuel, God with us, as Christmas draws close.

Popping Off

Art/music/video and other cool stuff that relate to the text

The Usual Suspects (movie, 1995)

A Generous Orthodoxy, by Brian McLaren (book, 2006)

Christmas under Empire

Lectionary Texts For
December 24–25, 2019 (Nativity of the Lord Proper I)

Texts in Brief
My dog ate my Bible!

First Reading
Isaiah 9:2–7

This is one of the most common non-Gospel texts read at a Christmas worship service. It is a key text that authors of the Gospel, Paul in the Epistles, and even Jesus himself refer back to in order to emphasize that Jesus is the one described here as coming. This "great light" breaks the bonds of oppression and ends hunger and violence. In particular, the text notes that David's kingdom will endure and will do so in peace.

Psalm

Psalm 96

A call for praise to the God of Israel, who is to be seen as superior to all other god-figures over anything else we might worship instead. It also calls us to spread the word about this God and that God will judge the world righteously.

Second Reading

Titus 2:11–14

This brief and often overlooked text packs a lot into a couple of sentences. It speaks of Jesus's time on earth as the embodiment of God's grace, reminds the audience that he came to reconcile us once and for all with God, and speaks to the anticipation of his coming again after his death and resurrection.

Gospel

Luke 2:1–14

Similarly densely packed, this text covers Mary and Joseph's travels to Bethlehem, the birth of Jesus, and the annunciation by the angel to the shepherds about the birth of the Messiah.

Bible, Decoded

Breaking down Scripture in plain language

Day of Midian—Midian is a son of Abraham, so Midianites are considered descendants who are supposed to be a part of God's chosen people. Though they have established their autonomy from Israel (establishing the territory also called Midian), Israel later conquers them, bringing them back into the greater nation of Israel.

Bethlehem—It is necessary in the Gospels for Jesus to be born in Bethlehem in order to fulfill the prophecy that the Messiah will be born there, as stated in the book of Micah.

Quirinius—Quirinius is the governor of the territory where Bethlehem is at the time of Jesus's birth. For the sake of grouping territory for the census—which the Israelites really hate having to do—the regions of Syria and Judah are combined into one under his oversight.

Points to Ponder

First Thoughts

Note that in this nativity story, there's no mention of kings. That's because they don't come along in the story until Epiphany, which comes after Christmas. Epiphany lasts for twelve days after Jesus's birth, which is where the twelve days of Christmas come from.

It's also interesting that the story in Luke makes no mention of how many shepherds are involved. We usually have three in the nativity scenes, likely because it lends some aesthetic balance to the setting. But it's not biblically based.

Finally, if you see a nativity set—especially at a church—with Jesus in the manger before Christmas, think about how weird that is. If the point of Christmas is to celebrate the arrival, and if Advent is about the anticipation leading up to that birth, shouldn't the manger be empty until Christmas day, much like we depict an empty cross on Easter?

Sometimes it's worth getting a new perspective on our traditions in order to help bring us more into the present moment so we really see what's in front of us, engaging it with our whole selves rather than letting ourselves get half-numb to the familiarity of it all.

Digging Deeper
Mining for what really matters . . . and gold

If we take the story of Jesus being born in Bethlehem literally, the Holy Family has no choice but to go there because of the census being taken. In this case, it's interesting to think that the Roman Empire—the very force that Jesus ends up standing up to, costing him his life—is an integral agent in the fulfillment of this biblical prophecy.

If we fast-forward to the end of Jesus's ministry (yes, I know it's not Easter), given that the Roman Empire also is the collective agent of his crucifixion, we could say that the "enemy" helped hasten the fullness of his becoming the Christ he comes to be.

It is not just the innkeeper who allows the Holy Family to stay in his stables who helps solidify the understanding of Jesus as a humble servant of the poor; the very opportunity would never have presented itself had they not been rejected repeatedly by the first innkeepers with whom they sought shelter.

It's a curious thing, this Jesus story. At every turn, there seems to be something pressing against the direction God desires for Jesus, and yet he emerges on the other side, not unmarked by the experience, but transformed in a way that seems like an even more complete picture of the Jesus who was prophesied.

This could reveal some uncomfortable things about God, depending on how we look at it. If God willed all of these things to happen, it's a pretty twisted way to show love to an only son. Or maybe Jesus is collateral damage in a larger story, with all of the means justifying the greater end of human salvation.

On the other hand, maybe people just do horrible things to each other sometimes. Maybe God doesn't intercede because if God did, these constant lifelines would ultimately prohibit us from growing. Or maybe suffering is more of an inevitability rather than a necessity. Maybe God knows that though we have the capacity to know and do better, we won't all the time. And maybe God can work in the midst of those worst moments of humanity too.

In the midst of a foreign occupation, faced with scandal, likely marital tension, potential poverty, far from home and absent a true resting place in a moment of greatest need, love, grace, peace, and hope still push their way through into the world. Yes, it's messy, painful, and not exactly what we expected, but it's beautiful regardless. It's irrepressible in its aim to transform, despite the fear and violence with which that transformation is met.

We may be able to change how it looks or the places where it's found, but love is insistent. It's inevitable. It simply is.

Heads-Up

Connecting the text to our world

When I met Amy some twenty years ago, she had been through a string of rough relationships. By the time I came around, she had resolved to be a "crazy cat lady," living alone in her apartment for the rest of her life. But love seemed to feel otherwise about that.

While I knew the night I met her that I would eventually marry her, I wasn't reckless or stupid enough to tell her that. We dated for a few months until it had gotten serious enough to have "the talk." We had come to that point where we knew there were only two ways this could go: forward, probably all the way, or it would end. I knew I loved her, but she wasn't sure she could hear it.

After a number of emotional talks, she seemed a little bit defeated. I figured that was a pretty bad sign, as if she was giving up. She looked at me with a mix of sadness and desperation and asked, "Why do you believe that I love you?"

"Because I love you," I said. I didn't think before I said it for once; it just came out. Of course, as soon as the words came out of my mouth, I started to cringe, worried that they had just sounded contrived and cheesy. But it was true, and it was all I had.

Sometimes, though not all of the time, one person can hold enough love to hold you both. That resolve in the face of helplessness, hope despite impending despair, can sustain two, even when just one can muster it.

I'm not always sure I love God well. Actually, I'm pretty sure it's a really lopsided relationship. But I know whatever it is I bring is good enough. How? Because God keeps on loving, even when I have the audacity to ask, "How do you know I love you back?"

Prayer for the Week

Be enough love for both of us, God, when I can't seem to hold up my end. I'll keep working at it, but don't give up on me.

Popping Off

Art/music/video and other cool stuff that relate to the text

The Cross and the Lynching Tree, by James H. Cone (book, 2011)

Nativity mural at Batahola Norte Cultural Center in Managua, Nicaragua, by Gerardo Arías (mural, 1994)

Why Did Jesus Suffer?

Lectionary Texts For

December 29, 2019 (First Sunday after Christmas)

Texts in Brief

My dog ate my Bible!

First Reading

Isaiah 63:7–9

A short offering of praise, noting that the salvation of God's people was only achieved through God, and that it came when they were at their most desperate. God pronounced them (the Israelites) as God's beloved and was their source of strength when they were weak.

Psalm

Psalm 148

Another, more effusive offering of praise. The author goes through a long list of everything—animate and inanimate—that should shout out to God in praise. It reads almost like the second creation story in Genesis. The point is that all things, both material and spiritual, are of God and owe their existence to God.

Second Reading
Hebrews 2:10–18

The first big claim in this text is that the sanctifier (Jesus) and the sanctified (us) are born of the same spiritual father (God). This is why Jesus considers us all brothers and sisters. The second is about what is achieved by Jesus's suffering and death: an atonement for human sin.

Gospel
Matthew 2:13–23

An angel tells Joseph in a dream to get his new family out of the area because of the planned assassination by King Herod. They stay in Egypt until Herod dies, which, the author notes, fulfills the prophecy that the Messiah would be called out of Egypt. Herod is so mad about their escape that he punishes the Israelites by killing all of their male babies younger than two. After Herod's death, Joseph and his family return but avoid their home territory because of a ruler they fear. They settle in Nazareth, which fulfills the prophecy that the Messiah would be a Nazarean.

Bible, Decoded
Breaking down Scripture in plain language

Horn—Ram or ox horns were symbols that represented power in ancient cultures like the one referred to in Psalm 148. It may suggest that all of this praise is spurred by a victory over an enemy or oppressor.

Archelaus—This governor's full name was actually Herod Archelaus but was probably listed as "Archelaus" to avoid confusion with Herod the Great, who was his father, or Herod Antipas, his brother. Antipas was the ruler over the territory where Bethlehem was at the time of Jesus's death, and Archelaus presided over Judea, to the south.

Ramah—A territory in ancient Israel occupied by the tribe descended from Abraham. It's noted specifically in this Gospel because after King Herod orders the murder of babies throughout the region in an effort to kill this new Messiah, there is of course pervasive mourning over the devastating losses. This, the author notes, fulfills the prophecy stated by Jeremiah that there will be weeping from mothers in the land of Rachel, Benjamin's mother.

Points to Ponder

First Thoughts

It may seem kind of weird to be talking about Jesus's suffering and death so soon after his birth. It certainly feeds the notion that Christians are pretty fixated on a suffering Christ. More on that in a minute.

Why we'd be talking about Jesus's death is explained a little bit more once we get to the Gospel, though, with Herod already trying to kill him before he's hardly drawn a breath.

The Psalms and Isaiah texts present a theologically interesting take on God, one that some Christians would label as heretical. So of course we're going to talk about it! This idea that all things, living and not, are of God and contained within God has echoes of what some might call a "panentheist" view of God. Whereas a pantheist way of thinking would be that God is in all things, panentheism says that all things are within God. The beautiful thing about this is that it eliminates this perceived division between the physical and metaphysical. It's all contained within God's holy embrace or, if you prefer, God's holy womb.

Digging Deeper
Mining for what really matters . . . and gold

If you're like me, you struggle with the common Christian claim that Jesus suffered and died to make good for all of our sins. And yet here we are, faced with it in the Hebrews text. No sooner do we celebrate the fat, little, happy baby Jesus than we jump right to the bloody, horrible part.

But it's important to understand that all of Jesus's life—birth included—is framed by death, or at least mortality. If we're honest, all of our lives are framed by the same thing. Life is precious in large part because it is finite. While we do risk losing sight of the significance of Jesus's life in focusing too much on his death, we can't ignore its importance either.

We also have a long-running and insatiable need to find an explanation for suffering. From the first book in the Bible, we're presented with the correlation between our sins and our suffering. Adam will labor and Eve will endure labor (the childbirth kind) because they sought to know the mind of God. David and the Israelites determine that their many misfortunes are because they've screwed up in God's eyes. So why do we suffer? One time-tested explanation is that we deserve it.

While I don't contest the idea that much of our suffering is brought upon ourselves, I will push back against the notion that God places suffering on us as a price we have to pay for offending God. Also, this exposes the problem of why Jesus, supposedly without sin, also had to suffer, just like us.

Kind of blows the whole "We suffer because God is punishing us" hypothesis out of the water, doesn't it?

So rather than reframing our entire understanding of the entirety of Scripture as a collection of texts gathered from imperfect people, recording glimpses of their imperfect efforts to understand and explain a perfect God, we try to make a suffering Messiah make sense. In this scenario, Jesus suffered and underwent death—entirely undeserved—in order to take on the weight of our collective sin and conquer death. Seems neat, straightforward, and consistent with all of the rest of the texts, right?

But we need to look more closely at the words toward the end of the Hebrews text. Hebrews 2:17–18 specifically:

> Therefore he had to become like his brothers and sisters in every respect, so that he might be a merciful and faithful high priest in the service of God, to make a sacrifice of atonement for the sins of the people. Because he himself was tested by what he suffered, he is able to help those who are being tested.

It doesn't actually seem to say here that Jesus's blood, suffering, or death particularly satisfied God in any way. In fact, the only mention of God is regarding Jesus's merciful and faithful service to the world for God. Yes, it does say that a sacrifice atones for our sins, but in the next verse it explains why that suffering was atoning.

Jesus was tested just like we are by both the prospect and the real experience of suffering. He would have been happy to take a pass on the whole agony-and-death thing; he said as much in the garden at Gethsemane. But although he was tempted to run away or fight back, he faced the threat head-on, refusing to waver in his commitment to living out his conviction that love was more important that even life itself.

Jesus was tested and prevailed because he was unmoved in his commitment. Love would redeem him, and us, even in the face of the worst moments imaginable. Maybe then—just maybe—we'd get it. Yes, God/Jesus really meant all that stuff. It wasn't just talk. It was actually enough to outweigh all of the pain of living and, even the prospect of death itself. The terrible beast was declawed, leaving something real but without power to be the Prime Mover in our existence.

Jesus finally knew it was possible and that the thing in which he placed all of his faith pulled him through. And now, thanks to him forging that path, he can show us how to get there. In doing so, Jesus's life is no longer framed by his death. His grasp of the true fullness of what existence is about is our new theological grammar, and it's liberating.

Heads-Up
Connecting the text to our world

My wife, Amy, and I were asked to sing at a funeral a few years ago that was particularly hard. Though we've helped out in many memorial services over the years, the ones where a young person is lost are by far the hardest.

In this case, a teenage girl was killed in a car accident, and of course her family was devastated by it. Their pain was palpable, and it was all we could do to hold it together through the service to try and offer what little consolation we could through music.

It's in our nature to try and explain, or at least respond to, death and suffering in a way that makes some sense of it. As a result, we tend to say things that we don't necessarily mean or that we think will be comforting that actually aren't.

Everything happens for a reason.

She's in a better place.

God needed another angel in heaven, so God called her home.

We've all heard these, and likely others, before. We may have even said some of them. But do we really mean what we're saying? Do we think there's a reason that a loving, merciful God decided that a teenage girl needed to die that day? And if we do believe she is in a better place, focusing on that overlooks the present suffering borne by the family left behind. And as for God feeling a need to add beautiful girls to his cabinet of heavenly curios, that's just cruel.

The fact is that suffering and loss are real, and they're terrible. And while we long for answers, there aren't always any to be found. Sometimes death is senseless, terrible, and unexpected. Sometimes it takes someone who doesn't seem to have done anything to deserve it. It's just awful, period.

Sometimes silent presence is the best thing we can offer. If we have stories about the best things the lost loved one brought to the world, those stories can offer some comfort. Even just crying along with those who mourn can affirm the fact that they are not alone in their pain.

But we don't always have to explain it. Sometimes tragedy and suffering just don't make sense. And yet love and life persist. Here we are, together, at least for this moment. That, in itself, is a gift.

Prayer for the Week

God, help me look deeper, past the hurt and tragedy. I don't need to ignore the reality of pain, but help me recognize that there are paths through it, with your help.

Popping Off

Art/music/video and other cool stuff that relate to the text

Contact (movie, 1997)

What Dreams May Come (movie, 1998)

Let It Shine

Lectionary Texts For

January 5, 2020 (Second Sunday after Christmas)

Texts in Brief

My dog ate my Bible!

First Reading

Jeremiah 31:7–14

After spending several weeks in Isaiah, we get this text from Jeremiah, which echoes much in the second half of Isaiah, namely that God is calling back the exiled people of Israel to be one nation again. God will provide for them, particularly the weak and marginalized, and they will be made whole as a nation.

Psalm

Psalm 147:12–20

This psalm refers back to the text in Jeremiah, noting that the good fortune and peace being realized under

King David is due to the promises God made to Jacob and his descendants, who make up the twelve tribes of Israel.

Second Reading
Ephesians 1:3–14

The theme in Jeremiah alluding to God's chosen people being part of God's beloved family continues here, noting like the psalm that all good that comes to us originates from God. It refers to Jesus as the one who both reconciles us back with God and also made God's will known to us. We are inheritors, as adopted children, of God's grace and mercy, and the reconciliation is intended to spread throughout all people and the rest of creation.

Gospel
John 1:(1–9), 10–18

The first nine verses set the tone for John, establishing that all beings were spoken into existence by God. It also speaks of the man to whom the Gospel is attributed, explaining that he, like Jesus, is sent from God. In the second half, the text adopts the images of light and family to describe both what Jesus brought into the world (the light that enlightens everyone) and that he was the living expression of God (the Word) in order for us to come to know God intimately.

Bible, Decoded
Breaking down Scripture in plain language

Ephraim—A son of Joseph, who was a son of Jacob. Ephraim represents one of the two tribes of Israel descended from Joseph; the other is Manasseh. Joseph is the only of Jacob's sons from whom two of the twelve tribes of Israel are descended.

Light—Of course you know what light is, but it's important to understand why this Gospel uses this imagery to describe God in particular. This text was written last of the four Gospels (about a century after Jesus), and it was a period when a religious strain called gnosticism was gaining popularity. Gnosticism proposes that God is a "divine spark" within the enlightened, but that it is inborn, only in God's chosen. So the contrast of John's Gospel claiming that God is the "light that enlightens everyone" is a direct challenge to the particularism of gnostics.

Points to Ponder

First Thoughts

It's interesting one of John's primary messages is to subvert the idea that God is to be possessed by a particular few, or that God shows favoritism. Consider that, until Jesus came along, the Israelites considered themselves to be particularly favored by God. Jesus's mission to reach out to gentiles, or non-Jews, was one of the more controversial components of his ministry.

The text in Ephesians plays a little bit of a balancing act, still touching on the theme of chosenness, while also establishing that we (meaning all of us) were chosen by God to be a part of this family in which God sees us through eyes of love, rendering our sinfulness impotent.

Another contrast between the themes in Ephesians and John and the themes in Jeremiah and the psalm is that God's forgiveness, love, or light has nothing to do with the current state of things. In the prophecy and the psalm, the promise of good news is a sign of God's favor. In the latter two texts, God's wide-open forgiveness and decision to relate to all of us in a parental sort of love is the good news.

Digging Deeper

Mining for what really matters . . . and gold

The fifty-cent word for a central theme in this section of John is *incarnation*. The notion that "the Word became flesh" is, in many ways, the Christmas story. And given that John has no nativity scenes, or any childhood takes on Jesus, this is most definitely a Christmas story. It is the ideal Epiphany text, which is the twelve-day period after Christmas we're in now.

Epiphany is usually described as the time in the church year dedicated to the wise men—or magi or kings, depending on who you ask—traveling to and meeting Jesus. But in a broader sense, epiphany is understood as a physical manifestation to any gentiles. While it's disputed by some scholars, most theologians and historians believe the wise men weren't Jewish. And though we don't think much of that most of the time, it's really important, especially this week.

Yes, the wise men traveled to Jesus, so it's not like he had a lot of choice about them seeing him. But the only reason they knew where to find him is because they were directed there—not by a voice, a pillar of smoke, or a map. They were taken there by a heavenly light.

In John, we get the explanation that Jesus wasn't the light itself, but rather he was a bearer of the light. In the nativity story, however, it is the light that points to the light-bearer. It's an interesting interplay, blurring the lines between the Divine and the human, just as the line between Israelites and everyone else is being blurred.

Siblings don't often have a lot of say about who is added to their family; that's usually more of a parental choice. It can get crowded, and no one really likes to share, if they have their choice to or not. But light doesn't discriminate; it shines on saints and sinners, Christians and non-Christians. Ultimately, dark can't do anything to hold it back. Light prevails, saturating all within its reach with a warm, comforting glow.

That's the enlightenment of epiphany.

Heads-Up

Connecting the text to our world

Back before we had portable screens and streaming media (cue the old-guy music), we played with more unsophisticated toys. One of my favorite activities was to take a jar out and hunt lightning bugs. People call them different things depending on what region they grew up in, but there's only one kind of bug I know of whose ass lights up at night.

Part of the fun was running around, trying to predict in the darkness where they'd glow next. The other trick was getting them into the jar without letting other ones out that we'd already caught. On a good night, I'd go home with a jar full of maybe a dozen or so lightning bugs to use as a living night light in my room. While my friends were content to pull their butts off and smear the phosphorescent guts on their faces like war paint, I loved the little guys. I wanted to keep them.

I would do everything I could do make them feel at home in the jar. I would put little bottle caps full of water in there along with some grass or maybe even a flower. I had no idea what they ate, but I figured some lawn clippings would do the trick. But as careful as I was with them, I would wake up the next morning to a pile of mostly motionless bug carcasses. It always bothered me, but apparently not enough to stop putting them in there.

After dealing with my postmortem distress one too many times, my mom sat me down and explained that these were wild animals, not meant to be captured and kept. But I had been a good bug-dad, I insisted. What else could they need?

What they needed to survive that I couldn't give them was freedom. They were made to wander, to cast a glow on other kids in other neighborhoods, too. The thing I had to come to terms with was that they weren't mine. While I could appreciate them, I couldn't possess them for myself. In doing so, the very thing I claimed to love was extinguished.

The urge to hunt lightning bugs never completely went away, although I finally stopped. Even today, at forty-seven years old, I have a twinge of longing to catch them when I see them popping in and out against the inky landscape on summer evenings. But then I let go, appreciating them simply because they are and not because they're mine.

Prayer for the Week

Help me be a light-bearer instead of a light-possessor.

Popping Off

Art/music/video and other cool stuff that relate to the text

"Brief Case" scene from *Pulp Fiction* (movie, 1994)

The Matrix (movie, 1994)

The Big Shift

Lectionary Texts For

January 6, 2020 (Epiphany of the Lord)

Texts in Brief

My dog ate my Bible!

First Reading

Isaiah 60:1–6

The prophet speaks of an earth-shattering light that bursts into this mire of darkness that had seemed intent on overtaking everything. It is so powerful that everything is drawn to it. Those at war now come together in awestruck peace, and the light brings abundance and life with it to all within its glow.

Psalm

Psalm 72:1–7, 10–14

The psalmist offers a prayer on behalf of their king and his people, wishing for peace, honor, bounty, and generosity for the poor. Like the light in Isaiah and Jesus in Matthew are portrayed, the psalm depicts a longing for a leader who will be a "king of kings," one who causes all others in power to kneel in respect and deference.

SECOND READING
Ephesians 3:1–12

Paul describes himself as a prisoner for Christ, as that is the depth of his commitment to the gospel message. Although he is helplessly bound to Christ in every way, he still sees the revelation of the mystery of what Jesus is about as a great privilege. While he does find power in his role in the way the gospel is playing out, he still considers himself to be a servant more than a figurehead. Part of the mystery that is revealed is that God's grace has been broken out of the tribal favoritism and is now available to everyone.

GOSPEL
Matthew 2:1–12

The wise men hear of the birth of a new Jewish king, so they come to Herod, the regional ruler, to ask about him. Herod, of course, acts intrigued but actually sees this as an insurgent threat and asks them to let him know when they find the newborn. They come to Jesus, bring him gifts, and then leave in secret, as they have been warned in a dream not to share Jesus's whereabouts with Herod.

Bible, Decoded
Breaking down Scripture in plain language

Midian/Ephah/Sheba—Ephah is a son of Midian, who is a descendant of Abraham. So this Isaiah text is describing a tribal territory identified with the tribes from Abraham's descendants. This is a region that would have likely been known as a source for frankincense and maybe myrrh. Sheba is a region known for its gold and spices. This ties them to the gifts described in the Matthew text.

Tarshish—A remote region used as an example to show how far away other rulers would come from to offer tribute to the king of the Israelites.

Gold/Frankincense/Myrrh—Gold is a symbol of royalty. This is a reference to the fact that Jesus will be seen as a king among kings. Frankincense is a perfume that would have been used in sacred rituals by priests, alluding to Jesus's role as a spiritual leader as well. Myrrh is an oil that was often used to anoint bodies at the time of burial, so this is a reference to the significance of Jesus's death.

Points to Ponder
First Thoughts

The Matthew text is a study in contrasts of how power responds to God's revelation in the world. The wise men are brought together by this news and drawn to this new king by this compelling celestial light, while

Herod—fearful of the loss of his own power—seeks to snuff out this threat to his authority. We see these diametrically opposite reactions to God's revealing truth all of the time. While some people allow themselves to be forever changed by it, others who refuse the opportunity to be transformed feel their only recourse is to respond with force and violence to extinguish any potential for real change in their lives. So the light of transformation in itself isn't enough; it requires a willingness of those of us it shines on to take it in and allow it to become part of us.

Digging Deeper
Mining for what really matters . . . and gold

We can see connections in this prophetic text to lots of other Scriptures, including the first creation story in Genesis and the first chapter in John's Gospel, both of which emphasize the imposition of light into darkness, not only pushing the darkness back, but also calling things together and into being. But we can't ignore that this comes up during the season of Epiphany. In particular, it's hard to ignore that the author talks about two of the gifts the wise men are said to have brought to Jesus, also described in our Matthew text. This is not a coincidence, of course, as Matthew is making sure we think back to that Isaiah text. Remember that Matthew is particularly interested in making sure the audience sees Jesus's arrival as the fulfillment of ancient prophecy about a coming Messiah.

But in this Epiphany story, it's easy to get hung up on the kings and their gifts. After all, they're probably dressed really well, and the swag they're giving to the

Holy Family is impressive. But they aren't what Epiphany is about, any more than the nations being drawn toward God's light are the point of the Isaiah text.

The point is the light that is drawing them all together.

This notion of a single source causing everyone to stop in their tracks, to reassess what's important in their lives, and to radically change course is remarkable. We rarely talk about it, but kings of different territories were not necessarily the best of buddies. Think of how often the different tribes and regions are in conflict throughout the Psalms alone. And in Isaiah, we've had two chapters replete with darkness, struggle, and conflict leading up to this. And now all of a sudden, light breaks through and everything changes.

It's all too easy to clean our hands of the Christmas business and move on to the next thing. I talked to a pastor just last week who noted that his church didn't even recognize Epiphany. Come December 26, the decorations were packed up, loaded out, and we were back to normal until Lent.

But we can't go back to normal; that's the whole point. The terms of our own individual lives and those we share in community have been, and are still being, rewritten. To revert to our old ways after the Christmas disruption is to deny the very meaning of the event itself.

The point wasn't the people in their Christmas best, nor was it the gifts, be they under a tree or in packs on the backs of camels. We have to stop, really look, and allow the awe of the big shift that has just taken place in the universe. Then we have figure out how we now become agents, or coconspirators in facilitating that shift from now on.

Heads-Up

Connecting the text to our world

My baptism was kind of a let-down, if I'm being honest. People asked me how I felt afterward, and while I put on a smile and said something I thought was appropriate, mostly all I felt was wet. What I remember most about the whole thing is how unremarkable it was, especially compared to what I had built it up in my mind to be.

I had heard stories of visions and voices and these profound senses of internal transformation that I just didn't have. I didn't see any doves either, and I was baptized outside so there was a much better chance. The biggest mistake was that I was waiting for some magical experience to descend onto me or permeate me from within, rather than looking at it more symbolically as the shifting point, the first step along a new lifelong path.

That path hasn't always been smooth either. There was my time of spiritual and religious exile, periods of tremendous darkness and suffering that I thought I would be exempt from after getting the holy dunking. But if I had really been paying attention to what imitating the life of Christ was really like at the time (keep in mind I was ten years old when I was baptized), I would have known better.

I have had some of those lightning-flash sorts of moments though, even if no one else may have recognized it at the time. It wasn't magical like a flaming, talking bush, but it left a mark. It was more like the "still, small voice" described in the Bible. It actually came through music, and what's really weird is that I was the one making the music.

I've written before about how, after a decade in exile from church and having been thrown out for my many theological heresies, I came back, albeit warily. After a while I accepted their invitation to sing, and that's when "the thing" happened. I didn't even know exactly what was going on, but I can look back and recognize that a few things conspired to make the change work.

My girlfriend at the time, who is now my wife of eighteen years, was patient but persistent in inviting me to join her in her small church community. They were easygoing but very clear in their invitation to have me share my music in worship. And finally, I lowered by defenses long enough to let the music pass through, which is how it always feels.

Little did I know that the music had a hitchhiker that made its way in under my radar.

It was grace in a way I can never quite articulate. It was the patient "yes" to every "no" I had used to justify why I was beyond repair and love when it came to God. It may not have been a glowing dove or a flaming tree, but my grace came in the form of an open door and a small circle of like-hearted searchers, all looking for belonging in a way that our tribal identities had never been able to satisfy.

It felt like home. It drew me in, and I have held on ever since.

Prayer for the Week

I'm hardly the poster boy for what a "good Christian" is supposed to look like, God; will you accept a work in progress?

Popping Off

Art/music/video and other cool stuff that relate to the text

How the Grinch Stole Christmas (movie, 1966, 2000)

The Jesus Shot

Lectionary Texts For
January 12, 2020 (Baptism of the Lord)

Texts in Brief
My dog ate my Bible!

First Reading
Isaiah 42:1–9

A description of the coming Messiah who will bring justice, but not in the way people are used to. He will be strong, but not brash or violent. He will be transformative but subtle. Nothing will dissuade him from his aim to share the wisdom he has been given by God to share. The final claim in the passage about why God should be believed in this promise is because other prophecies made before have already been fulfilled.

Psalm

Psalm 29

This description of the many attributes of God stands in strong contrast with the characteristics listed in Isaiah above that the Messiah will possess. It stands to reason, then, if this is how people see God, Isaiah would feel compelled to explain how unremarkable in appearance and demeanor God's coming messenger would be. Without a heads-up, it would be easy to miss him otherwise.

Second Reading

Acts 10:34–43

Peter distills Christ's gospel down into a few words: "God shows no partiality." Peter proclaims Jesus as anointed by God, as a judge and savior of all nations, as a healer, and as having risen from death by God's power.

Gospel

Matthew 3:13–17

This is the famous story of Jesus's baptism in the Jordan river by John the Baptist. In this abbreviated accounting (all four Gospels have their own respective baptism stories), John balks when Jesus asks to be baptized. John argues that it should be the other way around, since he is the one in need of cleansing, not Jesus. But after Jesus explains that this is necessary to fulfill the Scriptures' predictions of how the Messiah will come about, he agrees, after which the dove-like presence of the Holy Spirit descends on them both, and God's voice proclaims that Jesus is God's son.

Bible, Decoded
Breaking down Scripture in plain language

Nazareth—While we've talked about the fact that prophets foretelling a coming Messiah said he would come from Nazareth, it's worth noting that it wasn't a place held in very high esteem. It was far more of a ghetto than, say, Jerusalem, where one might expect a Messiah to come from. So this is another indication that Jesus is, and will be, a people's Messiah more than he is a savior for the wealthy and powerful.

Holy Spirit—The fancy way to describe the Holy Spirit is as one of the three manifestations of the triune God-head. If you're more confused than impressed by all that, basically it means that God is expressed in three ways (God-Jesus-Holy Spirit), and that this is one of them. So when you see a dove depicted in sacred art, it's usually meant to illustrate the presence of the Holy Spirit. Some consider the Holy Spirit the more "feminine" expression of God, while many consider the "Father" God to be more masculine.

Points to Ponder
First Thoughts

It's a bit of an ironic twist that, just after the passage emphasizes that God shows no favorites, the Bible points out that the resurrected Christ didn't appear to all upon rising but only to the few disciples who had been following him before crucifixion. It seems like either the author is trying to drive home the fact that the person who is the subject of these stories spreading like wildfire is the same person many encountered during his life, or the writer is still struggling with his own ego a little. Maybe it's his own way of trying to tell himself he's okay, even after denying the very Messiah they're now preaching about.

Fun fact: John the Baptist and Jesus are cousins. Imagine finding out your family of origin is in the prophet-and-Messiah business. No pressure!

The beginning of the Isaiah passage reads a lot like the ending of the Matthew text. This is likely another literary device to ensure, in case the audience hasn't gotten it by now, that they understand this is the person the prophet was talking about. Remember that fulfillment of prophecy is a really big deal to Matthew's author.

Another fun fact: this text in Matthew is the only place in the Bible where all three manifestations of God are present at the same time.

Digging Deeper

Mining for what really matters . . . and gold

The text in Acts this week is believed to be part of a sermon that Peter offered about the beginning of Jesus's ministry. It's also believed to be the last message he offered during his ministry. And while that's worth knowing (after all, if you were given a chance to say some last words, you'd probably want them to be important), it's just as important to understand who he was preaching to and where.

The preceding parts of this chapter in Acts tells the story of Simon Peter traveling to Caesarea, which has been established as the Roman capital in Palestine. So symbolically, if not literally, Peter has traveled to the heart of the empire to make this speech. Also, he has been in the house of Cornelius, who is a soldier in the Roman army. Granted, he had previously described Cornelius as someone who was pretty sympathetic toward Jews and who seemed to have a heart for the God of the Israelites, but this whole journey is a big risk.

This makes the introductory verses in this passage especially poignant; Peter is claiming that his God has come for them, his enemies, in spite of the fact that they actively persecuted and killed his own people. In fact, by this point there is no mystery surrounding Peter's fate, given his status among the disciples and the establishment of the new religious movement. He was preaching about life, radical grace, and forgiveness for all wrongs while staring death in the eye.

Within this handful of verses, Peter covers all the essentials those listening need to know to affirm that Jesus was who he said he was. He represents a God for all people and all pasts on earth; he embodies life, death, and rebirth all in one; and he forgives without reservation all who seek it. All they have to do is have the will to summon the humility to ask.

Heads-Up

Connecting the text to our world

I've come to believe that some people look at baptism almost like an immunization against death. We've all heard the "baptism isn't fire insurance" saying, but we shouldn't be fooled into believing it's a shortcut around death either. We still have to die, and that sucks.

There are those Christians who seem completely unafraid of death, usually because they've been baptized. In fact, it can get to the point that it seems like they're almost looking forward to it (weirdo alert!). While I'm as intrigued as anyone to know what lies beyond all I see, know, and experience here and now, I'm also not in any hurry to get there. I, for one, enjoy life and am content to have it last as long as possible, thank you very much.

So what does this "new life in Christ" even mean anyway? The easy answer is that no one who is still alive knows. But we do have glimpses to give us hints.

First, there's the fact that life itself can take a turn when it is informed by the infectious hope found in the gospel. I know that makes me sound like a big, fat Jesus head. But when we come to really believe the kinds of words offered in Acts—that God doesn't play favorites—it's kind of mind-blowing. While pretty much every religious organization in the world will claim they are a community for all, we as human beings suck at really holding all people in equal regard. So knowing that God sees beyond our limitations serves as inspiration to at least work toward that kind of approach to life, even if we'll never completely master it.

Second, we should consider what that "new life" looks like. There's a difference between being revived in your same old body, like Jesus did for Lazarus or Peter did for Tabitha, and undergoing resurrection. Being revived, while miraculous in itself, is more about bringing the body back to its previous state. You were alive, you died, now you're alive again.

But that's not entirely the story of resurrection. When Jesus was resurrected, he had undergone a transformation that had not been possible, it seems, when he was living on earth like one of us. There was a transcendence of the binds that hold us back, that hem us in and keep us separate from God. It was more like the resurrected Christ was both "here" and "there" at the same time. For you science nerds, it's like the idea in quantum theory of a particle being in two places at once. It's this cohesion of coexistent realities, this paradox that bridges the space between two disparate states.

The example that always helped this make sense for me was thinking about the multiple properties of light. Is light a particle or is it a wave? Really, the answer to that either/or proposition is "yes." Is the resurrected Jesus earthly or celestial? Is he flesh or spirit? Is he alive, dead, or transformed into something we can't entirely grasp?

Yes!

Prayer for the Week

Sometimes I think I can make things right on my own; help me have the courage to know better and to do better.

Popping Off

Art/music/video and other cool stuff that relate to the text

Quantum Leap (TV series, 1989–1993)

"Playing Favorites: The Problem with Blessings and Curses," from *Progressive Christianity* (blog post, February 1, 2018)

Give It Away, Now

Lectionary Texts For

January 19, 2020 (Second Sunday after Epiphany)

Texts in Brief

My dog ate my Bible!

First Reading

Isaiah 49:1–7

The prophet offers assurance about Israel's chosen place in the world. Though they are reviled by other nations, Isaiah assures them that God has a role for them and that leaders from distant lands will bow to them one day. All people will gather to Israel, and because they will be strengthened by God, they will serve as a beacon of salvation to the world.

Psalm

Psalm 40:1–11

The psalm begins with an offering of thanks for the many blessings God has given. The author notes that

God has saved them more than once and that God's gifts are innumerable. The second section notes that God doesn't want the types of sacrifices common within many religions, including Judaism to that point. Rather, what God desires is a sacrifice of self in service to God's desire for the world. The psalmist has been given a song of praise to sing to the world by God, and the passage ends with them asking for the protection and strength needed to spread the word.

Second Reading

1 Corinthians 1:1–9

Speaking to the church leaders in Corinth, the author gives thanks for them and the many gifts God has given them. Namely, God has given each of them the spiritual gifts necessary to share the gospel to all who will hear it, along with the strength to carry out their calling. It closes with a confirmation that this is a divine calling, as revealed through Jesus and his example.

Gospel

John 1:29–42

John the Baptist proclaims to everyone listening that Jesus is the one they have been waiting for. He explains that the only way he knows this is because God revealed it to him. John tells his own followers that Jesus is the one they've sought, so they follow him. When Jesus realizes they are, he asks them what they're looking for, to which they ask where he's going. Instead of answering directly, Jesus invites them to "come and see." Andrew, one of the two who are following Jesus, goes and finds his brother Simon to join them. When

Jesus meets him, he renames Simon Cephas, which translates as Peter.

Bible, Decoded

Breaking down Scripture in plain language

Sword—The imagery of a sword is used several times throughout Scripture, but in this case specifically it is meant to represent strength and protection.

Sosthenes—Sosthenes is the head of the Corinthian church. By claiming the authority of Paul as the head of their own church, the writer is effectively claiming to speak on the congregation's behalf.

Cephas—While translating as *Peter*, the meaning of the name is *rock*. This is a foretelling of Peter's role as the foundation of the church.

Points to Ponder

First Thoughts

It's worth noting that the book of Acts, which tells of the establishment of the early church, was actually written before the Gospel of John. Knowing that, this story is actually pointing backward in time, rather than predicting a future event.

There is a merging of contexts in these passages by using the symbolism of a rock. In the psalm, David claims that his strength and authority in leading the Israelites comes from God. Then in the Gospel, the disciple Peter is to be the strength and foundation from which this new religious movement will emerge. We should also remember that Isaiah speaks elsewhere of God offering a "cornerstone" on which his people's strength and prosperity will come, and Paul later calls Jesus the cornerstone that Isaiah was talking about. So we have Jesus serving as the hands, feet, and voice of God on earth, followed by Peter who will serve as Christ's hands, feet, and voice in establishing this new movement.

Digging Deeper

Mining for what really matters . . . and gold

We human beings have a bad habit of latching onto whatever is right in front of us. We want the "silver bullet" that will solve our problems and answer our questions. From the current political leader to the latest miracle gadget advertised on TV, we fall for the lie, over and again, that that next person or thing will be the answer we've been seeking. Then everything will be all right.

I'm guessing Isaiah had his share of acolytes who were all too ready to endow him with the mantle of messiah, were he to allow it. But he made very clear from the beginning of his ministry that he was a messenger, pointing the way to something else yet to come. King David likely had people trying to do similarly with him, especially given the tendency for people to conflate political power with an inherently divine nature.

John the Baptist worked particularly hard against the assumptions people kept having that he was the messiah too. He was just the way-maker, the messenger who had no further role or authority than that in the unfolding story. I'm sure that Peter and Paul (sorry, no

Mary to round out the music joke this time) had a few people who tried to hold them in higher regard than they believed was their right. But if they had learned anything from Jesus, it was that the whole story—though using them as instrumental pieces—was not about them.

Then comes Jesus, who John the Baptist announces to all around him is "The One." John urges his own followers to leave his side and walk behind Jesus instead. When they ask Jesus what he's up to, he doesn't answer them directly. Rather he invites them to see for themselves.

We conclude with Jesus empowering Peter, who is to be a critical disciple in forming the movement that will come after Jesus's death, to serve as the foundation on which the future of the movement will be built.

Think about that for a minute. The church will not be built on Jesus himself but rather on one to whom he gives the strength and authority to carry it out. Why Peter? Likely because Jesus understands that Peter gets the "it's not about me" part.

It doesn't seem particularly noteworthy to follow a guy who tells you to come and see what he's about only to have him give another follower a new name. Whoopee, right? But symbolically, it's a huge deal. Peter is serving as an example to everyone else. He—like the rest of us—is endowed with certain gifts and strengths. The key element is that those gifts are only truly realized when used by giving those gifts and that strength away.

Jesus set the story in motion; he left it up to us to keep the message on point.

Heads-Up

Connecting the text to our world

Siddhartha had it all: power, admiration, wealth, and a kingdom that would bend to his every word someday. He had been insulated from the struggles of the world his whole life until he ventured out, beyond his bubble of protection. It was then that he really saw suffering, which changed him profoundly. He realized that the things and the titles on which his identity had been built were not real; they had no true value to him anymore.

So he left. He went out into the wilderness to meditate under a tree, searching with the hope that the real meaning he sought would be revealed. It didn't happen right away, but he did stumble into the enlightenment he had hoped for. His eyes were opened. His spiritual gift was wisdom, clarity, vision. He could no longer see either himself or the world the same way again.

The irony of the story of Siddhartha Gautama becoming the Buddha was that he came into his full, true self by first becoming nothing. He shed his titles and his preconceptions about reality, about himself, and about what life's meaning was. To say it was life-changing would be understating it, given that he never went back to his old life, which now seemed relatively silly and pointless.

Instead, he committed himself to furthering his search for enlightenment and then to teaching others how to seek likewise. Plenty of times, people would try to place him back up on a pedestal, worshipping him as their new God, but he rejected their praise. If they were looking to him for answers, it was as pointless as their efforts had been when they looked within themselves.

Siddhartha became the Buddha first by becoming no one. He could have done anything he wanted with his newfound gifts, but he only wanted to use them to give them to others who would then do the same. It was the gift he valued most of all, but which he never truly possessed.

Prayer for the Week

I know I have gifts, even when I'm hesitant to admit it. Help me have the strength to claim them with authority and then use them to give myself and my story away.

Popping Off

Art/music/video and other cool stuff that relate to the text

"40," by U2 (song, 1983)

"The Healing Power of Telling Your Story," *Psychology Today* (article, November 27, 2012)

Pull Your
Head Out!

Lectionary Texts For

January 26, 2020 (Third Sunday after Epiphany)

Texts in Brief

My dog ate my Bible!

First Reading

Isaiah 9:1–4

This hopeful foretelling is an assurance offered to the nation of Israel that their long-endured suffering and time of darkness will soon end. Their dark times will become awash in divine light, and all that is now wrong will be made right.

Psalm

Psalm 27:1, 4–9

This psalm excerpt acts as a sort of response to the message in Isaiah, on behalf of the Israelites. It's a clinging to the assurance that God will, indeed, serve as protector, sustainer, and light, helping them prevail against adversity of all kinds. There's an emphasis on the psalmist's desire to seek God, and for God not to turn from them in their search.

SECOND READING

1 Corinthians 1:10–18

Paul is writing to stop the infighting within subgroups in the Corinthian church. Though he names several leaders with whom different groups of people have affiliated, apparently in opposition to one another, he says that they are all—first and foremost—with Jesus. This should hold them together far beyond any arguments or differences, which pale by comparison to the strength of their greater Christian bond.

GOSPEL

Matthew 4:12–23

After John the Baptist gets arrested for his ministry, Jesus flees to the territory referred to in Isaiah as Zebulun and Naphtali. Matthew makes a point that this is the fulfillment of that prophecy Isaiah spoke of when a divine light would appear to them. There, he recruits brothers Andrew and Simon Peter from their fishing jobs to come with him as disciples. He then recruits James and John, and they all began to preach and perform miracles in the region.

Bible, Decoded

Breaking down Scripture in plain language

Zebulun/Naphtali—These are two of the twelve tribes of Israel. They bordered each other from the west and east, respectively, and they were along the southern end of the Sea of Galilee. Both of these tribes were among the ten so-called "lost tribes" of Israel, which were separated from the rest of the nation of Israel after being attacked by the Assyrians more than seven hundred years before Jesus's birth.

Day of Midian—This is a strange one. In short, it's a day of recognition of the Israelites in Midian overcoming remarkable odds to vanquish enemy forces from their land with God's help. God orders them to take torches in clay pots and horns and, in a seemingly hopeless moment when their remaining army of only a few hundred is surrounded, they break the clay pots and blow the horns. The cacophony and the burst of light emerging from the broken pots freak out their enemies, who flee.

Chloe—Since this is the only reference to Chloe in the entire New Testament, it's hard to pin down for sure who she is. But based on the context, it can be assumed that she and those affiliated with her are likely one of the quarreling factions within the church at Corinth.

Points to Ponder
First Thoughts
In the Christian narrative, the light emerging from the broken vessels, leading to God's providence for God's chosen over the forces of evil, is seen as a predecessor to the coming "light of the world" that would emerge from this broken world, empowering God's people with the strength they require to face their oppressors.

From the beginning of the Gospel of Matthew, we can recognize that one of the author's top priorities is showing that Jesus's life fulfills many of the prophecies in the Hebrew Bible, or Old Testament. So while we often focus in this text on the new disciples, Matthew is more intent on connecting this story to the Isaiah text.

Finally, who can imagine factions within a church or denomination in conflict—right?! But seriously, this is a good reminder for all of us that while our many differences can tend to drive wedges among us over time, none of it is as important as the things that we have in common—namely, divinely inspired and informed love.

Digging Deeper

Mining for what really matters . . . and gold

The magic word for this week is *tribalism*. We see a story in Isaiah about some of these "lost tribes" that were overtaken by a larger army back in the day. But we have to wonder if this would have been possible if the twelve factions among the Israelites had stuck together to begin with. The phrase is "divide and conquer" for a reason, after all.

And here we are again in Corinth, with this small group of early Christians already drawing lines of division based on which evangelist they think is "doing it right." Never mind that they're in the heart of an empire that would just as soon see them eliminated altogether; instead, they're making themselves even more vulnerable than they already are over stuff that Paul suggests really doesn't matter.

Then we have Jesus in the Gospel text, who doesn't seem too intent on growing moss, or roots, in any one place for too long. Though this is very early on in his ministry, he's already onto his third location. He's the archetypal refugee, come to think of it. The only thing really driving him is his mission, far more than his familial ties, familiar surroundings, or cultural standards. God speaks, and he goes.

It seems to be infectious, too, because (at least in Matthew's telling) it only takes a short encounter for four guys to drop their livelihoods and go wherever he's headed. They see something more pressing, more compelling, and they don't think twice about responding.

This is what Paul is telling his handful of quibbling church folk. They're losing sight of why they are there in the first place. They're distracted by their all-too-human issues: the same ones that cause us to take our eyes off of the big picture.

At least in the psalm the author knows this is their tendency, and they ask God for help. Fortunately, no squirrels or pretty, shiny things come along in the middle of the prayer, or they might have never gotten to the good stuff at the end! But really, the example in the psalm is probably the best for us to bear in mind. Yes, God's light is all around us if we're really present to each moment and are intent on seeking it out. But too often, we bury our heads in the darkness of worldly minutiae rather than staying focused.

It probably makes sense, then, to ask God for a little help pulling our heads out of the shadows when we get distracted.

Heads-Up

Connecting the text to our world

It may not be technically a part of the biblical canon, but let's face it: *The Simpsons* TV show is on up there when it comes to prophetic wisdom. While they have no small amount of gastric-driven humor, the deceptively simple cartoon actually holds up a mirror to a lot of what works and (more often than not) what doesn't in our culture.

In one of my favorite episodes, Homer Simpson's boss, Montgomery Burns, realizes that despite all of his wealth and power, nobody really likes him. To remedy this, he embarks on a full-on charm offensive—as much as Monty Burns can, anyway—around Springfield to try to win people over.

When he gets to Homer, he pulls out all of the stops, offering to take him to Scotland on a trip. But clearly, Burns's efforts with Homer won't be easy. At one point, they're talking in Homer's car, and Homer notes that he's not one to be easily impressed. Immediately afterward, his eyes bulge (I know they always bulge, but more than normal), and he points out the driver-side window, mouth agape.

"Woah," he shouts, "a blue car!"

It's easy to sit back and laugh with a little bit of pity or contempt for the hapless, simple-minded Homer, but the reason it's funny is because we all have a little bit of Homer Simpson in us. We all have our blue cars that take our eyes off the road, despite the fact that we're pretty sure we are intently focused on the important things in life.

Hell, just as I was thinking about what to write in this section of the chapter, I grabbed my phone for a quick round of Toon Blast. Smirk if you want, but I guarantee I'm further along in the game than you, buddy.

It isn't easy to stay focused and not let the petty stuff of daily life become the things that define our days and end up pushing us apart. It's so easy to become "of the world" while trying just to be in it. But our real strength and source of greater impact comes from clinging to, and cultivating, the bonds that are greater than the sum total of our differences. We may not always be good at it, but God will help, if only we'll ask.

Prayer for the Week

I'm not so good at the spiritual discipline of staying focused on the big things that matter most, God. Help me pull my own head out of wherever it's stuck when I'm bogged down in the small stuff.

Popping Off

Art/music/video and other cool stuff that relate to the text

"Woah, a Blue Car!" scene from *The Simpsons*, season 10, episode 21 (TV series, 1989–)

"The Fall of the Berlin Wall in 1989" (YouTube video): http://tinyurl.com/y456um4a

The Moron Test

Lectionary Texts For

February 2, 2020 (Fourth Sunday after Epiphany)

Texts in Brief

My dog ate my Bible!

First Reading

Micah 6:1–8

During the first part of this text, the prophet is speaking on behalf of God, who is mourning the fact that God's people are straying in their devotion. God questions their good treatment to this point, reminding them of the many times they have been spared under divine protection and wondering why their faith is faltering in spite of this long-standing providence. The author then shifts to speaking for the Israelites, hypothetically asking God what they have to do to get right again with God, to which the author says they already know what is required: do justice, love kindness, and walk humbly with God.

Psalm

Psalm 15

The psalmist basically asks a question, and then answers their own question. They posit what is necessary to be fitting for God's presence, and though the answer is more detailed, it reflects the same virtues outlined at the end of the Micah text.

Second Reading

1 Corinthians 1:18–31

Paul must be getting tired of people looking for God in all the wrong places, because he's critiquing both Jews and non-Jews in their attempts to get to God through the wrong means. While the Greeks tend to take a more scholarly, intellectual approach to knowing God, the Israelites tend to ask for divine signs of God's presence in order to believe. But Paul says that the story of Jesus, which culminates at the cross, is the only sign and is all the wisdom that we need. Faith for the sake of itself is what God requires.

Gospel

Matthew 5:1–12

In one of his most famous sermons, Jesus offers what we now call the Beatitudes, or blessings for God's beloved people. He is "flipping the script" for all of those who seem to have it rough during this life, because God's light and mercy will shine on them in God's heavenly presence. So while this is comforting to the poor, suffering, and marginalized "others," it's also a veiled warning to the prosperous and comfortable that their success on earth is no indication of being in God's favor.

Bible, Decoded
Breaking down Scripture in plain language

Balak/Balaam—Balak, king of the territory called Moab, recruits Balaam (a mystic known for the power of his blessings and curses) to curse the Israelites so they won't be successful in a possible invasion of his land. God comes to Balaam and says he can only speak the words God gives him to say to Balak. At the moment Balak expects Balaam to curse Israel, he actually offers blessings on Israel. After Balak tells Balaam to get lost, Balaam tells Balak that one day the Israelites will defeat him.

Shittim to Gilgal—This is a reminder to the Israelites of the safety God offered them in crossing the Jordan from enemy-occupied territory over to the land of Canaan, where they would eventually be able to settle.

Points to Ponder
First Thoughts

I'm not a big fan of the country song "Jesus, Take the Wheel," but that's kind of what Balaam does in the Micah text. Yes, he has incredibly powerful gifts, but the key to his power is actually surrender. It's counterintuitive—much like most of the claims in these passages—but it's what God asks for.

It's interesting that Micah outlines three simple steps to a relationship with God so long before Jesus's "greatest commandment" comes along. So maybe it's not that God required so many rules to be followed, but then had a change of heart; maybe we're the ones that needed help getting untangled from our self-made theological mess.

Digging Deeper

Mining for what really matters . . . and gold

How do we come to know God? The short answer, according to the Scripture this week from 1 Corinthians, is that we don't. There's nothing we can do to finally "get it." And while Paul talks about the "foolishness of the cross," in a way, the real foolishness is in our efforts to try to understand the true nature of the Divine.

It's a lot like the old adage that the more we learn, the less we actually know. Rather than becoming masters of the material and metaphysical worlds through our intellectual prowess, real learning actually leads us to a deep level of humility about how incredibly little we actually understand. In expanding our reach, we actually become relatively small in the midst of an ever-growing universe of ideas, information, and inscrutable mystery.

In this respect, the cross itself, or rather the crucifixion, isn't foolish. Paul isn't saying that Jesus was ridiculous for having submitted himself to everything he endured. It's a typically biblical subversion of the status quo: the wise become fools, the mountains made low, darkness invaded by light, and so on. In the Beatitudes, the lowly are the great ones, which, by contrast, implies that the great and powerful will be brought down. In the Gospel according to Luke, this is called the "great reversal."

We also have to consider, though, how absurd it really is to focus on the cross as central to the evangelism efforts of the early church. It would be a little bit like trying to convince someone today that the essence of God's grace for humanity can be found in an electric chair. Most people find symbols of violence repulsive, so why in the world would we focus on a gruesome instrument of death and torture to share what we claim is good news?

It's what God does with the cross that is the real miracle. The amazing thing about the cross is that God takes our violence and turns it into mercy. God uses our bloodshed and channels it into an outpouring of love. Our darkness becomes God's light. Everything is turned on its end.

It's beautiful, confounding, and a little bit crazy. But if it was what we were already expecting, it wouldn't exactly be news, would it?

Heads-Up

Connecting the text to our world

My son decided today he was going to give me something he found online called the "Moron Test." Basically, it consists of a handful of questions that are deceptively simple, and the tendency is to overthink them rather than see the obvious answer right in front of us.

For example, one of the questions went along the lines of, "There are red, green and yellow buttons in front of you. Your goal is to press the red button twice, the green button twice, and the yellow button fourth. How do you do it?" Apparently lots of us will assume that we have to push the red and green buttons twice in a row (even though it doesn't say that), which of course makes pushing the yellow one fourth impossible.

There's something in our nature that causes us to unnecessarily complicate things and to overthink them until we're tied up in a philosophical knot. How many angels fit on the head of a pin? Whose doctrine of Communion is consistent with ancient church practice? Is the resurrection a literal event or does it represent something symbolic?

According to Paul, God is not impressed with our intellectual acrobatics and big, fancy words. Sucks for us writers, no?

It reminds me of the character Otto in a movie from the eighties titled *A Fish Called Wanda*. Though Otto fancies himself an intellectual, he isn't actually as bright as he tries to make everyone think he is. Sure, he can spout off a few literary quotes here and there, but if anyone looks just below the surface, they'll realize he isn't the brightest bulb in the chandelier.

Otto's ego is incredibly fragile, too. If anyone calls him "stupid," he loses his mind. That's because they have seen through his ruse. He is at risk of being found out for the fraud he really is. And such is the case, apparently, with so many who try to find more complex or sensational ways into a relationship with God.

The problem for a lot of us with faith is that we can't seem to accept that God's longing for us—and expression of it through the life and death of Jesus—is so simple. Micah says it, but we figure we're smarter than that and that there must be more to it than doing justice, loving kindness, and walking humbly through our lives with God.

But what if it's not? Grace can't be logically sorted out. God may not be sending any lightning bolts to rattle you into being faithful. You have all you need, say the texts. Don't end up being your own stumbling block.

Prayer for the Week

God, help me stay out of my own way and remind me that making things more complicated doesn't necessarily make them better.

Popping Off

Art/music/video and other cool stuff that relate to the text

"What Was the Middle Thing?" scene from *A Fish Called Wanda* (movie, 1988)

The Moron Test: www.TheMoronTest.com

Do "Sorry," Don't Say It

Lectionary Texts For

February 9, 2020 (Fifth Sunday after Epiphany)

Texts in Brief

My dog ate my Bible!

First Reading

Isaiah 58:1–9a (9b–12)

Isaiah is sharing God's dissatisfaction with the empty rituals and religiosity of the Israelites. While they do all the right things on the surface, they're not living in the spirit of what God intends (which we outlined from Micah last week). Though God hears their supplications and wailings about their burdens not being eased, God notes that their problems will lessen when they find it in their hearts to show the kind of provision and mercy to the least among them that God has shown them.

Psalm

Psalm 112:1–9 (10)

The psalmist's message can be summarized largely in the first verse. God's people aren't only to follow God's laws; they are to do so with a glad heart. If we say all the right things and perform the religious acts but with an empty heart, and if we don't allow the spirit of those commands to change how we act in the world, they're pointless.

Second Reading

1 Corinthians 2:1–12 (13–16)

Paul continues his contrast of human wisdom and spiritual, or divine, wisdom from the first chapter of 1 Corinthians. Maybe most striking is when he says that, had the authorities allowed themselves to discern Jesus's message on a level of spirit, and not intellect, they never would have crucified him in the first place. He continues by saying we will remain fallow with respect to spiritual gifts unless we practice spiritual discernment. Only then do we develop the fertile ground God requires to implant gifts of the spirit God desires for us.

Gospel

Matthew 5:13–20

Although Jesus has been described in recent weeks as the light of the world, here he is describing us as not just bearing that light but being it. In describing us as salt and light, he likens us to simple things that are of little use on their own; only once they are combined with something else do they realize their full value. The simplicity of these basic elements aside, we are charged with cultivating them and bringing them into their full potential within us. And he emphasizes that calling us to this isn't a heretical call to replace the old religious laws; rather, this is what the ancient prophets like Isaiah meant about right-heartedness and manifesting these spiritual gifts in our works.

Bible, Decoded

Breaking down Scripture in plain language

Salt/Light—You might have heard the phrase "familiarity breeds contempt." Given that we have on-demand light every minute of the day and given that our food today is saturated with loads of sodium, it's easy to lose the context of these symbols—salt and light—back in Jesus's day. When it got dark back then, unless you had the money for lots of oil, you were stuck in darkness. It was basically disabling until sunlight mercifully returned. Likewise, salt wasn't pre-injected into every meal and wasn't available by the pound in everyone's cupboard. It was a precious commodity that many people had limited access to. So these things would have been more special.

Sackcloth and Ashes—These were symbols used in ancient Jewish culture to express humiliation and repentance. Sackcloth was kind of like burlap today. It was made from goat hair and was coarse and really uncomfortable. Someone expressing themselves in an act of repentance—often done in a time of national crisis, which would have been seen as a result of God's anger—would usually sit in a pile of ashes, pouring some ash over their heads.

Points to Ponder

First Thoughts

The prophets seem to take the tough-love approach when it comes to their messages. Either they are coming down hard on their people for screwing up, or they're offering heartfelt hope during times of hardship, assuring the people that if they stay the course, things will get better. This is definitely one of those passages that falls in the former category.

This leads us to wonder how bad things really are at the church in Corinth by this point. Yes, we know from last week that there are lots of little factions arguing among themselves, but every community goes through things like that. But maybe it's getting worse than that. It could be that Paul recognizes the potential for this whole movement to start to fall apart if his fellow Jesus-followers don't keep their priorities straight.

How they got there, most likely, is by doing exactly what Jesus warns against in Matthew. We push those inherent gifts aside given to us from birth by God, opting instead for the skills and other things that the world seems to value more. But this leads us exactly in the direction the ancients foresee: toward division, struggle, and unnecessary, self-imposed darkness.

Digging Deeper

Mining for what really matters . . . and gold

This Gospel reading, most commonly known as the Sermon on the Mount, is one of Jesus's most famous monologues. It's also in the classic style of Jewish teaching, which helps to solidify his authority as a leader among his people.

The fact that he is described as being on a mountain is more of symbolic importance than anything to be taken literally. First of all, I've been to the region where Jesus spent much of his time in ministry, and it's not exactly the Rockies. In fact, several of the specific so-called mountains named in Scripture are little more than hills, at best. The fact that the setting is described as a mountain means that what's happening is important and that we should pay attention.

It also is meant to implicitly draw a connection between Jesus, Moses, Elijah, and the other great prophets, who often were described as coming down from mountains when they had wisdom to share from God.

Regarding the content of what Jesus says, this excerpt outlines all of the key elements he will address throughout his three years of active ministry. It's an outline of sorts for what is coming.

The audience for this sermon grows as it progresses. While it starts out only in the company of his immediate disciples, there is a larger crowd by the end. So the wisdom he is sharing is attractive; it compels people to draw closer to him because there's something about it that rings powerfully true on a deep level, beyond your traditional intellectual sort of knowing.

As noted above, the salt reference is important, particularly when said to his closest followers. Salt on its own is of little worth; it's only once it is added to something bigger that it comes to life and realizes its true potential. Likewise, light that doesn't shine on anything is relatively pointless. In this way, he's urging them not to get too comfortable in their close-knit tribe. Their job is to go out and plow new ground, so to speak, among those who they don't yet know.

Jesus rounds out his message by adding some context to his points. While his ideas aren't directly found in the ancient Torah, none of this is a repudiation of anything said there. Rather, his issue is more with how people interpret the old laws, focusing on the words, the rituals, and such rather than allowing God's law to thoroughly transform us.

Heads-Up

Connecting the text to our world

If I had a nickel for every time my kids say "I'm sorry," I'd be driving a Tesla instead of a used Nissan. They get to where they say it so much after getting off track or making a bad choice that I start to wonder if they even realize they're saying it anymore.

Of course there's only one real way to know, and that way tells me the "I'm sorrys" are ringing a little bit hollow.

More than nine times out of ten, nothing changes in their behavior after an "I'm sorry." In fact, sometimes they're doing the exact same thing again within a matter of minutes. And nothing says "I'm not really sorry" like not changing your behavior.

There's a long-standing debate within Christianity about the role of "good works" in our faith practices. In particular, following the Protestant Reformation five centuries ago, there was an emerging emphasis on salvation by grace rather than by works. This means that there is nothing we can do to earn God's mercy. It is given without condition because God determined it to be that way.

The problem with that is that a lot of Christians take that to mean that all we have to do is ask for forgiveness, regardless of what we did or didn't do, and we are all straight with God. To me, this is the religious equivalent of the empty "I'm sorry" that I get from my kids.

Granted, grace isn't something we can earn. If it was, it wouldn't be grace. It would be something more like a spiritual paycheck. But the outward changes are a reflection of deeper inner transformation taking place. So while just doing good works isn't the point, neither is empty prayer, going to church, or any other action unless the heart behind it is tuned into that spiritual drumbeat that calls us to greater union with the heart of God.

One day after the thousandth "I'm sorry," I stopped one of my kids and looked them in the eye. "Stop saying 'I'm sorry' to me," I told them, which caught them by surprise. "Do 'I'm sorry.' Show the change of heart you're claiming. And if you're not there yet, spend some time on that necessary heart work before letting your mouth get ahead of you."

Prayer for the Week

God, I know sometimes I say "I'm sorry" when I'm not actually doing "I'm sorry." I'll keep working on it.

Popping Off

Art/music/video and other cool stuff that relate to the text

Shawshank Redemption (movie, 1994)

Schindler's List (movie, 1993)

Un-Helicopter Parent

Lectionary Texts For

February 16, 2020 (Sixth Sunday after Epiphany)

Texts in Brief

My dog ate my Bible!

First Reading

Deuteronomy 30:15–20

Before the Israelites cross the Jordan into free territory, God offers a stark warning: love and obey me, and life will be long and abundant; stray from me and cling to false gods, and this won't last. This is the land God has promised to the descendants of Abraham, Isaac, and Jacob (a.k.a., the Israelites), but it's on them to make the covenant work.

Psalm

Psalm 119:1–8

The psalmist is echoing the sentiments from Deuteronomy, recognizing that goodness comes to those who follow God's commands. They then vow to do this, asking in return that God will not abandon them.

Second Reading

1 Corinthians 3:1–9

Because of the division and conflict he sees within the people of the Corinthian church, Paul likens them to the spiritual equivalent of babies. And like little children, they want more, which he says he can't give them until they've gotten a firmer grasp on the basics. He points out that although each of them claims various allegiances to spiritual leaders among them, all of those leaders are from the same source: God. So, he suggests, they should worry less about which person to follow and focus more on following the whole reason they came together in this mission in the first place.

Gospel

Matthew 5:21–37

Jesus pushes the religious envelope this week by doing the ancient commandments "one better." He goes through a series of "The Scripture says . . . but I say . . ." phrases, urging those listening to do more than follow the letter of the ancient law. They should also have a dramatic change of heart, until they get to the point that their actions no longer have to be directed by the written law because their heart guides them even more deeply toward the spirit behind the words.

Bible, Decoded

Breaking down Scripture in plain language

Abraham, Isaac, and Jacob—In the story of Abraham, God comes to him and promises him that his descendants will be as numerous as the stars. He is to be the start of the bloodline for all of the Israelites. All twelve tribes of Israel are descended from him and his family (including his son Isaac and Isaac's son Jacob).

Apollos—One of the original church leaders in Corinth. Given his name, he likely came from Greece. This might explain why there were factions divided between Paul's less scholarly, intellectual teaching and that of Apollos, who comes from the cradle of Western civilization, where much of modern philosophy originated.

Points to Ponder

First Thoughts

Although the letter in 1 Corinthians is attributed to the apostle Paul, note that it refers to him in third person midway through. This is because someone else most likely wrote this (and probably many or all of the other letters) on his behalf. The degree to which Paul had direct involvement in the creation of each letter is unknown, since it was also common practice to put someone's name on something as more of an honorific if the content was in the spirit of what they had said before. It doesn't necessarily mean they wrote it down, though.

It's important to understand the rhetorical technique of hyperbole that Jesus is using in the Gospel text. He doesn't actually want people to carve their eyeballs out if they stare too long at the pretty lady in the tunic. He's trying to make a point, which is that if you have habits, places, or cultural norms in which you find yourself slipping from gospel teaching, make a real change.

Digging Deeper

Mining for what really matters . . . and gold

In Jesus's recent teaching in Matthew, he's hit on a couple of important themes more than once:

First, ritual alone doesn't cut it. God doesn't need to be worshipped so much as God requires faithfulness and a transformed way of living.

Second, being in religious community is not the same as serving the least among you. In other words, just being nice to the guy at the church coffee bar on Sunday morning isn't as appealing to God as actively serving the poor and marginalized.

By now we've gotten that, but there's something more revealing here. Jesus is taking huge risks by urging people to take personal responsibility for their own morality and ethics. Aside from offering what opponents could—and will—easily argue is heresy against existing doctrine, he's largely discounting the authority of religious authorities on how God's grace is given.

If we think about it, it's this kind of talk that spells the beginning of the end for Jesus, even though this is still very early in his ministry. This serves not only as a religious disruption of the status quo but as a political disruption as well. Bear in mind that given the reality that Roman imperial forces are spread out all over the place, they have to depend on more localized systems to maintain order. This only works if the local authority figures agree to serve as the Roman proxy force, in exchange, of course, for special privilege and favor.

And what better way to control people than through religion?

It's not so much that it takes a lot of force most of the time to maintain this political-religious order, either. As Paul recognizes, people are all too eager to find a leader in their midst, but we see where that leads.

In the Deuteronomy text and the Gospel, we're presented with a starkly binary choice: live or die. Of course, given our modern Western sensibilities, we tend to individualize and personalize this, assuming it's talking about our own individual life. While I'm not discounting that exactly (though I think there's a difference between not truly living and no longer being alive, which is important to distinguish), we have to consider the way people thought back when these passages were written.

The communal collective was far more important than the individual, by and large. In fact, when sin is discussed in the Bible, it's often referring to a collective falling-short more than a single person's sin. Considered this way, we can see the physical manifestation of these life-or-death propositions taking form in Paul's letter to the Corinthians. They're clinging to authorities other than God's, and the result is inevitable death of the new community before it has even reached a more mature state of self-sufficiency.

We're still given a choice in this new model that no longer requires an intercessor to make us do the right thing. But people like Jesus and Paul trust that we will ultimately err on the side of faith and love, namely because they already have when it comes to us.

Heads-Up

Connecting the text to our world

We humans will destroy ourselves and our communities of our own volition given enough of a deficiency of foresight. Consider the debates about the impending environmental crisis or the fallout from the 2008 housing crisis, both of which stem from our attention getting diverted from what is truly right and onto false gods like consumption, greed, comfort, and immediacy.

Why doesn't God just slam on the brakes and set us straight again? Why would a loving God allow us to screw ourselves up so royally?

It's because that's what any good parent does, painful as it may be. As the father of two kids of my own, I know this struggle all too well. Anyone who has helped raise children can tell you how incredibly hard it is to finally let go and allow your kids to make their own choices and suffer their own consequences. The worst is when you see them steering themselves into a brick wall—hopefully not literally—and everything in you is inclined to jump in and keep them from making the mistake.

Sometimes, especially if the kid is still learning, or if the consequences are too grave, we still may end up getting involved to try and change outcomes. In the short term it may feel like we've done the right thing.

But over time, we tend to second-guess ourselves, wondering if our efforts to rescue are the familial equivalent of keeping our children emotional babies, like Paul talks about.

Sometimes we have to learn the hard way, or we'll never really gain the wisdom that can come from making it out on the other side of the bad choice. It sucks to watch, and it's no party to live through either. All the same, we all do it. The best thing we can do as caregivers is to give the kids we love all of the tools they need to have the best chance at success. Then they have to find their own imperfectly beautiful way to navigate through the world.

That's love.

Prayer for the Week

God, I'd ask you to keep me on the right path, but I guess that's my job. You've given me the tools; help me remember to use them wisely.

Popping Off

Art/music/video and other cool stuff that relate to the text

"Smart," from *Where the Sidewalk Ends,* by Shel Silverstein (book, 1974)

Parenthood (movie, 1989)

Takes Change to Make Change

Lectionary Texts For
February 23, 2020 (Transfiguration Sunday)

Texts in Brief
My dog ate my Bible!

First Reading
Exodus 24:12–18

God tells Moses to leave the Israelites he has led out of Egypt and go up to the top of Mount Sinai in order to receive the new Hebrew law. A cloud covers the mountain for a week before God speaks to Moses, calling him to the mountain's top, where he spends forty days with God.

Psalm
Psalm 99

This is a psalm of praise offered to God on behalf of the people under King David's rule. The so-called "City of David" is built on a mountain called Zion, which is where this psalm says the lord is particularly mighty. The psalm continues by recounting that this is the same God who led the Israelites out of bondage in Egypt under Moses.

SECOND READING
2 Peter 1:16–21

Peter asserts that their faith in Jesus being who he said he was is not based on hearsay or any other sort of word-of-mouth sensationalism. Instead, he says, he and his associates (in this case, James and John) witnessed the miraculous nature of Jesus in person. They also claim to have heard Jesus speak to them when they witnessed the event described in this week's Gospel text on top of a holy mountain.

GOSPEL
Matthew 17:1–9

Jesus takes Peter, James, and John with him up a mountain, where he transforms into a dazzling white figure, joined in brilliance by Moses and the prophet Elijah. Peter is in such awe that he asks Jesus if they can set up camp and live here in this holy place, but Jesus tells them their work is back down the mountain among the rest of the people. On their way back down, Jesus tells them not to tell anyone what they have seen until after he dies and is resurrected.

Bible, Decoded
Breaking down Scripture in plain language

Aaron and Hur—Both men are companions of Moses who have helped him in the past. When the Israelites were in a battle with the Amalekites and God told Moses his people would keep winning as long as he held up his hands, Aaron and Hur held his hands up for him when he got tired. Once again they're backing him up as proxy leaders while he is with God on Sinai.

Forty—The number forty often represents periods of being lost or adrift in the Bible, like when Noah survived the great flood that lasted forty days. It also reflects the period of exile in the desert (a "lost time") of the Israelites after their exile from Egypt. So this is generally a time of transition or great change that is coming but isn't yet complete.

Seven—This number is considered in Scripture to be the number of God, principally because of the Genesis story in which God rested on the seventh day after completing creation.

Points to Ponder

First Thoughts

While there are speculations about on which mountain the transfiguration took place, it's never explained in the Bible. Some scholars argue it is likely Mount Hermon, namely because some events prior to this in the Gospels take place there, plus it's the highest mountain in the region, standing at nearly ten thousand feet.

The event in Matthew is part of multiple so-called "Messianic secrets" in the Gospels. These are times when something happens, but Jesus tells those with him not to tell other people. While there are many times when he performs miracles in front of people who don't know him yet, they are generally done as acts of compassion rather than to prove he is the son of God. This is likely because he wants people to believe simply because of who he is, not because of what he can do for them.

Digging Deeper

Mining for what really matters . . . and gold

There are several worthwhile areas we could focus on this week. First, there's the matter of so many things happening on top of mountains. No, this isn't because God gets better reception when we're up high. It's because these places are special and set apart. It might also be because people felt that God was above them in heaven, so being on top of a mountain did get them closer to God. There's also the fact that it takes intentional work to get up there. No one just accidentally happens across the top of a mountain; you have to want to get there.

So when something takes place on a mountain in the Bible, it's begging for our attention, because something special is happening.

Next, while there's commonality in all of these things happening on mountaintops, there's also an important distinction to be made among the three stories in Exodus, Psalms, and Matthew. Each of these accounts depicts some sort of covenant, or holy promise, between God and humanity. In Exodus, the covenant forged on Mount Sinai is based on the law. In the psalm, the covenant (though not specifically explained here) on Zion is between God and David, as this is where God wants David's city to be built. This time, though, the covenant isn't one of law; it's a covenant based on grace.

Finally, we have the bond forged in the Gospel text. Jesus shares something very special and revelatory with his disciples but binds them to secrecy. This time, the covenant is based on real, human relationship.

If we consider this, it's a sort of Holy Trinity of sacred connection with God.

You may be wondering what this has to do with transfiguration. I tend to think of the "transfiguration event" a little bit differently than I've heard it taught before. Some focus on this being evidence that Jesus is holy. Others focus on the secret part, emphasizing the importance of faith being based on something other than visible signs of the miraculous. Still others talk more about our tendency, like Peter, to find something sacred and want to keep it all to ourselves, or to remain in retreat from the challenges of daily life.

But let's consider what's really going on with Jesus. It's not really explained, nor does it seem to serve any real practical purpose. No fishes and loaves, no dead being raised . . . not even any water to wine! I noted elsewhere when thinking about Jesus's baptism that it's the only place in the Bible when God, Jesus, and the Holy Spirit all come together.

But what if it's not?

We know Jesus is transfigured, but into what we're not sure. Maybe his companions in white can give us a clue. Jesus, who is a real flesh-and-blood person in relationship with Peter, John, and James, is joined by Moses, whose bond with God is one based on the law, as we noted. Elijah is a great prophet, so maybe his role is to hand over authority now to Jesus as the patriarch prophet of the faith. And remember that prophets don't get their gifts by way of the law. Like David, they receive their blessings from God by grace alone.

So we have all three expressions of God here, especially if we consider "God the father" to be representative of the god of laws. Elijah can be an expression of the holy spirit, who is an expression of God's grace in our midst. And both of these expressions now come together in Jesus, the man who embodies them all.

Yes, Jesus is transfigured, but it's because God is the very essence of transfiguration. God is change, and any encounter with God evokes similarly radical change in those who bear witness. If Jesus is, indeed, God in the flesh, then the event of transfiguration isn't really that remarkable. What's more important is that his transfiguration has a transforming effect on James, John, and Peter. They can't unsee this, can't unknow it about Jesus. But by taking part in it, they are part of the ongoing transformation God is intent on in the world. As long as they come down from the mountaintop, they have the opportunity to pass that transformation along to everyone they meet.

Heads-Up

Connecting the text to our world

My wife, Amy, had a theology professor who used to drop little rhetorical gems on his classes, sometimes without entirely explaining them. One of my favorites that he tossed out there one day was "It takes change to make change." The way the phrases would just hang there was a little bit like a parable in that they would be illuminating, but we just weren't always sure what exactly was having light shed on it.

I've thought about that one a lot since then. I've decided that what he meant was, in order for change to come about in the world, we have to change personally first. In other words, transformation or transfiguration is an inside-out job.

I can't exactly endeavor to make the world into a kinder and more compassionate place if I'm not willing to become kinder and more compassionate myself.

If I want to see greater acts of charity in my community, I should most likely start by being more charitable.

If it were possible, I think I'd prefer a world in which I could just direct the kind of change I think we all need, while not having to do the grinding soul-work of taking such a mandate on myself. But even if this wasn't what her professor meant, he's still right:

It takes change to make change.

Prayer for the Week

Help me remember that part of my covenant with you is to allow myself to keep changing because you are change, God.

Popping Off

Art/music/video and other cool stuff that relate to the text

"Up to the Mountain," by Patty Griffin (song, 2007)

The Sacred Mountain (Parahi te marae), by Paul Gauguin (painting, 1892)

Road
Not Taken

Lectionary Texts For
March 1, 2020 (First Sunday in Lent)

Texts in Brief
My dog ate my Bible!

First Reading
Genesis 2:15–17, 3:1–7

God warns Adam against eating from the tree of the knowledge of good and evil, or he'll end up dying. A serpent tells Adam and Eve that they won't die if they eat from it but instead will know the mind of God, and their eyes will be opened. They eat from the tree, their eyes are opened, and they realize they're naked and cover themselves in shame.

Psalm
Psalm 32

The passage is an expression of relief for having been unburdened of their sins. The author recalls how they were consumed with guilt when they failed to come to God in humble search of forgiveness. The burden was thankfully lifted once they asked. It notes that God is both teacher and protector to all, and that we shouldn't let our stubbornness get in the way of asking to be forgiven.

Second Reading
Romans 5:12–19

Paul observes that if God can forgive Adam, our forgiveness should be relatively simple. After all, Paul suggests, by introducing death into the world, the deaths of everyone since then are on Adam's head. Then Paul contrasts the condemnation of all through Adam with the salvation of all through Jesus.

Gospel
Matthew 4:1–11

At the end of Jesus's forty days of solitude in the desert, the devil appears and tempts Jesus to use his power for himself, which Jesus rejects. He then urges Jesus to test God's devotion to him, to which Jesus quotes the Scripture about not testing God. Finally, the devil appeals to Jesus's greed, offering him the world if he will worship the devil. When he rejects this, the devil leaves and angels appear.

Bible, Decoded
Breaking down Scripture in plain language

Selah—A word indicating a holy pause from reading. The idea is to leave space into which the holy spirit can enter in order to inspire our reading.

Devil/Adversary/Serpent—There are a lot of words used throughout Scripture to describe different evil forces or inclinations. More important than what name is used and the theology behind the notions of existential evil spirits is how the evil involved appears to work. Note that nothing is forced by an outside "other." Instead, it is the impulses or desires already existent in the person that are stoked. So whether we believe evil exists "out there," "in here," or is some combination of the two, it lacks any agency, at least in these texts, absent human agency and will.

Points to Ponder

First Thoughts

The way I think of the story this week in Genesis 2 is that it is the day humanity lost our innocence. The serpent didn't entirely lie to Adam and Eve. It told them their eyes would be opened, and they were. But when we are innocent and naïve, we don't yet realize the implications of that. Knowing evil in the way it came to us wasn't exactly a welcome ability.

It's interesting that in the psalm, the asking for forgiveness is not being done for God's sake. God isn't the one bearing the burden for the transgression. Considering this, humbling ourselves and asking God for forgiveness is an important act of self-care.

It seems convenient in the Romans text to blame Adam for all of our woes, but I think we have to be careful not to defer responsibility. While the story of Adam may be the prototype of sin in our faith tradition, part of the healing process with respect to sin and forgiveness is taking personal responsibility. While it would be nice, I don't think saying "I'm sorry, Adam made me do it" is what is necessary.

Digging Deeper

Mining for what really matters . . . and gold

This Romans text is a tough one this week. It's been used by lots of theologians in different ways to assert Christian doctrine. In particular, Augustine employed this letter to assert what we call the doctrine of original sin. In a nutshell, this doctrine says that we all are bound to sin ever since Adam because (at the risk of sounding like a third-grader) he started it. Therefore we can't help but sin since Adam messed it up and set us all on this course of inevitable transgression.

Poor Adam. All for some fruit! If only my kids were so eager to eat whole foods.

In all seriousness, this one concept has led to an awful lot of things in Christianity that have been very harmful. For one, there's the idea that our sins somehow aren't entirely our own responsibility. It's like we're deferring partial blame on some guy named Adam, who may or may not have ever literally existed. Either way, anything that allows us to shrug off full responsibility for our choices doesn't avail us in full to the potential for healing through divine forgiveness.

Second, we have movements in Christianity that emerged from leaders like Calvin who point to such texts and contend that we human beings are inherently depraved. Said another way, we're fundamentally inclined toward wickedness instead of being inclined to goodness.

If ever there was an ideal formula for individual and collective self-hatred, there it is.

I think we've missed the mark with all of this. Consider the stories in Genesis and Matthew as a study in contrasts. In both cases, temptations creep in, and in both cases, they are very real. Actually, maybe we should say the temptation bubbles up, because while both narratives portray evil as some external adversarial force, we're self-aware enough to admit by now that we have the capacity for evil within us all the time. This is driven by both a basic instinct for self-preservation and also the insatiable appetite of the ego.

Though these stories were written many centuries apart, the adversary character is remarkably consistent. This is because each of us contends with our own desires, no matter the culture, age, gender, or economic status. But just because it's inextricably part of each of us doesn't mean we get to shrug our shoulders and blindly follow anywhere it leads.

The difference between these stories is in the decision made by the person involved: consent versus resistance. In standing firm in resistance to his desire, Jesus didn't kill it forever. Like the story says, it just retreated for the time being. It was temporarily weakened but not forever beaten. From then on, though, Jesus knew he was in control of his own desires, or at least how he responded to them.

It brings to mind the Robert Frost poem "The Road Not Taken," in which he offers the now-famous lines:

Two roads diverged in a wood, and I—
I took the one less traveled by,

And that has made all the difference.

We always have more than one road when it comes to desire. The one we choose makes all the difference.

Heads-Up

Connecting the text to our world

I'm not in a twelve-step program, but I have more than enough addicts in my life to know my way around the twelve steps. One thing some people misunderstand about how groups like Alcoholics Anonymous approach addiction is that they don't let the addict off the hook. I've heard it argued that if you call alcoholism a disease, you're divesting yourself of your own choices.

Far from it.

The truth is that some people can drink and will never feel the compulsion to keep going. They can stop and walk away. Others come into the disease gradually, wading in incrementally until they suddenly realize they're drowning. Still others will know they're hooked the moment they open that first beer. It's chemical, neurological, emotional, and psychological. But there's no debating that the substances in question affect us differently.

If we think of sin as a sort of disease we're all born with, I think it's a helpful corollary. No, I can't help having this thing as a part of me, but how I respond to it is on me. If I have a cold, I can either rest, drink fluids, and dose up on vitamins, or I can eat junk food, pound a six pack of soda, and stay up all night with friends.

I don't owe my body any apologies for getting sick sometimes; it happens. But if I mistreat my body, especially when my immune system is compromised, I owe my body a big, fat "I'm sorry."

Then I have to go about mitigating the damage I've done with my choices. In twelve-step programs, the very first step is admitting you lack full control over the situation. Again, this is not a divestment of responsibility so much as it's a cry for help. We also still have to confront the reality of the harm we've done and have the humility to ask forgiveness within the twelve-step system. Notice that asking forgiveness is not the same as just saying "I'm sorry." You invite a person to offer you grace; whether they give it to you is up to them.

That's vulnerability.

The good news is whenever we come to God with the question "Can you forgive me?" the answer is always the same. It may not always be the case with other people, but the only part that's on us is admitting the transgression and asking for forgiveness. That in itself yields a great burden lifted, even if the relationship remains beyond repair.

Finally, there's no endgame in a twelve-step program. As soon as you get through step twelve, you start back over at one again. Such is the way with sin. While we're never done with it, we're all the wiser the next time such a choice comes around, and we know the grinding work ahead if we make the same choice again.

Prayer for the Week

Help me know the difference between the two roads, to be willing to own my choice, and to have the humility to admit it when I take the wrong one.

Popping Off

Art/music/video and other cool stuff that relate to the text

"The Road Not Taken," by Robert Frost (poem, 1916)

Twelve Steps and Twelve Traditions, by Bill W. (book, 1953)

Pull Me Back

Lectionary Texts For
March 8, 2020 (Second Sunday in Lent)

Texts in Brief
My dog ate my Bible!

First Reading
Genesis 12:1–4a

God told Abram to go to a land God would lead him to and that God would bless him, his descendants, and all who honored him. God promised Abram that a great nation would come from his bloodline. Abram took Lot and left his homeland and family in obedience to God.

Psalm
Psalm 121

The psalm continues in offering the assurance of protection and blessing to the nation of Israel (the nation descended from Abram) that began with the promise God made to Abram in Genesis.

Second Reading
Romans 4:1–5, 13–17

This text offers two sets of contrasting ideas. First, it clarifies that, while some things of the earth are earned through work, God's grace is not one that can be earned. It is grace simply because it is given freely and without condition. Likewise, we can't earn God's favor by adhering well enough to religious laws. As the author has seen, suggesting God's favor can be earned leads to pride, judgment of others and, more broadly, what they call *wrath*. Evidence that grace is unearned is found, the text says, in the story of Abram (who God renames "Abraham" later in his story), who is blessed beyond imagination only because God chooses to.

Gospel
John 3:1–17

Nicodemus, a Jewish religious leader, recognizes that Jesus has a special bond with God that no one else has. This, Jesus responds, is possible for those who are born of spirit and not just in physical form. Nicodemus is baffled by this, wondering if he is supposed to reenter his mother's womb to be reborn, but Jesus explains this is a different kind of birth. He claims that God's will is unbound by any other limitation, and that his special connection to God is for the purpose of leading others to a similar relationship.

Bible, Decoded

Breaking down Scripture in plain language

Son of Man—This is one of many titles used to describe Jesus in the Gospels. What exactly the title means is widely debated, but given the talk of flesh and spirit, and also given Nicodemus's recognition that he is indeed special in the spiritual sense, it could be Jesus's way of emphasizing that while he is connected uniquely to God, he is also utterly human.

Nicodemus—While Jesus often butts heads with the Pharisees, Nicodemus is somewhat of an exception. He concedes at least that Jesus is special and that he understands God in a way no one else can. Still, he is still skeptical about the things Jesus tries to teach him. So while he is further along than many of his other peers, he still struggles to let go of old ways of thinking in order to embrace this new wisdom in its entirety.

Points to Ponder

First Thoughts

It's easy to focus on the incredible blessings that God is offering to Abram in Genesis, while overlooking the gravity of what's being asked of him. God is telling him to walk away from everything he knows and loves, without even telling him exactly where he's going. Equally remarkable, at least in the way the story is told here, is how readily Abram drops everything and just goes. It's a whole lot like how the disciples respond in the Gospels when Jesus finds them and tells them to set everything aside to follow.

Oh, and let's not forget that Lot, Abram's nephew (apparently the only relative who made the guest list), goes as well just based on what Abram tells him. He didn't even get the word directly from God like Abram. Talk about faith!

I find the idea of Jesus being fully human both comforting and sometimes kind of troubling. On the one hand, it's reassuring to think about God being so intent on connecting with humanity that God wanted to fully experience the human condition. It takes the compassion of God down to a deeply empathetic level.

On the other hand, it would be convenient if Jesus wasn't human, because it also implies that if he can achieve such remarkable things in his life, so can I. If he was just God and not human, I might have more of an excuse for not getting any further along my spiritual path than I do.

Digging Deeper

Mining for what really matters . . . and gold

This week we're shifting from Matthew to the Gospel of John, which is a dramatically different read. If Matthew is the equivalent to a "Just the facts, ma'am" telling of the Gospel, John is steeped in symbols, poetic accounts, and a sometimes maddeningly indirect way of talking about things.

Just consider how Jesus responds to Nicodemus throughout the text. He doesn't answer a single thing directly. Instead, he seems to drift off into platitudes that only adjacently relate to what the Pharisee is talking about. That's the Jesus of John's Gospel for you.

But let's back up. Given that there is a ton of symbolism in John, we have to consider little details and whether they mean anything bigger. The fact that Nicodemus shows up to see Jesus could be nothing more than a demonstration of the fear Nicodemus has of being found out by his peers for his curiosity about this new rabbi. But given how much John's Gospel already has talked about dark and light up to now, we have to wonder if this is a statement about the degree of doubt Nicodemus has about Jesus, despite his earnest words.

If so, Jesus would certainly know this, which might explain why he doesn't bother responding to the empty praise from the Pharisee. This isn't to say that Nicodemus can't believe, or that he is working angles in an effort to set Jesus up. But at the least, it seems like he may have strong reservations about how legit this guy is.

Maybe this is important for us to see, though, especially in the same week when we have Abram so readily setting his entire life aside to follow God's direction. Perhaps Nicodemus's struggle or skepticism is an indication that we don't all come along at the same pace. If we did, would Thomas have had to ask to feel Jesus's wounds after the resurrection? Sometimes doubt lingers, even when much of us really wants to believe.

The hopeful ending to this segment of Scripture is in Jesus's assurance that God's relationship with the world is founded on love, not on wrath. Given the stories we have throughout the ancient texts in the Hebrew Bible, it's easy enough to go full-on John Edwards and believe we are little more than sinners in the hands of an angry God. Jesus dispels this, though, stating that the prime mover, and the connective tissue in this collective divine-human body, is love.

Refocusing on Lent through a lens of love might turn our experience on its end. Consider how this time of penance, reflection, humility, and self-sacrifice is informed by this point of view as we walk slowly but certainly toward the terribly difficult moment of crucifixion.

Heads-Up

Connecting the text to our world

My wife, Amy, was meeting with a boy in elementary school at our new church in Colorado who had decided to get baptized. And while he understood why we do baptisms, I don't think he had ever seen one done in person.

As Amy began to explain to him how the whole thing would go, his eyes got really big. "You know that if you held me under when you put me underwater," he said, "I would die."

She wasn't exactly expecting that. Instead of trying to gloss over it or explain his reservations away, she invited him to keep going. "Tell me more about what you're thinking," she said.

"Well," he said, looking down at the table, "when you put me under, my eyes are closed and I'm not breathing." He looked back up at her. "It's like I'm dead."

"Do you think I would hold you under?" she asked.

"No," he shook his head. "You'll pull me back up, and then I can open my eyes and breathe and everything again. I can come back to being alive."

"That," said Amy to him, "may be the most perfect description of what baptism is about that I've ever heard." She assured him that he was right, and that she would be with him the whole time, helping him and guiding him through. He was a little bit nervous, especially since he didn't know how to swim. But he trusted her to take care of him, so he agreed to go ahead with it.

What profound faith that little guy showed. He was venturing into the unknown, into something where he would be utterly vulnerable and dependent on someone else to care for him to bring him back after he was lowered into the waters. He trusted because he had faith that she cared about him.

Maybe more important than that was that he knew he was worth saving.

Prayer for the Week

This being reborn thing is an ongoing process. It's entering into darkness, where I'm helpless and a little bit lost. But I'll try as long as you'll find me.

Popping Off

Art/music/video and other cool stuff that relate to the text

"Nicodemus, the Mystery Man of Holy Week," from *The Washington Post* (article, March 17, 2013)

Study for Christ and Nicodemus on a Rooftop, by Henry Ossawa Tanner (painting, 1923)

Lent Is Weird

Lectionary Texts For
March 15, 2020 (Third Sunday in Lent)

Texts in Brief
My dog ate my Bible!

First Reading
Exodus 17:1–7

The Israelites get really thirsty along the way to the new promised land and protest to Moses about it. They get mad enough that Moses appeals to God for help. God orders him to take some elders and the staff he used to strike the Nile river, go ahead of the group, and strike a rock, which will then produce water.

Psalm
Psalm 95

The psalmist refers to God as the "rock of salvation," claiming God is king above all other gods. Then the voice switches to God speaking, warning people not to test God as the Israelites had done. God claims here that, because of their faithless complaints, the Israelites are required to wander the desert for forty years before settling in the land promised to them.

SECOND READING
Romans 5:1–11

The first emphasis is that it is our faith alone, and nothing else, that allows us access to God's grace. Further, we are cautioned to live with a grateful heart even when we struggle or suffer, since enduring these hard times sharpens our character and resolve. This, in turn, is our source of hope beyond circumstances. One of our greatest sources of hope is in knowing God loves us completely and sacrificially, even when we don't love God back.

GOSPEL
John 4:5–42

Jesus asks a Samaritan woman for a drink at a well. She is surprised that he would speak to her since he is Jewish and Samaritans are considered unclean. Through their conversation, it becomes clear that he knows of her checkered past, and yet, she comes to believe he is the Messiah. She goes to tell others about him, at which point the disciples return to him with food. He explains that this is where they need to minister. Some people come to believe Jesus is who he says he is based on the woman's testimony, and others believe after hearing from him directly. They stay there to evangelize for two days.

Bible, Decoded
Breaking down Scripture in plain language

Rephidim—One of the sites where the Israelites camp following their exodus from Egypt. While there, they are attacked by the Amalekites, but the Israelites (led by Joshua) overcome them. The origins of the name are questionable, but most understand the name Rephidim to mean something along the lines of *support*, *rest*, or *refreshment*.

Massah and Meribah—Translates as *proving and strife*, given that this is where the Israelites test God. Because of this lack of faith that God will sustain them, they undergo four decades of struggle in the wilderness.

Sychar—The name can mean either *liar* or *drunk*. We can assume, given the history of the woman Jesus talks to, that this is a reference to the character of the people living there. Not exactly the most upstanding people in society. On top of that, they're not Jewish either, which should make them people to avoid anyway, according to Jewish law.

Points to Ponder
First Thoughts

We see an example this week of God's chosen people being held to a higher standard than non-Jews are. This isn't necessarily because God sets conditions on the Israelites that don't apply to anyone else. Rather, the Israelites have experienced God's mercy, grace, and protection firsthand, so this lack of faith suggests that their fidelity is somewhat conditional or even self-serving.

On the other hand, the Samaritan woman and her community members have messed up plenty but haven't yet encountered the gospel like this. When they do, their eyes open, and all past transgressions are relegated to history.

This doesn't mean that they can do whatever they want now. Once they know better, God will expect more of them as well.

Digging Deeper

Mining for what really matters . . . and gold

For some, Lent is a time of self-imposed deprivation. Those of the Catholic faith avoid certain foods, while some Protestants select something on their own to cut out or limit during the weeks leading up to Easter. Still others dismiss Lent, enjoying the excesses of Mardi Gras at the beginning, ignoring the rest.

The idea behind this time of want is to help remind us both of how much we do have the rest of the year, as well as turning our minds and hearts toward God whenever we recognize the absence of whatever we're avoiding during Lent. This is a time of year when little is growing and, if those in a preindustrial society hadn't planned accordingly, they might be without even the most basic staples by now.

And yet the days grow steadily longer: thus the root of the word *Lent*, which refers to the lengthening of days.

The provision of spring is not yet here, but there are signs around us every day that, just like last year and the year before that, it will soon be here. This, even for those outside the Christian faith, is a source of hope. The key thing for us to remember is not that the hope is for the current circumstance, per se, but rather that despite our longing, there is a promise that will most certainly be kept.

Those who focus more on their rumbling stomachs instead of the promise of what is to come can easily fall into a state of grudging tolerance. We look around ourselves and see what seems to be endless cold and dark, scarcity and near-death. It's easy to miss the handful of minutes of added daylight or the upward creeping of the thermometer when the present moment is less than desirable.

It's especially hard when we think we're nearly out of the worst of it and that inevitable Arctic front hits. The Israelites have similarly gotten over the elation of freedom, especially now that they are faced with a more pressing need. The thirst is real, but the real suffering in the situation comes from a lack of vision.

It's in our moments of greatest personal need that our focus often folds inward. Our perspective narrows and any discernment of signs of hope, or even just the memory of past promises kept, fades dimly into the backdrop. In these moments, the absence of God feels as real as our thirst. But it's not so much that God has left us as we have chosen to stop seeing.

Contrast this with Jesus, who has just traveled a long way from wherever he came before. He is tired, hungry, and thirsty: a sort of trifecta of elements often leading to self-absorbed negativity. Despite this, his focus is still outward, intent on connecting with people in a way that affords them the sort of divinely inspired vision he enjoys, which, while not immediately meeting his physical needs, robs them of their ability to lead to suffering and loss of faith.

There will be times of darkness and want. A life in the path of Christ hardly offers us a shortcut around this. What it does provide is a strength of spirit that transcends the transient, fickle weakness of the flesh. The challenge, then, isn't to offer up empty, hollow words of gratitude when we really don't feel it. The call is to look beyond the current situation to the greater promise.

That is the curious, weird, but necessary gift of Lent.

Heads-Up

Connecting the text to our world

If we want to see the dark underbelly of someone's core animal nature, deprive them of the basic necessities of life. Better yet, pit them in competition with others for a limited—or even shrinking—resource.

It's easy for us to claim faithfulness in times of plenty. It's also easy to judge others who have less for lacking the same piety or dignity we believe we have. We see racism flourish in situations where basic human nature and survival instinct kick in, although the issue is principally economic rather than race-driven.

The Israelites were quick to judge others who didn't act as they did, forgetting maybe that they, too, had quickly lost their grip on who—and whose—they were when their basic needs were challenged. And yet this is exactly where Jesus wants them to be.

If we are now the hands and feet of Christ in the world, where does that lead us then? To the legislature to argue for stricter no-tolerance prison sentences? To fortify ourselves against the threat of losing what is rightfully ours? Or toward the heart of need itself?

We don't have to travel to Syria, Somalia, or even the southside of Chicago to find such want (although there's plenty to be found in those places too). And while it may be tempting to go there and preach about how "Jesus loves you" while people are hungry or scared for their lives or those of their children, Jesus set a different example. When more pressing needs got between him and his message reaching others, he met them where they were, feeding them or healing them first.

No one wants to hear about God's love when their stomach is rumbling. There's time enough to tell people about God's love, especially after we've shown them.

Prayer for the Week

God, help my mouth not grumble just because my stomach does. Help me hold on to the God-inspired vision that hope in spite of circumstances is the taproot to a more meaningful relationship with you.

Popping Off

Art/music/video and other cool stuff that relate to the text

"Mealtime Prayer" scene from *Talladega Nights* (movie, 2006)

Slumdog Millionaire (movie, 2009)

When Vision Fails

Lectionary Texts For

March 22, 2020 (Fourth Sunday in Lent)

Texts in Brief

My dog ate my Bible!

First Reading

1 Samuel 16:1–13

Saul is upset that God rejects his son, Samuel, as the next king of Israel. Instead, God sends Samuel to meet Jesse, from whose lineage the next king will come. Jesse presents his sons, but God tells Samuel the next king is not among them. When Samuel presses Jesse, Jesse notes that his youngest son is out caring for the sheep. Jesse has him brought to Samuel, and God tells Samuel that David is to be king.

Psalm

Psalm 23

The author offers a prayer to God as their sustainer, comforter, guide, and protector. They express certainty that as long as they remain in God's presence, they will continue to be blessed. They refer to God anointing their head with oil, which indicates that this is David speaking.

Second Reading

Ephesians 5:8–14

Paul calls on his audience to remain in the light of Christ, rather than dwelling in secrecy and darkness. In fact, he urges them to bring to light the misdeeds of their colleagues done in secret. The passage closes with a reference to Isaiah, in which the prophet cries out for all sleepers to awaken to the light of God.

Gospel

John 9:1–41

Jesus's disciples wonder what a blind man they encounter did to deserve this punishment from God. Jesus says that he did nothing but rather that it is an opportunity to reveal God's power. Jesus makes mud from earth and spit and puts it on the man's eyes, then tells him to wash them in order to see. When others ask how he can now see, he tells them about Jesus. But the religious leaders condemn this act since Jesus performed the miracle on the Sabbath. While they claim Jesus is a charlatan, the healed man holds fast to his belief in

Jesus being of God, so they kick him out of the temple. Still the man proclaims Jesus is of God.

Bible, Decoded
Breaking down Scripture in plain language

Jesse—An Israelite shepherd and farmer, Jesse is the grandson of Boaz and Ruth, ancestors of Jesus. Jesse's eighth son, David, is anointed by God to be king of Israel. This is consistent with the prophecy from Isaiah that claims the Messiah will come from the family "tree of Jesse."

Ramah—Birthplace of Samuel, where he returns after participating in the anointing of David as the heir-apparent of the throne as king of Israel.

Pool of Siloam—A spring-fed pool along the southern edge of the city of David, or Jerusalem. The pool was a critical source of drinkable water for the city. It is noted in Scripture at least seven centuries before Jesus's birth, but likely was a primary source of water, and therefore life, during David's reign.

Points to Ponder
First Thoughts

There are some potential parallels between David's anointment with oil and the baptism of Jesus. The oil on someone's head was a means of consecrating their role as particularly chosen by God. And while Jesus was anointed by God, this was a spiritual anointing. Similarly, John the Baptist speaks of baptizing people with water (a cleansing), though the baptism by way of the Messiah will be a baptism of the spirit, cleansing us from the inside out.

While it's easy in the Samuel text to focus on David, consider how hard it had to be for Saul to have to go and consecrate David as the next king, especially after assuming that the faithfulness of him and his family would lead to God naming his son, Samuel, as king.

Whereas in Samuel, the passing-over of Saul's son for the crown has nothing to do with his devotion to God, the Gospel text presents Jesus asserting that the blind man didn't suffer his condition because of a lack of faithfulness. It seems that the point here is that misfortune comes to good people, just as good things sometimes come to those who haven't necessarily earned it in our eyes.

Digging Deeper

Mining for what really matters . . . and gold

In the Gospel story this week, it's interesting to consider the circumstances in which this healing happens. First of all, the man has been blind since birth. So this lends new gravity to the "Sleeper, awake!" reference from back in Isaiah that Paul makes in Ephesians. This awakening from a life of literal darkness into a world awash with light will certainly be stunning. Even once his eyes start to work, his brain has no way to process everything he is now taking in.

We could hardly blame him for wanting to close his eyes again, just to get his bearings. Anyone who has lived in a community of deep, persistent mutual accountability can attest that the degree of exposure required is vulnerable and can be a little bit exhausting. Who, after all, hasn't wanted to turn the lights of truth back off and crawl back in bed?

Still, the blind man acts out of faith. Even without seeing this strange man who is smearing spitty mud on his face, he does as Jesus commands, going to the pool of Siloam to clean off the same mud this guy just put on his eyes. So while we can't know the heart of the blind man for sure, it's possible that this blind man, who dwelled in darkness his whole life, was already "awake" in the spiritual sense.

It's also worth noting that, while in most cases someone asks Jesus to heal them or he asks them if they want to be healed, such a conversation never happens with the blind man in John. As for why, Jesus makes it clear; this act of healing isn't being done as an act of mercy but instead to prove he is the son of God. This is a significant break from the other Gospels, and especially from the first Gospel, Mark, which was written two to three generations prior to John's Gospel and includes more than one example of Jesus performing his miracles in complete secrecy.

Either Jesus or the author of John has a different agenda in this case than just compassion. Jesus says that the act is done so that the kingdom of God can be known, but by whom? The blind man acts in faith before he sees results, so to speak. Instead, the ones whose eyes need to be opened are the temple leaders. Though their blindness isn't a physical one, it is a lack of access to the spiritual reality, right before them, largely because they think they have this whole "faith thing" already nailed down.

The Pharisees are blinded by ego, by certainty, by religious legalism, and by the comfort of their agreement with the Roman authorities that serves them well at the expense of the Israelites. It may sound strange, but the healed man is little more than a prop or an object lesson in this story. He is a tool in a greater act of religious and political subversion.

Jesus didn't forget it was the Sabbath; he was a devout and knowledgeable Jew. He is inviting the conflict on the very subtext of what he knows is keeping the religious powers from truly knowing what God is about. Just as the text says: those who think they see clearly actually are the blind ones. Jesus is the light that provides the opportunity for real sight; it's up to the witnesses whether they will open their eyes to it.

Heads-Up

Connecting the text to our world

I've written in a previous volume of this series about a movie written by Oliver Stone and starring Val Kilmer back in the late nineties that nearly nobody care about called *At First Sight*. Kilmer plays a man who has been blind since birth, but some modern medical innovations afford him the gift of sight. The problem is that he has no way to process the new stimuli. He has to go about learning what visual cues match up with which words and nonvisual sensory experiences he's known his whole life.

Even as he starts to develop a foundational visual vocabulary, though, he struggles. He can't tell the difference between an apple and a picture of an apple. He gets easily overwhelmed and occasionally blindfolds himself to return to the comfort of familiar darkness.

The movie particularly struck me because I was in the middle of my own graduate studies about visual processing and the autism spectrum. I was especially intrigued by a condition called prosopagnosia, more commonly called *face blindness*. In the most severe cases, you could speak to someone with this disorder, leave the room, and come back five minutes later and they wouldn't be able to recognize you at all.

They can see you. They see your eyes, nose, mouth, hair, and cheekbones. That isn't the problem. The breakdown is in something called gestalt visual processing, which is the process in the brain where we take all the puzzle pieces that compose a face and assemble them together into a cohesive, single thing. Before that happens, the face (at least in our minds) is just an assortment of unrelated parts.

This is the point at which sight becomes vision. Sight, after all, is of very limited use if we can't make sense of the input. We don't have to have a neurological disorder, though, to have these moments when our sight is intact but our vision fails. The stumbling block can be assumptions, stereotypes, previous experience, assumed knowledge, or a number of other things. But seeing just isn't enough.

Sleeper, awake!

Prayer for the Week

God, sometimes my own sight gets in the way of my vision. Help me see things as they are and should be, rather than how I assume they are.

Popping Off

Art/music/video and other cool stuff that relate to the text

At First Sight (movie, 1999)

The Man Who Mistook His Wife for a Hat and Other Clinical Tales, by Oliver Sacks (book, 1985)

Spiritual Zombies

Lectionary Texts For
March 29, 2020 (Fifth Sunday in Lent)

Texts in Brief
My dog ate my Bible!

First Reading
Ezekiel 37:1–14

By this point, the Israelites have lost all hope and are spiritually dead. So God takes the prophet to a valley filled with bones of long-dead people and orders him to command them back to life with God's power. After they are resurrected, God likens this rebirth to the kind of spiritual rebirth of the Israelites, promising Ezekiel that their time of being lost will soon end and they will reclaim a homeland.

Psalm

Psalm 130

The psalmist is grateful for God's short memory for his sins, knowing that if he was held to account for every one of them, he—like everyone else—would be unworthy of God's mercy. But he urges his fellow Israelites to cling to hope in God's provision, just as they can have hope in God's limitless forgiveness.

Second Reading

Romans 8:6–11

Focusing only on the physical world around us and our own immediate needs robs us of real living. We are invited instead to claim life by not being controlled by our desires, sins, and physical limitations. If we seek real life of the spirit as exemplified in Jesus, we embrace life, regardless of our physical state. It is a sort of resurrection that death can't overcome.

Gospel

John 11:1–45

Mary and Martha beg Jesus for help for their brother, Lazarus, who is sick. Jesus contends that the illness won't lead to death, and he stays where he is for two more days until after Lazarus dies. When he decides to go back to Judea to the site of Lazarus's burial place, his disciples worry about his fellow Jews killing him. But instead of fearing them, he notes that where there is spiritual darkness is exactly where they should go. In Judea, he tells Martha that her brother will live again. She assumes he means he will rise when the second coming happens, but he means he will come back to physical life. Jesus calls Lazarus out of his tomb, and he comes out, causing witnesses to believe Jesus is the Messiah.

Bible, Decoded
Breaking down Scripture in plain language

Ezekiel—Ezekiel is the prophet who brings both welcome and unwelcome visions to the Israelites. While he foretells of the destruction of Jerusalem, he also sees when they will go back to Israel and he predicts the rebuilding of the so-called third temple in Jerusalem. He is believed to have lived during the Israelites' period of captivity under the Babylonians in the southern territory of Judea.

Lazarus—Lazarus of Bethany's resurrection is considered one of the seven signs offered in the Gospel of John as evidence that Jesus is the son of God. This miracle moves a vast number of people to follow Jesus, which the Jewish priest Caiaphas sees as a threat. This sign of Jesus's growing influence is a tipping point that leads to the decision to have Jesus arrested and crucified.

POINTS TO PONDER
First Thoughts

In last week's Johannine Gospel story, Jesus gives sight to the blind. This week, he gives life to the dead. These seven miracles in John shouldn't just be seen as "evidence that demands a verdict" about Jesus's divinity. They should be understood as the manifold ways in which God's presence in all of our lives brings us from a state of zombie-like survival to rich, meaningful, and full living.

The passage in Romans gives us the road map for how this is achieved—setting aside our focus on physical, selfish matters and reorienting our priorities to focus on the indwelling of God's spirit within us. Resurrection, then, isn't something reserved for the corpses in the tomb or dry bones in the valley. We don't have to wait for Jesus to call us out of the tombs of our own creation. Consider the Gospels our standing invitation out into light and life with God.

Digging Deeper

Mining for what really matters . . . and gold

There's a lot we can take from the story about Lazarus, well beyond the words at face value. True, we can be content to see the miracle and claim this as our evidence that Jesus was who he said he was. If we stop there, though, we miss a lot about what the author of John assumes we know or wants us to come away with.

For starters, this is the only Gospel in which this resurrection story appears. While this is the first time Lazarus of Bethany is introduced, it seems clear that he and Jesus are close. This would explain why the last time Jesus and Lazarus are seen together is at a feast not long before Jesus is arrested and sentenced to death.

The symbolism of this is no accident; John's author is drawing a distinct parallel between Lazarus's death and resurrection and that of Jesus. If we don't consider this, we are met instead with a sort of lazy Jesus who just doesn't seem to get motivated to fulfill Mary and Martha's request until they (not to mention their brother) have had to suffer through the brutality of his death and burial.

However, Jesus waits two days, which may be significant. While we can't be sure, this may be a way of the author foreshadowing the death and resurrection of Jesus, after lying for two days in his burial tomb. Consider, also, that it is Mary and Martha who host Jesus for one of his final meals, anointing him much like one would do for a dead body. In these stories, life and death are not so clearly distinct; the line is blurred, the veil very thin, between one and the other. This helps us make sense of why this story would come up in the lectionary calendar as the final Sunday before Good Friday and, of course, Easter.

It's also noteworthy that this is the final straw for the religious and political leaders, leading them to conclude that this troublemaker, would-be Messiah needs to die. In fact, they want to kill off Lazarus because his very existence is stirring the Jews to seek out and follow Jesus. In all of the other Gospels, it's the story of Jesus cleansing the temple of moneychangers that leads to his arrest, but in John, that story is early on in Jesus's ministry, taking place just after the wedding at Cana.

Like the healing of the lifelong blind man last week, the resurrection of Lazarus is done—as Jesus himself states—as an act to reveal Jesus's true nature to those living in the darkness of unbelief or ignorance. It is also, like last week's miracle, an act of religious defiance and political subversion. He knows that he is in the belly of the proverbial beast in Bethany, with a lot of Jews unhappy with him—namely, those thick with the Romans.

Jesus does this on purpose, knowing full well where it will likely lead. In some ways, we could just replace the name "Lazarus" with Jesus in this death-and-resurrection scene. It is even the women who bear principal witness to the miracle, just like women found Jesus's tomb empty.

We might wonder why Jesus isn't running away, steering clear of the most dangerous place he could go. Clearly there is need for his miraculous power elsewhere, so why here, why now?

As he often does, Jesus walks the talk he offers in his ministry. He doesn't ask anything of anyone he wouldn't be willing to undergo himself. Yes, death is a likely response when we confront these indominable powers, and yes, it will be painful. Even Lazarus still smells bad when he arises from his tomb! Paul sees clearly why Jesus is doing this; he has his mind and sights on something well beyond what he will suffer to get there. His heart is intent on matters of the spirit, regardless of the price to the flesh.

Our call is to go and do likewise.

Heads-Up

Connecting the text to our world

I can't help but picture Lazarus like Westley in *The Princess Bride*, who is brought back to life (albeit gradually) by a pill concocted by someone named Miracle Max. Not long after Fezzik and Inigo Montoya shove the miracle pill down his lifeless throat, Westley's eyes pop open.

"Why won't my arms move?" he asks.

"You've been mostly dead all day," says Fezzik. The next several scenes portray Westley's various body parts coming back to life, but only one at a time. It turns out being mostly dead really sucks.

It's too easy to go through life mostly dead, animated corpses who are little more than spiritual zombies. For some, the awakening is dramatic and sudden; for others, we come to it gradually, a little bit at a time.

Unlike Westley, we don't have a pill from Miracle Max. What we do have, though, is Jesus's example of how to live both spiritually and physically however long we have. Jesus spends even his final days feasting, healing, and being in loving relationship with others. He won't let his imminent death take away from his present life. Sure, he could spend the waning hours poring over his choices, freaking out about his fate. At that point, though, he might as well already be dead.

Instead he lives life abundantly, regardless of his future or physical state. Sounds a lot better than being mostly dead to me.

Prayer for the Week

Sometimes I walk around mostly dead. Help me stop waiting for the miracle pill and realize I have all I need to really live, here and now.

Popping Off

Art/music/video and other cool stuff that relate to the text

The Princess Bride (movie, 1987)

"Black Knight Fight" scene from *Monty Python and the Holy Grail* (movie, 1975)

God
Takes Sides

Lectionary Texts For
April 5, 2020 (Palm Sunday)

Texts in Brief
My dog ate my Bible!

First Reading
None

Psalm
Psalm 118:1–2, 19–29

The psalmist offers a general call to worship, followed by words of effusive praise to God. These begin as individual offerings of praise and move into a corporate gesture of gratitude. The key phrase is in verse 22, which likely is in reference to David, a shepherd of lowly status becoming the leader of Israel by God's hand.

Second Reading

None

Gospel

Matthew 21:1–11

From Bethphage, Jesus sends two disciples to the edge of Jerusalem to bring him a donkey to ride on, along with its young colt. The disciples and onlookers treat him like royalty as he enters the town, laying down palm branches and their coats along the path. They shout thanks to God, and his entry causes such a stir in town that everyone is talking about his presence as the prophet that word had spread about.

Bible, Decoded

Breaking down Scripture in plain language

Festal Procession—A parade of celebration, usually ending in a feast. This psalm usually is read along with the fourth cup of wine at the Passover feast, which was a time of thanksgiving and celebration for God's protection and provision.

Hosanna—The word can be understood as a more generic expression of praise, celebration, or joy, but it can also be translated roughly to mean "save us."

Daughter of Zion—This phrase is used often in Scripture, usually either in reference to the city of Jerusalem or more specifically to the temple in Jerusalem. In some cases, especially when used in the plural (daughters of Zion), it can be understood as referring to all of the Israelites collectively.

Points to Ponder

First Thoughts

Psalm 118:22 is one of the most quoted texts from the Hebrew Bible in the New Testament. While it first appears in the writings attributed to the prophet Isaiah, it is quoted here in this psalm in reference to King David. But in the New Testament, it is a reference to how Jesus, who is rejected by the world, is used by God as the foundation for salvation for all.

There's some powerful symbolism in the fact that while this psalm is read during a celebration when God spares the children of the Israelites from death, it comes in the same week when Jesus—God's own son—is marching headlong toward his own death.

Our observation of Palm Sunday should also always be tinged with the profound humiliation, suffering, and brutal death of Maundy Thursday and Good Friday. This lends a lot of gravity to the use of all of the praise and attention Jesus receives here, since in only a few days, he is in a completely opposite situation.

Digging Deeper

Mining for what really matters . . . and gold

This Gospel passage depicting what is commonly called the "triumphal entry" has been interpreted a thousand different ways. Let's consider one political perspective, as well as a less-commonly considered theological one.

Politically, we have to remember that this is happening just before Passover, which has two points of focus: Jews entering the city to offer sacrifices in atonement for sin, and the people's celebration of their liberation from Egyptian bondage. We also need to know that Pontius Pilate, the region's Roman governor, doesn't actually live in Jerusalem. Instead he lives in Caesarea, a city sixty or so miles away that would have been much friendlier to non-Jews.

Though the Bible focuses on Jesus's entry into the city, it's necessary to understand that Pilate would also have been entering the town from another direction but to much the same sort of fanfare. And while the Roman powers required that they be praised as liberators and saviors, his presence there during Passover was meant to remind the people of Israel that while free of Egyptian captivity, they were still under occupation.

Lest they forget, he was there to make sure they knew who their masters were.

Enter Jesus, presented with similar cries of praise and emblems of royalty. Imagine how this looks to Pilate! It is a direct subversion of the power the Roman forces claim over Jesus and his people. And while the authority of Rome was claimed through coercion and bloodshed, Jesus's authority came only from God, given freely by those following him.

This was real power, and it was unsettling to the people in charge. Something would have to be done.

The means by which Jesus claims authority leads us, too, to the theological implications in this and the Passover story. Where, if at all, do we find good news in stories of the slaughter of babies or the torture and death of an innocent man? If we bear in mind that the slaughter and crucifixion were acts carried out by people and not by God, it begins to become clear.

God bears empathy for the suffering, the marginalized, and oppressed. God suffers with us. God's heart breaks for the death of anyone, let alone innocents, but we are afforded the freedom to act on our own. Even when it is in direct opposition to God's own way.

Amid that, God responds to those who call on God for mercy. It may not always look how we think it should, but we have to remember that we lack the vision and imagination of God. God responds to the Israelites' call for safety at Passover, and God responds again when they call out "hosanna, save us!" on Jesus's entry into Jerusalem.

God is on the side of all who seek God. No exceptions. This is expressed not with weapons of war but through the cross, which represents the culmination of God's outpouring of love in response to suffering. It is the "yes!" to all of our cries of "no!" It is compellingly attractive, not coercive. It invites but never forces itself.

The cruciform symbol of divine love at all costs stands as a reminder that divine love remains on our side, advocates on our behalf, even when we are intent on killing God.

Heads-Up

Connecting the text to our world

It may be weird to draw parallels between Jesus and Britney Spears, but here goes.

I was a little bit too old to have any interest in the music of Britney Spears as she hit her spectacular heights of popularity. That, and I was more of a metal-and-grunge guy, and she decidedly isn't in that vein. I was old enough, though, to watch the spectacle of her stardom from a sort of arms-length perspective. What I saw was both fascinating and horrifying.

Popular culture took this young girl, barely out of puberty, and put her under some of the most intense scrutiny a person could endure. We mythologized her, sexualized her, and nearly deified her as her star rose to the upper echelon of media celebrity.

She was on every television and radio and in every magazine found along the checkout aisles at the grocery store (it was a little bit too early to blow up on digital and social media in the earlier parts of her career). And then she snapped.

The pressure to produce, perform, and live up to these inhuman images people had built up about her came crashing down on top of her, a young woman just trying to keep up with the insanity around her. She shaved her head in a rebellious act of defiance against the icon that was her public persona, and, after a few too many distasteful public outbursts, she disappeared into solitude and treatment.

The public loved this at least as much as we devoured the celebrity at its height.

Philosopher René Girard developed what is now known as the "scapegoat theory" regarding how we relate to people with great wealth, power, or status in our culture. In short, the only thing we love more than building them up is tearing them back down. It's a sort of bloodlust that reveals all too much about the darker parts of human nature.

In short, the concept goes that we idolize these figures, elevating them to unrealistic levels in our imaginations. In a way, they represent the transcendence of our own depravity and utter humanity. They represent someone who has magically found the shortcut around suffering and want. Then, when we inevitably come to the realization that they were human the whole time, we feel betrayed. So for that, we sacrifice them.

With Jesus, the situation is a little bit different, of course. It's not his humanity that caused us to turn on him. From fear of retribution from the government to the reality that the kind of liberation and salvation he came to offer wasn't exactly what a lot of us had in mind, he revealed the true nature of our own humanity. And in that way, it is similar.

We may not literally crucify our celebrities today; their crucifixions are more figurative. Suffice it to say that we haven't changed as much as Jesus would hope.

Prayer for the Week

Help me come to terms with my own imperfections and all-too-human failings. Help me also see the beauty of the image of God in both myself and in everyone else.

Popping Off

Art/music/video and other cool stuff that relate to the text

"10 Years Ago Today, Britney Spears Shaved Her Head," in *The Daily Dot* (article, February 16, 2017)

The Scapegoat, by René Girard (book, 1989)

Deathless Hope

Lectionary Texts For
April 12, 2020 (Easter Sunday)

Texts in Brief
My dog ate my Bible!

First Reading
Jeremiah 31:1–6

An account of the prophet's vision for the reconciliation of Israel. Yes, many died under the sword of captivity, and many were lost in exile for years. But now is the time for what was lost, abandoned for dead, to be reborn, and with abundance.

Psalm
Psalm 118:1–2, 14–24

The psalm begins with a call on Israel to shout out in affirmation of God's unending love. There is a recognition of God's punishment for wrongdoing in its past, but now there is cause for celebration as the Israelites are being redeemed. It concludes with the metaphor of the rejected builder's stone (which is referenced in the New Testament more than once) now becoming the foundation upon which a new way will be built.

Second Reading
Colossians 3:1–4

For those reborn in the likeness of Christ, our minds should always incline themselves to the sort of things Jesus called us to, rather than matters of the flesh that bind us to the life of our past.

Gospel
Matthew 28:1–10

The two women named Mary go to visit Jesus's burial site when an angel appears, telling them that he has risen. They're ordered to go and tell this to the disciples and to have them all go to Galilee, where Jesus will meet them. On their way back to deliver the message, Jesus appears to them and tells them the same thing.

Bible, Decoded
Breaking down Scripture in plain language

Ephraim—A centrally located and mountainous region in what became the new nation of Israel. Symbolically, it was the heart of the new promised land and might have been considered particularly holy, given its elevation. It got its name because the Israelites tribe of Ephraim previously occupied it.

Galilee—While a lot of Gospel stories take place in and around Galilee, one reason Jesus might have said he would appear to the disciples there is because they would be at less risk there, without the Jewish authorities in Jerusalem around, who likely were keeping a close eye on the disciples and would have been especially concerned about any gatherings of them all together.

Points to Ponder

First Thoughts

This is one of many times when the direct parallel between the nation of Israel and Jesus is drawn. The Israelites were the physical body of God on earth, so this notion of the followers of Jesus becoming the resurrected Christ in the world would have been very familiar and founded in their ancient wisdom.

It's interesting in the Gospel text that though the ones who were petrified with fear were the male guards, it was the women the angel told not to be scared. In fact, the angel says nothing at all to the guards. Maybe the guards were afraid because they saw with different eyes, whereas the women were looking for something beyond what the men could have recognized.

Digging Deeper

Mining for what really matters . . . and gold

Everyone knows this story, so we won't belabor the parts you practically know by heart. Let's focus instead on the people who would be considered the supporting cast in the narrative leading up to Jesus's death: those who abandoned Jesus. More important, let's reflect on both why they turned away from him and how, if at all, they respond later to this. I know it seems like a strange angle to take when we're talking about new life, but how we respond to the path to the cross also informs much about how we respond beyond it.

First, we have Judas, who seems to act out of greed. Though I'm sure he is aware of the risks to his well-being if he stands by Jesus, this also isn't the first time Judas has been focused on money. Another example is when he freaks out about Mary anointing Jesus's feet with expensive oil. Though he claims his motives are pure (he argues for how many of the poor could be fed with the money the oil costs), this betrayal of Jesus for a handful of silver suggests he belied the truth.

After asserting fiercely that he would cling to Jesus until death, we see Peter crumble when faced with the very real threat of a similar fate. He realizes what he's done a little bit too late.

While we don't see the other disciples actively deny Jesus, we do see them falling asleep against Jesus's command in the garden at Gethsemane. This allusion to their weakness of character is evidence enough to realize they won't be there when it matters.

Pilate literally washes his hands of responsibility, allowing someone to die who he knows is guilty of no crime, because of political expedience. The crowd (if we agree it was primarily composed of leaders among the Israelites who were complicit with Roman rule) called for Jesus to die out of opportunism and lust for keeping their power.

The guards at the cross taunt Jesus and have a lot of fun at his expense, likely because if they saw him as truly human—let alone the son of God—their work of one crucifixion after another, day in and day out, would have been unbearable. Their denial of his humanity, then, helps them maintain their own sanity and sense of self-worth.

We know nothing of how the people in power end up seeing Jesus and their actions against him, given that there is no follow-up from Pilate or the Jewish leadership about any moments of clarity or disbelief. Judas's eyes are opened, and he responds to his role in the systemic betrayal with suicide. The centurions' eyes are opened at the moment of Jesus's death, and these same people who had just killed Jesus claim him as the world's salvation.

Peter, on the other hand, confronts his shame but does not let it become him. Ultimately, he becomes the foundation from which the movement of those following Jesus post-resurrection is built. Without him, we might not be here today.

God let flourish the entirety of humanity from two sinful people in a garden. God empowered a broken man to lead the people of Israel as king. God called a drunk to save the few bits of creation that would endure the great flood. And God uses his own betrayers and the killer of his beloved faithful (Paul) to build the movement that would transform the world forever.

What sort of resurrection, then, might this same God have in store for us?

Heads-Up

Connecting the text to our world

Some might be surprised to learn that Rev. Martin Luther King Jr. actually challenged the doctrine of bodily resurrection, which many consider essential to their identification with Christianity. While he was studying at Crozier Seminary in 1949, he wrote a paper in a systematic theology class about Christian doctrine, finishing the paper with his thoughts on resurrection.

"They [early Christians who knew Jesus] had come to see," wrote King, "that the essential note in the Fourth Gospel is the ultimate force in Christianity: The living, deathless person of Christ. They expressed this in terms of the outward, but it was an inner experience that led to its expression."

He went on to remind people of two distinct differences between our current culture and that of the early Christians and pre-Christians. First, they had no exposure to contemporary science, and so, the idea that the physical world was bound in large part by certain scientific properties was completely foreign. King also stressed that the people who experienced Jesus's resurrection knew Jesus in a way we never will; they lived, ate, slept, and struggled through ministry with him. And while their faith was hardly perfect, it plumbed depths that we can hardly know.

We also internalize our experience of faith a lot more than the early ancient Christians did. Their belief that the spirit, ministry, and collective body of Christ was inextinguishable was expressed outwardly, which in this case comes in the form of resurrection.

It's interesting that King, a man whose ministry continues to reverberate throughout the nation today, met with such an eerily similar fate as Jesus. And not to suggest that he was a second messiah, but Rev. King has, indeed, left behind "the living, deathless person of King," to borrow his own words.

It is definitely fitting that Martin Luther King Day is celebrated around the time of Easter every year, because he is yet another chapter in the ever-growing story of resurrection in our midst. Whether or not flesh comes back to life, the promise of hope, unconditional love, and a bending of the arc of history toward justice will not die.

Prayer for the Week

As often as I turn from you, God, you never seem to turn from me. Even when I'm sure you've abandoned me, it turns out to be the other way around. Use me in the ongoing and unfolding resurrection story.

Popping Off

Art/music/video and other cool stuff that relate to the text

"What Experiences of Christians Living in the Early Christian Century Led to the Christian Doctrines of the Divine Sonship of Jesus, the Virgin Birth, and the Bodily Resurrection," by Martin Luther King Jr. (essay, November 23, 1949)

The Resurrection of Jesus: John Dominic Crossan and N. T. Wright in Dialogue, edited by Robert B. Stuart (book, 2006)

No Lost Causes

Lectionary Texts For

April 19, 2020 (Second Sunday of Easter)

Texts in Brief

My dog ate my Bible!

First Reading

Acts 2:14a, 22–32

Peter, along with his fellow disciples, speaks to a crowd of Israelites about Jesus's death and resurrection. He begins with an accusation that they knew of the plans to have Jesus killed and didn't do anything to stop it. He goes on to quote King David in the Psalms, who speaks of one sent by God who can conquer death. Peter asserts that Jesus is the one sent by God that David was talking about, since they now know of Jesus's resurrection.

Psalm

Psalm 16

A psalm proclaiming faithfulness to the God of Israel alone. David attributes his success as king to that faithfulness and implies that the ones he defeated lost because they worshipped the wrong God. It concludes with thanks to God for being spared, be it from being conquered or because of his own sins, closing with a reaffirmation of praise now and always to God.

Second Reading

1 Peter 1:3–9

The author talks about how those who embrace the resurrected Christ story are blessed with divine inheritance that is eternal, as compared with any earthly inheritance they would get otherwise. The text notes that even though those listening have suffered plenty, they have survived it all because they have remained faithful. They are particularly blessed because they have faith even though they didn't witness the things firsthand that the disciples did.

Gospel

John 20:19–31

The disciples are meeting in secret for fear of their own people turning on them when Jesus appears to them. He says that he is sending them out to continue the ministry that God had sent him to offer. He gives them spiritual gifts that endow them with many abilities that Jesus had possessed, like forgiving sin. Thomas, who wasn't with them at the time, later questions their account of this encounter, so they bring him to Jesus. Jesus allows the still doubtful Thomas to feel Jesus's wounds to know it's him. When Thomas finally believes it, Jesus says that people who can have faith without concrete evidence are blessed more abundantly than those who need proof.

Bible, Decoded
Breaking down Scripture in plain language

Hades/Sheol—While these terms are sometimes used interchangeably, they have very different backgrounds. Hades is a belief from Greek Hellenism, named after the god Hades, lord of the underworld. In Hellenism, this underworld is not a place of punishment but rather a place where all who die will dwell after physical life is over. Sheol, however, is a concept from ancient Judaism. Though it is also a place of rest for the dead, it is considered to be a temporary holding place until God returns to call them back to literal, physical life.

Thomas—We don't hear a lot about Thomas, unless it's in reference to this account of his tentative encounter with Jesus. What we hear less about is his ministry after this experience. It's generally accepted that he traveled east into the region we now know as India. There are still monuments to his ministry in various places around India, and in fact he is considered by Catholics to be the patron saint of that country.

Points to Ponder

First Thoughts

It's curious that one thing David condemns pagans for in this psalm is for "drinking offerings of blood." Meanwhile, Communion is celebrated regularly in Christian worship, with many congregations proclaiming the sanctified wine as being the blood of Jesus, which we drink. Yet another example of how subsequent cultures adopt and adapt symbols and myths from preceding cultures, much like the post-Jesus Israelites referred to what they had known as Sheol by a more recently introduced term from a "pagan" culture.

Also, while it's easy to overlook if we're not careful, the ending of the passage in John is important, as it explains why these gifts are given to the disciples. They're not empowered with miraculous abilities to overthrow the government or to win people's hearts to follow them. The sole purpose is to lend more compelling credibility to their claims of Christ as Messiah for those who struggle to believe. So even though Jesus sees Thomas's need for proof as a disappointment, he also understands that it's an inevitable part of human nature all too often.

Digging Deeper

Mining for what really matters . . . and gold

We have to be careful not to rush to judgment of Thomas in this week's Gospel. Aside from the inevitability that we all have our doubts from time to time (for me, it's a staple of my spiritual discipline), we just read about the rest of the disciples being skeptical too. In the story of Jesus appearing to Mary Magdalene, she went to tell her colleagues right away. But maybe because she was a woman, maybe because they hadn't seen any physical evidence, or maybe because they were scared or even in shock after Jesus's death, they dismissed her claims.

Nevertheless, Jesus came to them. Not only that, but he also gave them immeasurable gifts of the spirit. Granted, this wasn't to aggrandize themselves so much as it was to continue the ministry Jesus had started with them, but they were gifts, nonetheless. Also, he went, quite literally, to where they were and met them there. He knew they were too afraid in Jerusalem to be open to his presence, so he appeared to them in Galilee.

While Jesus may have longed for a world in which everyone believed truth when they came into contact with it, he also knew better. Further, he accommodated that doubt and even worked with it. Likewise, he didn't give up on Thomas, even though he may have shaken his head at him, kind of like we do to a kid just before we drop a "What did I just say?" on them. And following this experience, the one who hadn't believed without seeing became a means by which many who never knew of Jesus came to embrace him.

There's no such thing as a lost cause in the kingdom of God, only works in various stages of progress.

Heads-Up

Connecting the text to our world

Comedian and satirist Stephen Colbert came to fame by playing his now infamous role as a fictitious alter-ego who was a combative, narrow-minded pundit who found facts too inconvenient to bother with. While prescient now, his coining of the word *truthiness* was pretty funny at the time. Basically, he would assess the degree of truthiness of any claim based on how well it already aligned with what he believed.

Facts be damned; if something opposed his existing worldview, it had no truthiness.

Now we live in what some call a post-fact reality. Calls of "fake news" are hurled in all directions, while we find ourselves increasingly hardened in our ideological trenches, continuously reinforced in our preferred way of thinking by custom-tailored echo chambers, curated for us by social media.

Recently, I listened to a TED Talk podcast episode in which the speaker described how good voice-manipulation software is getting. To provide an example, he took several dozen audio clips on a person talking about nothing in particular, fed them into his computer and then typed whatever message he wanted. In seconds, an eerily accurate mashup of the real person's voice uttered the words he told it to say. To make things even creepier, he added visual manipulation software that was able to cull through images of the person online, then make a recreation of that person's face speaking the words he wanted.

My daughter bought a virtual-reality headset for herself with money she had saved up and let me try a game where I got to ride a roller coaster through a prehistoric wilderness, overrun by scads of dinosaurs. By the end, my stomach was queasy, my palms were covered in sweat, and she laughed at the way I was gripping the couch cushions for dear life.

It wasn't long ago that the litmus test for believing something was seeing or hearing for ourselves. So now what?

There are achievements of modern science that people in Jesus's day would have chalked up to acts of the Divine. We can even bring brain-dead patients back to full function, and even replicate an organism from a few strands of genetic code.

Is there room for miracles anymore, and if so, would they have any chance of changing the way we see the world, let alone how we think about God?

Jesus understood the frailties of our overdependence on first-person sensory experience. Not to say that he knew that nearly two billion of us would now be using Facebook on a daily basis, but he understood human nature far better than we knew ourselves.

Faith that is affirmed by observed evidence can just as easily be undone by countervailing observations. Ultimately, faith is not so much a decision as it is a commitment to an idea, an investment in a way of living that frames everything else we do. It may smack of questionable truthiness to some, but real faith isn't rooted in fact; it's founded on hope.

Prayer for the Week

I know you don't give up on me, God, but help me have as much faith in myself as you do in me.

Popping Off

Art/music/video and other cool stuff that relate to the text

"Doubting Thomas," by Nickel Creek (song, 2005)

"The Word—Truthiness" scene from *The Colbert Report*, season 1, episode 101 (TV series, 2005–2015)

We > I

Lectionary Texts For
April 26, 2020 (Third Sunday of Easter)

Texts in Brief
My dog ate my Bible!

First Reading
Acts 2:14a, 36–41

This week's Acts passage starts like last week's, with Peter accusing his fellow Israelites of turning their backs on Jesus. When they ask what they should do now, he urges them to repent and be baptized. About three thousand people do as he says.

Psalm
Psalm 116:1–4, 12–19

The psalmist is faithful to God because god has been faithful to them. There's reference to lifting the cup of salvation in a ritual of worship, which will later be reflected in the Last Supper performed by Jesus with his disciples.

Second Reading

1 Peter 1:17–23

Here, too, Peter encourages people to submit themselves to God to liberate them from the burden of the sins of their ancestors through Jesus. He is apparently speaking to those who repented and were baptized, because he reminds them that because they did this, they are born again.

Gospel

Luke 24:13–35

Cleopas (a.k.a. Simon) and someone else are walking to Emmaus when a stranger joins them and asks them why they're so distraught. They explain about the loss of Jesus as their prophet and how they are distressed that he hasn't returned to them. The stranger chastises them for not having faith in what the prophets said would happen, and they invite him to stay with them for dinner. When the stranger breaks bread for them, they suddenly recognize him as Jesus.

Bible, Decoded

Breaking down Scripture in plain language

Emmaus—Exactly where this town was is not clear, but it is believed to have been along a road out of Galilee and probably on the way to Jerusalem.

Cup of Salvation—This is a reference in multiple places in Psalms, which represents both a figurative and literal cup. On what the Psalms call the "table of infinite love" (God's table), the cup of salvation offers an abundance of grace that we can drink in. This is ritualized at tables, like at the Passover meal, with a chalice that represents the holy promise between God and God's people. When we drink it, we are doing so as an act of worshipping God, while also taking this promise to heart and letting it become a part of us.

Points to Ponder

First Thoughts

We can see Peter the evangelist already emerging at this early period after Jesus's death. Clearly, Peter was convicted by his experience, and the effect of his exhortations to others is powerful.

While the rituals with the cup and bread at the Last Supper are part of Passover, they are also symbols and part of a ritual that was practiced at other times outside of Passover. In particular, the cup being lifted toward God and drunk from is an act of worship expressing our own recommitment to the promise references in this psalm both that God made with God's people and that the people made with God. The covenant was particularly solidified with the salvation of the Israelites from their fate under Egyptian rule.

Once Jesus employs these elements, he is still speaking of the same covenant. However, the salvation or liberation he is concerned with isn't with respect to physical salvation but rather salvation of the spirit through liberation from the burden of sin.

Digging Deeper

Mining for what really matters . . . and gold

It's interesting how many stories from Luke involve travel along a road. From the Holy Family's travel to Bethlehem to this walk to Emmaus and many others, Luke is always trying to take us somewhere. We see this narrative device carry over into Acts, which many scholars think was written by the same author or authors as Luke. Think about how similar the story of Paul encountering Jesus on his travels toward Damascus is to this week's account with Cleopas.

In this version, the men Jesus appears to are blind to his identity, but then the proverbial light blinks on at the table. For Paul, he can see (or at least he thinks he can), but it's only when he loses his physical sight that he really can see clearly. Leave it to Luke to jump all over symbolic studies in contrasts or reversals. He's all about them whenever he can be.

To that end, consider the meal after the trio's journey to Emmaus. Before that, it's almost like Jesus is playing with them a little to see what the nature of their hearts is. Remember, the passage doesn't actually say that they don't recognize this stranger; actually, it says they're kept from recognizing him. So maybe Jesus is disguising himself on purpose. If that's the case, who can blame them for being blind to his real identity?

It's also kind of funny that when Jesus plays dumb with them and asks why they're so bummed out, they treat him kind of like my kids do when I don't know the joke behind the latest meme lighting up Instagram. This guy must have his head in the sand not to know why they're in distress!

Back to the table: keep in mind that this stranger is their guest. They invited him to stay with them, which kicks into play a whole host of social rules that would normally be assumed by host and guest, one of which is that the host or hosts would always serve their guest. Leave it to Jesus, though, to turn that on its head and jump right in to serve them instead. This continues in the theme of the many "great reversals" that are so commonly identified throughout Luke.

The guest becomes the host, servant becomes master. God of all creation reveals that true nature by becoming like a host or server to a world of God's own making.

What is not stated here explicitly, but is most certainly implied, is that those who embrace this good news that turns everything on its head are to act likewise. We come into our greatness by lowering ourselves to nothing more than beloved servant of our fellow sisters and brothers on God's behalf.

Or maybe we should say, nothing less.

Heads-Up

Connecting the text to our world

Some new research has found fascinating trends in the direction of our economy, especially among millennials. For some time, we've realized that fewer young people are as interested in owning their own car, which was the brass ring for every teenager when I was growing up. More teenagers now don't even care much about getting their driver's license.

Among young couples and families, the notion of buying a home and gradually upgrading to your dream house is a fading reality too. More young families are content to live in smaller, simpler settings, or even to rent indefinitely. The push to earn more than our parents and grandparents is less important, and there's even a shrinking emphasis on the "they who die with the most toys, wins" ethos, which some saw as a core identifier of the capitalist-driven American dream.

Signs point us toward a dramatic shift away from a material-driven economy and toward an experience-based one. More specifically, shared experiences like meals out and shared vacations are considered more desirable than that new gadget. An entire subset known as the sharing economy is giving rise to everything from Airbnb and Uber to Meetup and Spinlister, which allows you to loan out your stuff to others in exchange for you borrowing theirs when you need it.

While we pushed so fervently toward building our own custom-built, private worlds, there's a push-back against that trend that suggests we may need each other more than we thought. There are even apps now that allow you to invite strangers to dinner parties at your place, or for you to join new people in their homes for a meal. We crave connection, and we long to break bread with each other.

We were made by God to be interdependent. One way we encounter God is through these experiences with each other. That's not to say that a guys' weekend in Vegas is necessarily a holy moment, but as Jesus said, wherever two are more are gathered . . .

There's a hunger for setting down old values and embracing new ways of thinking and living together. Slowly but certainly, we're awakening to the lack of nourishment in what we thought would fill the void within us. Jesus points the way to the substance we're looking for here; we come together, serve our neighbor, and go out to preach the gospel of "We-over-I." When we do this, God will meet us there at the table.

Prayer for the Week

God, help me always remember that "we" is more important than "I," and that serving is more of my call than I may think.

Popping Off

Art/music/video and other cool stuff that relate to the text

The Dinner at Emmaus, by Caravaggio (painting, 1601)

Walk to Emmaus event by Upper Room Ministries (ongoing): emmaus.upperroom.org

When Doing Right Sucks

Lectionary Texts For

May 3, 2020 (Fourth Sunday of Easter)

Texts in Brief

My dog ate my Bible!

First Reading

Acts 2:42–47

Those who repented and joined the way of the disciples began to do everything communally. They sacrificed individual possessions for the common good, worshipped and ate together, and learned in community. The more they did all of this together, the more people came to be a part of this new movement.

Psalm

Psalm 23

This is a well-known psalm of gratitude about being able to live through even challenging times without fear because of the confidence of never being abandoned by God. There are, again, references to coming to the table, and in this case, the table even includes those who we may have seen before as a threat.

Second Reading
1 Peter 2:19–25

Those who suffer because of their beliefs are to be encouraged, because they are afforded endurance to withstand such struggle by the God they serve. We are also reminded that this was part of what would inevitably come by following in the way of Jesus, but that this also means we don't go through it alone. God gets it.

Gospel
John 10:1–10

There is no shortcut to being a part of what Jesus calls us to. It's a path of work, struggle, and occasional heartbreak. God knows the difference between those trying to fake our way through it and those who are really invested. We're reminded not to be distracted from our mission by empty promises of the easy way around. It will be difficult, but it leads where we want to go.

Bible, Decoded
Breaking down Scripture in plain language

Valley—We think of valleys most of the time as pastoral, calming places to be. But in the Bible, this is not the case. We've talked several times about how mountains and the events that happen on them represent sacred moments. These are times when the subjects are very close to God. When we see valleys, the experience is just the opposite. This could be an existential struggle with doubt, or it could be that real-life hardships make us feel far away from God. But this Psalm assures us that God is there, as well as on the mountaintops.

Sheep—We think of sheep as stinky and dumb (they are), but back when these texts were written, they were incredibly valuable. And as we know, they're one of those animals that aren't predators, and they are very faithful to their shepherd. Also, they hold together, as their strength is in their numbers. So being called a sheep then wasn't the insult it is today, when we value individualism so highly.

Points to Ponder

First Thoughts

The type of community emerging in the Acts text reminds me a lot of the Mennonite communities, who share nearly everything in common. When someone needs a new home or barn, they come together to build it. If someone needs an extra horse or tool, it's provided. And both worship and many meals are community events. The main difference I see is that while most Mennonite communities are fairly closed off from the outside world, this one in Acts is bringing in new people all the time.

I once heard a pastor preach on Psalm 23 at a funeral, who took the angle that the rod and staff were used to beat people into place, and that the image of God preparing a table before our enemies was so they could grovel while watching us feast in victory. Suffice it to say this isn't what I think we're supposed to take from this! Amazing what some folks can do to Scripture when left to their own devices and agendas.

It's clear that by the time the passage from 1 Peter was written, the honeymoon phase of following this new way was over. It would be interesting to find out how many of the thousands who joined in while the community was growing and feeling good stuck around once this valley time came along.

Digging Deeper

Mining for what really matters . . . and gold

There's some weird stuff in this text from 1 Peter. First, we have to struggle with the idea that the author seems to be condoning slavery! Passages like these are the kinds of references the Christian church of the American South used to justify continuing to own people stolen from Africa like livestock. And while we can talk all day about how the slaves of ancient Near East culture (this would have taken place in what is now Turkey or thereabout) were treated, that's not what the author is trying to say.

The radical part of this Scripture is the fact that the author is speaking directly to the servants at all. This was a major breach of protocol in this culture. Custom dictated that anything intended for the household was to go through the man as head of the household. So this is someone not interested in social conventions.

It probably indicates that this group of early Christians were meeting in secret, so that their masters or other officials wouldn't discover them. They were taking some real risk in assembling at all, and based on this call in verse 18 to serve masters well, we could reasonably assume there's grumbling in the group about quite the opposite. In fact, there may be rumor of a rebellion against these pagan masters.

Hang on, 1 Peter's author says. There's something larger at stake here, bigger than the individuals involved. This Christian movement, while growing, is still new and could be snuffed out by the powers that be if they're inclined to. In that case, there would just be more bloodshed, and the movement would be effectively dead. So although what is happening is wrong, and despite the suffering of these servants, they're urged to keep their focus on the longer game.

This is little consolation for those who have to go back to their master's house and get treated like crap. On the one hand, they're told they're precious, beloved children of God. In the real world, though, they're practically nothing. Suffice it to say that this is a "valley time" for these Christians. And while following this path of Jesus doesn't afford them the shortcut around the struggle that they might prefer, they are asked to find comfort in the fact that God—as expressed in Jesus—has been there.

God went through the valley. God was next to nothing. God surrendered to the darkness, knowing there was something beyond it. The reason God would take this journey isn't for God's own sake; it's for ours.

Stay the course. Push forward. Don't lose sight of what matters.

Heads-Up

Connecting the text to our world

We've all had dark-valley times. I know I have.

I was so excited about my next book coming out that it was practically all I thought about. It was finally with a major publisher, coming out in hardback and with a small army of publicists behind it to push me into the rarified air of being "kind of a big deal."

Then the publishing house decided to close the division that was publishing my book before it even came out. They still put the book out but didn't do anything to publicize it. Combine this with the fact that they were gridlocked in negotiations with the biggest online bookseller in the world, which meant that said bookseller showed all of their titles as unavailable in retaliation.

In that same year I was also diagnosed with epilepsy, and then hypertension. Suffice it to say that that year officially sucked. Here I was doing what I had felt called to do, but everything was falling apart. My book was a failure, my body was betraying me, and the prospect of hitting the best-seller list faded back to the stuff of daydreams.

The thing is, I wasn't doing it for the right reasons anymore. I was doing it to feed my own ego rather than to further the ministry Jesus had started two thousand years ago. That's not to say that God made my book fail and made me sick because I got a big head; I don't believe God engages humanity that way. But it helps to explain why I felt as alone as I had ever felt during that time.

I felt forgotten, not just by the public; I felt forgotten by God.

It turned out not to be the case, fortunately. I was the one who had forgotten my calling. I had gotten too comfortable with using my work to point toward myself rather than toward God. So when I found myself in the belly of the dark valley, my only company was my own self-interested aspiration.

To make a long story short, I lived to tell about it. I may not be competing with J. K. Rowling for book sales, but I like to think I achieved something greater: finding work with purpose.

Prayer for the Week

It's really easy to give in to my own impulses, even when they lead me in the wrong direction. Help me remember what matters.

Popping Off

Art/music/video and other cool stuff that relate to the text

"Long Road out of Eden," by The Eagles (song, 2007)

"Jesus Walks," by Kanye West (song, 2004)

One Big Family

~~~~~~~~~~~~~~

Lectionary Texts For

May 10, 2020 (Fifth Sunday of Easter)

Texts in Brief

My dog ate my Bible!

First Reading

Acts 7:55–60

Stephen, preaching the gospel to a crowd, has his teaching rejected by them. The crowd drags Stephen to the center of the crowd and begins to stone him to death. Stephen cries out to God to take him and not to hold this sin of killing him against his persecutors. The leader of the mob is Saul, who later becomes Paul the apostle.

Psalm

Psalm 31:1–5, 15–16

Here we have the king seeking refuge and protection by God from his enemies. There's a re-upping, of sorts, in pledging fidelity to God, concluded by asking God to stay close.

SECOND READING

1 Peter 2:2–10

Speaking to the early Christians in what is modern-day Turkey, Peter teaches them to be made holy from the inside out by God. Although they are seen as cast-offs and less than equal in the eyes of other people there, they are reminded that they are the foundation of a new thing being created by God. The world doesn't see in them what God sees, and for this, they should hold fast to their faith.

GOSPEL

John 14:1–14

The disciples are eager to see God for themselves to help bolster their confidence that they've made the right decision in following Jesus. Jesus, though, is surprised that they would ask this, since he has told them that by knowing him, they know God. God lives within him and is reflected in his life. So if they truly "get" what Jesus is about, they also understand the true nature of God. If they can't simply stand firm in this understanding, he offers to perform yet another miraculous work to convince them.

Bible, Decoded

Breaking down Scripture in plain language

Royal Priesthood—These Jesus-followers aren't just called the royal priesthood to make them feel better. Back in this time, priests stood as the go-between for God and humanity, and so they were as close to seeing

God in the flesh as people would ever get. If you were part of this priesthood, you were reflecting that same God image to others, which was both an honor and a great responsibility.

Philip—Philip was one of the original twelve named apostles in the Gospels. He appears this week in part because he is part of this movement of Christianity east, later evangelizing in Greece and what is now Syria.

Points to Ponder

First Thoughts

It's worthy of note that there are some parallels between this killing and that of Jesus. Not only is he killed for his ministry, but his last acts include calling out to God and begging forgiveness for his killers. In Jesus's story, one of the guards sees Jesus for who he is; in this case, we have Saul (soon to be Paul) who experiences his conversion experience after this.

Then we have a statement in the psalm that we also hear at Jesus's crucifixion. As Jesus breathes his final breaths, he quotes the central theme of this psalm: "Father, into Your hands I commend my spirit." It is one of two times that Jesus is said to have quoted the psalms from the cross.

In 1 Peter, we have another parallel between Jesus and his followers in reference to the early Christians, who were the "rejected stones" of their culture. As Jesus was referred to as the builder's stone that was rejected that becomes the cornerstone of God's new creation— first described in the prophets—now these followers are the continuing body of that same Christ.

Digging Deeper

Mining for what really matters . . . and gold

A lot of us may not know much about Stephen, but he's a really important figure in the early church. For starters, he is considered to be the first martyr of the Christian church. So his death is meant to serve as inspiration to others that following this movement through, even to our own demise, is a sacred cause.

This also represents a movement—quite literally—of the proto-Christians away from Jerusalem and further east and north. Jerusalem will no longer be the central nervous system of the messianic Jews. Part of this is because of what Stephen does. Understanding this will also help us understand why this crowd turns on him so readily.

Before preaching the message delivered in this Acts passage, Stephen has taken a really bold stand against the Jewish leadership in Jerusalem. Not only does he accuse them of murder, he also says they have broken Jewish law and stand in direct defiance of God.

No wonder these people want to kill him!

By this point, Stephen is a marked man. He is seen by Romans and Jews alike as an enemy of the state. Still, he holds fast to his calling, speaking his truth all the way to his final moments. The literary device of him using the same words that Jesus did at his death is less about what literally happened and more a way to highlight that he really fulfills the calling to which Jesus invites us. He gets it.

As for Jesus speaking words found in the Psalms, this is another tool of midrash employed to make a point. Obviously, he didn't have a transcriber there or anyone who likely would have remembered what he said word for word, let alone reported it years (or even decades) later to the authors of the Gospels. The significance here is to draw a direct line from Jesus to the bloodline of David, which of course takes us all the way back to Abraham.

We were promised that the Messiah would come from this lineage, so this is a gesture of promises kept.

But what about Stephen? He's not from the line of David, and as far as we know, Jesus had no kids. But now, the holy lineage continues not through blood but by the inspiration of the spirit. As far as God is concerned, Stephen's heritage is as legitimate as David's or Jesus's. Later, we have Paul join the family, and it continues to grow.

All of this helps us understand why Paul talks so much about living in a spirit of divine adoption. Family is really important to them. And whereas we might say today that our friends are like family, it carried a lot of weight in those times. It meant everything.

Heads-Up

Connecting the text to our world

Sometimes you can't prepare yourself for the things that come to you in ministry. It's a sacred invitation to be a part of some of the most intimate parts of people's lives, during both good times and bad.

This was one of the bad times, and yet heartbreakingly beautiful.

A single mother in one of our previous congregations had a young son, about four years old, who was on the autism spectrum. Though he could engage the world around him more than some on the spectrum, he was nonverbal. Like many people who can't express themselves with words, he could melt down in frustration on occasion, or simply because his senses were overwhelmed by input.

Having a son on the higher end of the spectrum (and she would argue a husband on it, too), Amy has both a special understanding and a heart-space for this boy, who we'll call Jonathan. She and Jonathan developed somewhat of a bond, at least in as much as he did with anyone, and she was patient and gracious with any attention he allowed her to give him.

Jonathan's mother worked to support her son and herself during the day and had limited resources to find special care for him. She ended up entrusting him to a home-based daycare system run by women who may or may not have been licensed, but it was all she could afford. Things were fine until one day she came to pick him up and Jonathan had bruises along the side of his face. The caregiver dismissed it as the result of a fall, which little kids do a lot. But when he came home with bruises around his neck, she knew there was a problem.

She brought Jonathan to Amy to talk about what to do, and it was clear that he had been the victim of abuse. It's not uncommon for untrained caregivers to lose their tempers with an autistic child, but abuse is abuse. Amy's heart broke when she saw him.

Amy knelt down to look more closely at him when his eyes connected with hers. Not only that, he opened his arms wide, inviting a hug. While Amy's usually good at putting on professional appearances until she gets home, she couldn't hold back her tears this time.

Despite the hurt done to this innocent little boy, and in spite of the veil of separation often holding him back from connection with the rest of the world, something beautiful occasionally still broke through. Love persisted, and it had been made all that more beautiful by withstanding the damage done to it.

Prayer for the Week

I want to trust that love persists in spite of the pain that accompanies it. Help me believe it.

Popping Off

Art/music/video and other cool stuff that relate to the text

Rain Man (movie, 1988)

It's All Relative, by A. J. Jacobs (book, 2017)

Holy Jell-O

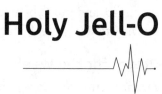

Lectionary Texts For

May 17, 2020 (Sixth Sunday of Easter)

Texts in Brief

My dog ate my Bible!

First Reading

Acts 17:22–31

Paul speaks before the elders of Athens, offering them praise for their faithfulness to their own religion. He notes how prominent their places of worship and tributes to their gods are throughout the city. Instead of condemning them for being pagans, he notes that they have one edifice that stands in honor of "an unknown god." He claims that this unknown god is the God of Israel, revealed through Jesus. This God is the source of all creation and life. And while God offers mercy for those who didn't know better before, now God calls all to turn toward this new path.

Psalm
Psalm 66:8–20

The psalmist calls on all to offer praise to God because although they've been put through a lot, they have endured and have emerged on the other side of it. It's now time to fulfill the promises made to God when they were struggling and asked for relief. The psalmist offers to speak of their own faith to any who will hear it, because they believe that their own delivery from adversity means their faith can be a beacon to others in need.

Second Reading
1 Peter 3:13–22

Peter emphasizes to the early Christians that they should remain faithful even when they find it hard or are persecuted. In other words, suffering will come, but endure it for the right cause. By holding fast to our conviction in what is right, we're given the endurance we need to withstand suffering. If we abandon what is right to get out of harm's way, we're left enduring the burden of having turned on God to save ourselves, which is in itself suffering.

Gospel
John 14:15–21

Jesus is starting to talk about his departure to be with God. He doesn't want this to discourage his followers from staying strong in their faith and in living out the way to which they have been called by Jesus. Living in this way is a means to express our love of God, opening ourselves up for God to love us back. In this bond with God through the covenant of love, Jesus continues to have a presence with his followers.

Bible, Decoded
Breaking down Scripture in plain language

Areopagus—In Greek, this word literally means *big piece of rock*. No, Paul wasn't preaching to stones; in this case, it was also the name for the elders' council in a Grecian community. The origins of the term aren't entirely clear, but it's possible that this council was considered foundational to the stability and order of the community. They heard public matters related to criminal and religious issues, in particular. It was similar to the senate within the Roman Empire.

Advocate—The "Advocate" referred to in the John passage is the Holy Spirit, or the third manifestation of God in the Trinitarian understanding of the Divine. In essence, it is the power of God that Jesus possessed, but free of the physical limits of humanity that bound Jesus. The particular choice of this name suggests that this spirit is not only for support but also to help be a partner in how we present ourselves to God.

Points to Ponder
First Thoughts

If you didn't already notice, there is only one reading from the Hebrew Bible section of our Scriptures this week (from Psalms). Although there's not an explicit reason given for this, it's probably because the focus at this point in the church year is on the transfer of responsibility to represent this "new way" from Jesus and his small circle of disciples to all others who have been touched by this ministry. We're witnessing the birth of something new, another resurrection of sorts: Christ in corporate form.

Sometimes Christians get into arguments about whether faith or good works are more important in our identity as Jesus-followers. Paul notes in the Acts text that God doesn't need us to perform certain acts of worship or goodness, so much as these gestures are an outward expression of an inward state—as described in John—which opens us up and prepares a space in our lives for God to connect with us. So while acts of worship and mercy are beneficial in the real world in some sense, it's also about a sort of spiritual conditioning.

While it's already noted above in the Acts summary, it's worth emphasizing how Paul goes about speaking of his new belief system in the presence of others who don't think like him. Nowhere in his words or tone is there any preemptive judgment or condemnation. In fact, he praises their faithfulness and simply offers to add something more that they already seem to be seeking in their faith practices.

Digging Deeper
Mining for what really matters . . . and gold

We don't talk as much about the Holy Spirit as we talk about Jesus or God, the Father/Mother. That's because there's at least as much mystery surrounding what exactly the Holy Spirit is as there is any real clarity. In one scene, it's a dove. In this Gospel text, the Holy Spirit is an advocate. We hear throughout the Bible about breezes blowing and still, small voices, but as soon as we try to pin down the Holy Spirit, it seems to slip out of grasp.

So I guess the Holy Spirit is kind of like Jell-O.

It's worth noting that in John Jesus says this spirit is "another Advocate," meaning that this continues an existing relationship already forged by Jesus himself. So the emphasis he's trying to make here is that though he's leaving soon, they won't actually lose anything, provided that they have faith in the bond that has been set between them and God.

But that's easily overlooked, especially considering what's happening here. Yes, this text comes up after Easter, but in the Gospel text Jesus is actually getting ready to be arrested soon, which of course leads to his death. The disciples know this, too, and they're probably not very happy about it. If they had their way, they'd cling to Jesus for the rest of their lives. But, Jesus says, that's not the point.

The relationship they have with him is actually a relationship with God. While they may love Jesus the man, it's God he's always been pointing to. So what, is the Holy Spirit supposed to be like our invisible Jesus-friend-substitute now?

I get the sense that the relationship is the Holy Spirit. The bond created between the human and Divine is itself the Advocate working on our behalf. It is the relationship that evokes mercy and love from God, and that keeps us open to accepting it.

Consider how differently we act toward someone with whom we have a relationship. We tend to be far more patient and slower to judge if we have history with them. That's because we know them more intimately, and that deeper knowing, while not eliminating our judgment all together, sets it in a contextual relief in which it doesn't tend to stand up against our love for that person.

In short: love wins.

Heads-Up

Connecting the text to our world

I get pretty passionate about politics. I have probably a half-dozen politically oriented sources in my daily newsfeed, which I'll admit I check multiple times a day. If I couldn't justify it as part of my work, I'd be the first to say it was a bit of a problem.

With that passion come some pretty strong feelings though, both about issues I feel are important and about the personalities behind them. In fact, I've noticed that the more we enter into this new digitally networked reality, the more that individual personalities seem to matter in politics. Whether someone comes across as likeable and trustworthy can be more critical to electability than policy positions.

It also means that when we like or don't like someone in the political world, it becomes a big deal. Combine this personality-driven politics with my innate passion for it, and you can imagine how I end up feeling, both good and bad, about our esteemed leaders.

It's all too easy to create avatars of these people with whom we have no real relationship and to develop all manner of fictitious narratives in our imaginations about what we would say to them given the chance. Not all of it is always fit for prime-time air either, at least in my case. In fact, I have on more than one occasion, expressed a litany of less-than-Christlike epithets toward certain people in power toward whom I have . . . let's say intense feelings.

A friend recognized this issue in her own congregation recently, and how it tended to get affirmed and amplified, given the common political bent of the vast majority of the attendees in the community. And as a good pastor would, she saw this as a growth opportunity for all of them.

The next week, she brought in a picture of the person who was the object of such resentment and criticism, only it wasn't a snapshot from any of the recent headlines. Instead, it was a photo of him as a little boy. She set it up in the fellowship hall and left it there for a few weeks. Her intention was to help those who found it all too easy to dehumanize him and see him as somehow less-than as a real, vulnerable, beloved child of God.

None of this took any political position on anything, and yet a lot of people had a really hard time with this. The reason was because it punched a hole right through their justification for tearing him apart (which felt good and in which they felt perfectly justified). After all, who would say such things to a little kid?

Over time, the venom dissipated, and they even began to pray for the leader. It wasn't easy, but it wasn't about the leader himself in the first place. It was about retaining the orientation of their own hearts, opening them up to the ever-present bond to all of creation (yes, even him) that is predicated on love, and love alone.

It's hard, it's vulnerable, and sometimes it's really unsatisfying. If Jesus can pray for his own killers while fighting for his final breaths, we should be able to muster a similar fortitude in our own context.

Prayer for the Week

God, help me have the resolve to pray for the people I can't stand.

Popping Off

Art/music/video and other cool stuff that relate to the text

Sense8 (TV series, 2015–2018)

Contact (movie, 1997)

A Lower Power

Lectionary Texts For

May 24, 2020 (Ascension Sunday)

Texts in Brief

My dog ate my Bible!

First Reading

Acts 1:6–14

Jesus's disciples ask him if he will now reconcile the tribes of Israel and bring them back to power, but he says such things aren't necessary for them to know. They will, however, receive God-given power now that his time among them is complete. He ascends to be with God. While they stare into the sky, two "men in white" ask them why they are looking for Jesus this way. So, they retreat to a hidden upper room and prayed.

Psalm
Psalm 68:1–10, 32–35

This is a prayer of longing that God might rise in power in a way that causes the faithful to rejoice and their enemies to wither in fear. The psalm then shifts to thanksgiving for the provision God has provided, particularly for the most vulnerable. It ends with praise to God for God's sovereignty over all, and for affording power to God's faithful, who are likely to prevail over enemies.

Second Reading
1 Peter 4:12–14, 5:6–11

Peter's audience continues to be persecuted for their beliefs, but he compares their present suffering with the suffering Jesus underwent. This, he says, can be cause for joy because it helps them to know Jesus even more intimately. They are asked to resist and endure the hardship, with the assurance that they will be restored and empowered by God in time.

Gospel
John 17:1–11

Jesus calls out to God to bring him back to God, as it was before creation, because his work on earth is now done. Jesus assures God that his followers now recognize that the spiritual gifts they have and the renewed hope and faith they are experiencing are from God, as Jesus has shown them. Finally, Jesus prays for God to hold his followers close and to give them protection in his absence.

Bible, Decoded
Breaking down Scripture in plain language

Olivet—The name literally just means *place of olives*, though we tend to know the scene of Jesus's ascension more commonly as the Mount of Olives. Not surprising that such an event takes place on a hill or mountain, given our many stories up to now that involve experiences of the human and Divine intersecting on mountaintops.

Men in White—We're not told exactly who these guys are, but whenever we see people dressed in white robes in the Bible, it tends to mean they are heavenly, not earthly, residents. But this doesn't necessarily mean they were angels either, since it was believed that the saints also lived in heaven. Given the appearance of Moses and Elijah with Jesus before, it might be reasonable to assume that it was them in this case.

Points to Ponder
First Thoughts

You might notice that this week, Ascension Sunday, is the seventh Sunday after Easter. As noted in other studies, the number seven is significant in Judaism, as it is a symbol of divine perfection. It might also refer back here to the creation story, in which God rested on the seventh day after creation was complete. This may be meant to symbolize to us that Jesus's work on earth was complete, too, and that it was time to retreat.

It's also worth noting the similarity between the two men in white who ask the disciples why they are looking skyward for Jesus and the men in white who ask the women at the tomb why they look for Jesus there. It seems to symbolize the disciples' need to cling to what was, rather than looking forward toward what can become.

Digging Deeper
Mining for what really matters . . . and gold

Technically, the ascension was celebrated three days ago, which marked forty days after the resurrection. So for all you Bible nerds, feel free to scoff at the theory about the number seven above. Again, this is a biblical number that often indicates a state of transition, or a "no longer here but not yet there" situation. Usually, though, something is given birth to on the other end of the forty days.

In the case of the flood, the earth was remade. After the forty years of exile, the Israelites came into their promised land, where their kingdom of Israel would be reestablished. This is also one reason that Lent (the period before Easter) lasts forty days: because Christ is being reborn, remade, or reimagined on the other side of the cross. So here we have another forty, at the end of which Jesus is leaving his disciples and is being reunified with God to be one and the same with the Father/Mother/Source.

Jesus isn't the only one being remade, though. This sets an expectation for the followers of Jesus left behind to be the presence of God in the world that will give birth to this new thing, with this new God-given authority and power. Talk about a passing of the baton! This is no small thing.

It's also not what Jesus's disciples had in mind. After all, they were still waiting around for him to restore the kingdom of Israel like the good old days so that they could reign over these other now-minor powers. They wanted to be the shining example on a hill that shone down on everyone and to whom everyone came in supplication and surrender. They wanted that sort of power.

This is not the power they're given, though. They're left down below to contend with the loss of their leader and beset on all sides by those who would rather see them extinguished.

God gives to God's people in abundance, but all too often it's not what we think we want or need. As I've been known to say (especially to my kids), God help us if we all get everything we want. Saint Mick Jagger of the Holy Rolling Stones put it well:

> You can't always get what you want,
> But if you try sometimes, you might find you
>   get what you need.

Heads-Up

Connecting the text to our world

Nelson Mandela was not always a pacifist. After finding his efforts to change his society with nonviolence fell short of his expectations, he joined the South African Communist Party, with whom he created a militant organization bent on bringing down the all-white South African government by any means necessary. For his insurrection, he was sentenced to life in prison.

He spent twenty-seven years of his life in a jail cell. No doubt he prayed for some providential delivery from his captivity or for some uprising to finally drag the leadership down from their positions of power over the majority-black population. But none of that happened. For more than three decades, he sat, waiting, praying, and doing all he could to cling to hope.

In the 1990s, Mandela was finally released. Given his time as a political prisoner, advocating for his people's rights, his profile as an icon of black liberation grew, yielding a movement around him that the government could not ignore. Ultimately, as you know, apartheid did indeed fall, and Nelson Mandela became the first black president of South Africa.

One of his first acts as president was to meet with his former captors and to try to find a way to work with them. While many in his cohort objected fiercely, he had come to realize that turning the tables on the white leadership was akin to what Walter Wink referred to as changing the rulers, but not the rules. Nelson Mandela knew that real transformation had less to do with who was in charge and everything to do with real, profound healing and reconciliation.

Mandela and his leadership team committed to a ceremony of forgiveness for their white oppressors, which ultimately has been instrumental to the maintenance of peace and general prosperity in the country. Though far from perfect, the cycle of violence and oppression was broken, all without bloodshed.

None of this happened on his initial desired timeline or with his anticipated methods. But in God's time, and in God's ways, something even better emerged from the shadows, bursting into brilliant light that shined over all people.

Prayer for the Week

Help the limitations of my own imagination and heart from holding back the limitless potential for hope, healing, and justice in the world.

Popping Off

Art/music/video and other cool stuff that relate to the text

"You Can't Always Get What You Want," by The Rolling Stones (song, 1969)

Nelson Mandela Foundation: nelsonmandela.org

People, Get Ready

Lectionary Texts For

May 31, 2020 (Pentecost Sunday)

Texts in Brief

My dog ate my Bible!

First Reading

Acts 2:1–21

The disciples are gathered in a home when a sound like wind sweeps through. There's a glow above each of them, and they start speaking in different languages. People gathering in curiosity assume they're drunk; others believe it is the presence of the holy. Peter refers to the prophet Joel, noting that this descent of the Holy Spirit would happen and give spiritual gifts to all who followed God's way. There would be dramatic signs of transformation and disruption on earth, and many would come to God.

PSALM

Psalm 104:24–34, 35b

A psalm of observance that God is the source of all life, death, creation, and destruction. Creation and life follow in God's presence, and they crumble and wither away in God's absence. Because of this awesome, unmatched power, the psalmist will praise God until their days have ended.

SECOND READING

1 Corinthians 12:3b–13

There are lots of spiritual gifts, but they all come from the same source. No gift is lesser or greater than another; in fact, they all work interdependently and in concert with each other, just as we should. This common ground within the embrace of the Holy Spirit binds us together beyond any differences that might otherwise separate us.

GOSPEL

John 20:19–23

Jesus meets with his disciples, who are retreated in hiding. Rather than justifying or indulging their fears, he endows them with spiritual gifts to go back out and serve the world as he had done. They will now be able to forgive sin with God's power, but it is their choice whether to offer forgiveness.

Bible, Decoded

Breaking down Scripture in plain language

Divided Tongues, as of Fire—No, the disciples aren't on fire. This glow around them signifies the presence of the Holy Spirit.

Last Days—This is a widely argued phrase in Christianity, sometimes interpreted as "end-times," "end of days," and by others, "later days." For some, this portends the end of the earth; for others, it is a foreshadowing of the destruction of the temple in Jerusalem, which Jesus himself predicted. But this translation of "last days" does not appear in all translations of Scripture. In some it is understood to mean something closer to "later on" or "in the future."

Points to Ponder

First Thoughts

While we focus on the text in Acts as a testament to how God gives God's faithful spiritual gifts, it's hardly the first time it has happened. For example, in the John text this week, Jesus (before he has called for his disciples to have the Holy Spirit [a.k.a., the "Advocate"] with them when he leaves) breathes the gift of forgiving sin on them. Even further back, in the book of Numbers (an alternate text we didn't cover this week), God's spirit descends on Moses and his followers, endowing them with spiritual gifts.

There are two reasons this Acts text is particularly important this week. First, it signifies what many call the beginning of the movement in earnest that will become the Christian church. Second, it is the first reported example of gifts of the spirit being given after Jesus's death and ascension.

Finally, it's important to consider that these gifts also come with an expectation of a call to action. These aren't the kind of gifts that are self-serving or that stand to further our wealth or status in the culture. On the contrary, employing these gifts in public will often be controversial and even dangerous to their own well-being. The gifts are more like giving someone the necessary equipment to undertake a journey we're sending them on.

Digging Deeper

Mining for what really matters . . . and gold

Most people spend much of their time and energy focusing on the descent of the Holy Spirit and its effect on the disciples, which is understandable. But in our effort to look in unexpected places to allow Scripture to speak, let's consider Peter's response to the crowd instead.

The audience that has gathered is both intrigued by this transformation and also cynically critical. They dismiss the bizarre phenomenon as the result of too much partying. Apparently they weren't around when the spirit rushed through like wind and the disciples lit up like Roman candles.

Or maybe their eyes weren't open to that part.

We've heard before about how such a presence is only encountered by those receptive to it. If they're not fit and ready, they may have experienced nothing more than this group of guys jabbering spontaneously like they were hammered. In that case, their question makes perfect sense: What does this mean?

Peter is really coming into his own here, quoting the ancient prophets much like Jesus would have done to give credence and historic context to his words. He cites Joel, who predicted such a time would come. We can divide up his response into sections, or movements, based on what he says that Joel actually doesn't.

First, his citation of Joel at the beginning is actually a paraphrase. While the actual text from Joel just starts with something more like "after this . . .", Peter is much more definitive about this being the end of something. What it's the end of, we're not sure. It could be (as many Christians have interpreted) a prediction that the world would soon end. Or it could be referring to the end of an era, as the world prepared to emerge into something entirely different.

In our context, at least, this new era would be a post-Jesus movement, inspired by him but without him physically present to guide his followers. As we noted last week, this was both scary (what do we do now?) and exhilarating. They were no longer limited by how far their leader could go; now they were being sent out everywhere.

Second, while he refers to slaves just like Joel does, Peter adds that God calls them "mine." So whereas slaves previously have been seen as little more than property, like sheep or trade tools, now they are beloved possessions and creations of God, just like the rest of us. God is laying claim to the humanity of those whose humanity we had ignored. This is a sort of gauntlet laid down before the disciples and others to now do the same.

Finally, while Joel doesn't say precisely why these spiritual gifts are given, Peter does. According to him, all gifts of the Spirit are for the purpose of prophecy. As we've noted before, though some interpret *prophecy* as predicting the future (often with horrible, scary imagery), the role of a prophet is to be a divine agent of revelation. They are helping to make clear to others what God has already made clear to them.

And just in case we're not convinced Peter himself is a prophet, he concludes with some of that trademark horrible, scary prophetic imagery. Though this isn't necessarily meant to be taken literally, he's making the point that this change that's around the corner is big. It's a shift in thinking and living that will change pretty much everything.

The message underlying the prophecy all of the disciples are now intended to share: People, get ready.

Heads-Up

Connecting the text to our world

Religion is no stranger to upheaval and even division. Keep in mind that the temple in Jerusalem, which was considered the nerve center of the Jewish faith, wasn't just destroyed once. It fell twice, was attacked over fifty times, and changed hands more than forty times. So Peter's claim that some big change was around the bend likely would have been met with excited anticipation by some but with exhausted eye-rolling from others.

Yes, the Israelites were more than tired by now of being an occupied people, but considering their history, it wouldn't be surprising if some would rather leave well enough alone. Sure, they were under another government's control, but who has the energy for another fight? Then along come these troublemaking Christians, challenging not only the Roman Empire, but also the religious status quo within Judaism. Enter: more division.

Fast-forward a thousand years to what is known in history as the Great Schism, when the Christian churches of the East and West split apart, divided over orthodoxy. While there's no real rancor between Eastern Orthodox and the Western church these days, the two weren't reconciled either.

Five hundred years after that, Martin Luther pushes back against the Western Catholic Church's insistence on serving as an intermediary between God and God's people. From this came the Protestant Reformation.

Now, as articulated by theologians and historians like author Phyllis Tickle, we may well be on the verge of a new thing, which some call the third great awakening. In her book *The Great Emergence: How Christianity Is Changing and Why*, Tickle contends that organized religion goes through these kinds of huge disruptions every five hundred years or so. Think of it as a sort of institutional house-cleaning or a breaking out of the Spirit from the bonds of institutionalism that have formed around it in a sort of gilded sarcophagus.

This means we're due. What this will look like, we can't be sure, but the disciples had no idea what the new movement they would help give birth to would look like either. Paul and Peter couldn't have possibly imagined the church of today when they were writing these letters to their colleagues. Yet here we are.

What's next is up to God.

Prayer for the Week

God, help me use what you've given me to be part of the new thing you're creating. Allow me to be a steward rather than a barrier.

Popping Off

Art/music/video and other cool stuff that relate to the text

"People Get Ready," by Curtis Mayfield (song, 1965)

The Great Emergence: How Christianity Is Changing and Why, by Phyllis Tickle (book, 2012)

Trust Fall!

Lectionary Texts For
June 7, 2020 (Trinity Sunday)

Texts in Brief
My dog ate my Bible!

First Reading
Genesis 1:1–2:4a

This is one of two creation stories in Genesis: the one without Adam and Eve in it. It lays out a poetic account of the origin of all creation and a theological justification for holy rest, or Sabbath.

Psalm
Psalm 8

This psalm of effusive praise marvels at the works of God's hand described in the Genesis text. And while it places humanity below God in stature, it places us above all else. In fact, it suggests we are to be stewards over the rest of creation, as we are as near to God as possible in the material world (at least at this point).

SECOND READING
2 Corinthians 13:11–13

Paul closes his letter to his colleagues in Corinth. Just in case they've forgotten, or have already started fighting again, he reminds them that maintaining their cohesion as a group is the most important thing. They are to embrace each other with the same sort of peace that is offered to them by God. In fact, they are to show each other the love of family by offering greeting with a "holy kiss."

GOSPEL
Matthew 28:16–20

This is the scene where the disciples encounter Jesus at the meeting place where he told them to go, near the sea of Galilee. Some of them are in worshipful awe while others are skeptical. He commands them to take what they have learned, seen, and been given and to go out throughout the world to bring people to this new way of following Christ.

Bible, Decoded
Breaking down Scripture in plain language

Holy Kiss—This type of kiss was common among people (specifically of the same sex) of this time and culture. It's known as the "kiss of peace" and symbolizes brotherhood or sisterhood.

Dominion—The literal meaning is to rule over something. Unfortunately some who call themselves *dominionists* take this to mean that the planet—or even the universe—is our personal playground or trash can. Rather, in the time when this was written, ownership over something else that was living came with many rules of protocol for care, respect, and stewardship. It was a responsibility, not just a gift.

Points to Ponder

First Thoughts

The Genesis text raises many challenges for biblical literalists, while addressing many overarching theological and existential questions if considered metaphorically. It takes on many age-old human curiosities, like: "Why are we here?" and "How did we get here?" It also makes the case for rest, because in as much as we are to act in accordance with God, we honor and even imitate God when we hold the Sabbath day as sacred for rest.

The psalm continues addressing these big human questions by taking on: "What is our purpose?" In this text, we serve as divinely ordained ambassadors to manage and care for all else on earth. It presents humanity as superior to animal life (and natural resources) but also as responsible for its care, sustainability, and balance. To take the mantle of the first without also accepting the second is irresponsible.

Not unlike the position God leaves humanity in as stewards of creation, Paul leaves his fellow Christians in charge of the faith movement in this region. While he is positive and inspiring in his farewell, the fact that he feels he has to remind them to stick it out together suggests he may have his doubts if they can pull it off.

Oh, and is it just me, or does anyone else hear the end of the Matthew text being narrated by Obi-Wan Kenobi?

Digging Deeper

Mining for what really matters . . . and gold

For those who aren't part of the Catholic or Anglican traditions, the notion of Trinity Sunday may or may not be something they've heard of. And while we all know about the whole Father-Son-Holy Spirit construct of the Trinity, we may not be entirely clear about the importance it is supposed to play in our daily faith lives.

While there is mention of God throughout the Bible, who many people refer to as "Father" (though Jesus's term is more like "Daddy" or "Papa"), there's no explicit naming of the triune Godhead anywhere in the Bible. That's because the notion of that being central to our theology didn't come along until centuries later. Since then, many Christians—and especially Protestants—have tended to diminish the role of the Trinity in worship, study, and their imagery of the Divine.

That's why we may be left scratching our heads about why these texts speak to the Trinity. The short answer is: because no Scripture does exactly. And while the expression of the three-in-oneness of God in the Trinity can be helpful in allowing us to imagine more than one expression of God, we Protestants don't feel like it's a central enough doctrine in many cases to hinge our entire identity on. For us, rather, it's a way of helping us think of God in different ways: human, divine, and . . . something else.

This brings us to the Matthew passage, which isn't usually thought of as a trinitarian passage at all. In fact, it's usually called the Great Commission text, because it's when Jesus orders his disciples to go out and make disciples of all nations. For many Christians, this is the justification for everything from embedded conversion-based mission work abroad to knocking on strangers' doors to the Crusades so many centuries ago.

Unfortunately, we can't "make" anyone a disciple. This is one of many places where the translation to English may have done more harm than good. In our postindustrial mindset, we think of "making" something as creating something out of nothing, or at least giving relatively worthless elemental parts real value and function. And while this may resonate with much of what we teach in evangelism, it's a pretty strong value judgment—assuming those we're reaching out to are worthless until we make them truly worthwhile.

The King James translation reads as "teach all nations," which is at least gentler on first blush. However, it still suggests that we know something they don't, almost like we're doing them a favor, and that smacks of colonialist religion.

Going back to the Greek, it's more helpful to think of *disciple* as a verb; it's something we are to be rather than something we make. Remember that we're not the makers in this relationship; God is. God made humanity to begin with, and Jesus made these common laborers into disciples. Now they're to go abroad.

Rather than converting people per se, the Wartburg Project suggests it's more helpful to think of this as an act of gathering, or attraction. If these disciples really have been transformed from the inside out, it should be fairly obvious, especially to people where they've never been. Wouldn't that attract attention, maybe invite questions? It's an age-old tension between evangelism being an act of attraction versus one of promotion. In one, we try to seek out and make others more like us. In the other, we are more like Christ, and in doing so, others are drawn to it just as these men were drawn to Jesus.

The one consistency in all translations of this text is the notion of "going." There is a call to action that, given the spread of the gospel accounted for in the rest of the New Testament, took hold in them. And not just in the ones who believed right away in this transformed Jesus they encountered; even the skeptics ultimately fulfilled this call. Jesus didn't argue or advocate for himself to make them believe he was who he said he was. He depended on the compelling truth of what already had awakened within them.

Regardless of what they thought of Jesus in that moment, they all heard the voice and call of God. Moreover, they responded. That's what mattered most to Jesus.

Heads-Up
Connecting the text to our world

Anyone who has been to a corporate training event, or who has seen a movie making fun of corporate training events, knows about the trust fall. It's an exercise to build community cooperation and (not surprisingly) to grow trust among the team members. Basically, one person is either blindfolded or closes their eyes, faces away from the group, folds their arms and falls backward with no way to see if they'll be caught by their colleagues or not.

You can always find the ones who struggle to put their fate in the hands of others, because they'll end up taking a self-preserving step backward as they fall, or they can't do it at all. The whole exercise involves a sort of social contract, all parts of which have to work together or it falls apart.

Then there's Daniel Tosh.

The highly irreverent, boundary-pushing comedian had a show called *Tosh.0*, on which he would play viral web videos, usually of people doing something stupid and hurting themselves, and then he would make fun of them. But as he realized he had to keep the show fresh, he started to insert himself into the scenes.

One of the funniest skits involved Tosh walking up to various unsuspecting people or crowds, turning away, spontaneously yelling "Trust fall!" and tossing himself backward into them. While the fast-thinkers usually caught him, sometimes the results were hilariously disastrous.

The thing that made it funny was because it pointed out, intentionally or not, that acts of trust require an agreement and an investment on all sides. You can't just decide to fall backward anytime, anywhere and expect people to catch you. In fact, everyone can end up getting hurt. You have to build the trust through communication and relationship first, after which such an exercise actually makes sense.

Just saying "trust fall!" isn't enough, nor is it enough to walk up to a stranger and say "trust me!" That part takes time and work. And both sides will change in the process, hopefully for the better, while learning more about themselves and each other. It's not as funny, but it makes sense, which Daniel Tosh usually doesn't.

Prayer for the Week

Help me be trustworthy, so that trust is given to me, rather than having to ask for it. And when you say "go," help me trust enough to do it.

Popping Off

Art/music/video and other cool stuff that relate to the text

"Surprise Trust Fall" skits from *Tosh.0* (TV series, 2010–2014)

The Divine Dance: The Trinity and Your Transformation, by Richard Rohr (book, 2017)

The Other Side of Suffering

Lectionary Texts For

June 14, 2020 (Second Sunday after Pentecost)

Texts in Brief

My dog ate my Bible!

FIRST READING

Genesis 18:1–15, (21:1–7)

Abraham is visited by three men, who he recognizes as God. He invites them to stay and prepares a meal for them. While eating, one of them tells Abraham he and his wife, Sarah, will have a child, even though they're really old. Sarah scoff at this, but by the time Abraham is a hundred, they have a son, who they name Isaac, which means *laughter*.

PSALM

Exodus 19:2–8a

Once the Israelites enter the Sinai region (the peninsula region northwest of Egypt), Moses speaks to God on a mountain, where God tells him that God will consider the Israelites to be a holy nation of people if they will stay faithful to God. Moses explains this to the elders, who tell the rest of the Israelites. Everyone agrees to do as God tell them.

SECOND READING
Romans 5:1–8

We are made right and holy, the author says, because of our faith in God. In suffering for our faith, it says, we can actually be grateful because of what comes from it. Suffering gives us endurance, which forges our character and makes room in us for hope. And since hope is independent of present circumstances, it can't be taken from us. This hope, it claims, is based in the faith that God will commit to us to the point of death, even when we don't really deserve it.

GOSPEL
Matthew 9:35–10:8, (9–23)

In going out to other communities, Jesus encounters more needs than he can meet on his own. So he commissions the disciples to help him, giving them the ability to heal and cast out evil, as he already did. He orders them not to take money with them or to accept payment for their work, but rather to depend on the hospitality of others to subsist. When met with hostility or indifference, they're ordered to move on. But if they're welcomed in as guests, they are to stay with their hosts and bless them. They're ordered only to do this among their fellow Israelites for now. They're warned they'll be brutalized for their work, but they should stay strong.

Bible, Decoded

Breaking down Scripture in plain language

Oaks of Mamre—The Oaks, or Oak, of Mamre is actually different from the region called Mamre, which had been around a lot longer. The Oaks of Mamre was considered to be a holy place, also called the Oaks of Abraham, because of this story of God's miracle performed here for Abraham and Sarah. It's also where Abraham builds an altar after Lot leaves. Metaphorically or poetically, it's important to know that such oaks were ancient. When they died, they would remain standing, and a new sapling would spring up next to the old tree, connected to the old root system, which gave it life.

Rephidim—One of the Israelites' stops in their journey from Egypt to the yet-to-be-seen promised land. While they are camping at Rephidim, they are attacked by the Amalekites. But led in battle by Joshua, and with God's providence, they defeat the Amalekites, advancing then to Sinai.

Points to Ponder

First Thoughts

This is the beginning of the time in the church year when the lectionary starts doubling up on Scriptures as "first" and "second" readings, sometimes giving us five or six texts to cover. But to keep my publisher from killing me and to keep this book from being a thousand pages long, we'll opt for alternate texts when they're suggested along with a psalm.

Interesting that this story about Abraham appears this week instead of last week, which was Trinity Sunday.

Though the text doesn't specifically say if one of the strangers is God, or if all of them are, this is one example in Scripture the doctrine of the Trinity comes from.

In the Romans text, the word that seems to jump out is *boast*. This is one of a few examples of the word choice showing up in the epistles, or letters, in the New Testament. It also appears in the Hebrew Bible texts. Boasting was actually considered culturally acceptable in Jewish culture. However, it was only proper when it was about something or someone else not directly connected to you. In this way, the type of boasting Paul is calling for is more like celebrating or affirming another's virtues or achievements. No humble-brags need apply.

We should note that while, in other stories, Jesus pushes the disciples to reach out specifically to non-Jews, this time he wants them to stay among their own. Even then, he says—or maybe especially because of this—he knows they'll be persecuted. Fortunately this never happens in congregations . . . right?

Digging Deeper

Mining for what really matters . . . and gold

The passages seem to work together this week, if from different perspectives. First, they're all about propagation of some sort, be it by birth, appointment, or evangelism. Something that starts small will grow, but only in God's time and God's ways. Second, there's a lot about hospitality and engaging the stranger this week, whether we're the host or the guest.

In Genesis, the entire encounter is predicated on Abraham following the cultural rules of hospitality, which compel him to treat strangers who happen by more indulgently than he might himself or his own family. Not only does he make room for the guests, he makes a sacrifice for them. Only then does the stranger speak of the gift they will soon have.

In Exodus, the Israelites are the very definition of strangers in a strange land. Suffice it to say that their presence is less than welcome in the region. In fact, their lives have already been threatened twice just since leaving captivity in Egypt. And yet, in remaining faithful, they will live into the blessing that awaits them on the other side of their present suffering.

Paul's letter lays out the map from suffering to standing awash in the blessings of God. Again, not an ideal path, but one that his fellow Christians are reminded is worth the trouble.

Finally, in Matthew, Jesus is sending his disciples out to do the work they're called to do, even though he knows it won't be easy, to say the least. But, he says, this is what it is all about, so to give up when it's hard for lack of faith in the result would be shortsighted.

Back in Genesis, we need to remember that this isn't the first time Sarah and Abraham have been promised children by God. In fact, God told Abraham his descendants would be as numerous as the stars in the galaxy. Yet here they are, about to enter into their second century with no kids. Of course they remember the promise, but at some point to hang on to hope starts to feel foolish. Sarah's had to endure decades of watching others around her grow their families, likely many generations over. It's understandable by now that the suffering of unrealized expectations is too much for her to deal with.

But as Paul points out, and Jesus reiterates, we don't give up and abandon hope because the situation sucks. In fact, we're told, it will suck, no doubt. So to work through it, we have to recognize that our expectations for outcomes aren't the same as hope. In fact, our expectations may be the very thing that challenges our hope the most.

Expectations are too easily dashed against the rocks of suffering, while hope is the nourishment that sustains us through it. In faith, we find the hope we need, but to get to it, we have to lay down our expectations.

Heads-Up

Connecting the text to our world

Amy and I have friends who have wanted kids for a long time. As their community, including us, grew from couples into families, and even some into (albeit young) grandparents, their spare bedroom remained empty. For years, we would ask them how their efforts were faring, from supplements and natural methods to leaning on the assistance of science.

For one reason or another, nothing worked. After long enough, they stopped bringing it up, and we stopped asking. The desire hadn't gone away; if anything it had grown as the years passed and the chances for viability of a baby waned. Most of us had assumed they had just stopped trying all together, finding contentment in the fullness of their lives as they were. Their work was fulfilling, their friends plentiful, and trips us child-encumbered folks couldn't afford to take let them see the entire world.

One evening after Thanksgiving, Amy noticed there was a new voicemail waiting on her phone. I was sitting nearby reading when Amy checked the message, her eyes widening, hand going up instinctively to cover her hanging-open mouth.

"Oh my God," she looked at me, beaming, "Dave and Julie are going to have a baby!" It took a minute to sink in, given that he's nearly fifty now and she's pushing forty-five, but it was true. The baby was healthy, and they had waited until all appeared to be pointing toward a spring birthday to share with anyone.

It's hard to know how much they really expected to ever get pregnant, but regardless of the odds, they never stopped trying. I don't know if the baby will be a boy or a girl, but either way, my vote is that they name the baby "Isaac."

Prayer for the Week
I get my hopes and expectations confused all the time, God. Remind me to set down the latter so I have room in my heart for the former.

Popping Off
Art/music/video and other cool stuff that relate to the text
"Childbearing: Why More Women in Their 40s Are Having Babies," in *USA Today* (article, May 19, 2018)

The Curious Case of Benjamin Button (movie, 2008)

Feeling Green

Lectionary Texts For

June 21, 2020 (Third Sunday after Pentecost)

Texts in Brief

My dog ate my Bible!

First Reading

Genesis 21:8–21

Sarah is jealous of Hagar and Hagar and Abraham's son, Ishmael. She tells Abraham to send them away now that he has Isaac, and God tells Abraham to do what Sarah says. He sends them away, and when they run out of water, Hagar abandons Ishmael, unable to watch him die. But God reveals a well to her and tells her not to worry, that God will make Ishmael's descendants numerous like Isaac's. Ishmael becomes a man of the wild and marries an Egyptian woman.

PSALM/PROPHET

Jeremiah 20:7–13

Jeremiah is dealing with an existential crisis. He's become a joke to everyone he prophesies to, but if he tries to stay quiet, the urge to speak out is agony for him. He asks God to punish those who are making him a laughingstock among his peers, so they will respect what he is saying to everyone. But also he wouldn't mind seeing them suffer a little.

SECOND READING

Romans 6:1b–11

While grace has no limit, Paul cautions that this isn't a license to do whatever we want. As he has said before, we are supposed to die to sin like Jesus died, which should remake us in a new image. It's only by doing this that we can hope to find real liberation from the ever-present bondage of sin and temptation. If we do this, we no longer live for worldly things, but for God alone.

GOSPEL

Matthew 10:24–39

The disciples are facing persecution for their ministry, but Jesus offers them encouragement. While their enemies can hurt them physically, they can't harm the disciples' souls, which are forever guarded by God. We're more important to God, and known more intimately, than all the rest of creation. In this we should find confidence that God is on our side, no matter what happens. Jesus knows that there will be division about this new way of thinking, which isn't part of the Jewish tradition,

but it's the ministry the disciples are called to, regardless of the cost.

Bible, Decoded
Breaking down Scripture in plain language

Hagar—Abraham's concubine who gave birth to a son
by Abraham named Ishmael. While a concubine in
those times could have been an indentured servant
who served the patriarch in many ways, including sexu-
ally, it could also connote a relationship that couldn't be
officially formalized for any number of reasons, including being from different cultures, religions, or social
statuses or because the man was already married. So
although the man could only be married to one woman,
he could have multiple "life partners."

Beelzebul—While the name *Beelzebub* has become
more commonly known in contemporary culture, this
is actually a sort of typo. Instead, the name is Beelzebul,
which means *lord of the flies*, and he is known as the
prince of the demons. Many people conflate this with
various names and imagery we have for Satan, Lucifer,
or the devil.

Points to Ponder
First Thoughts

In his letters, Paul uses Ishmael and Isaac metaphorically as representative of both the old and new covenants
God has with God's people. So Ishmael (who is considered wicked by some in Christianity, though he did seek
forgiveness) is a symbol of a covenant based on the law,
while Isaac (a.k.a., the "true" patriarch of the Israelites and

the ark of the covenant) is the bloodline that represents this new covenant through grace as revealed by Jesus.

Digging Deeper

Mining for what really matters . . . and gold

Not to excuse the reaction people have to the disciples' teachings in their own community, but it's understandable if we think about the history there. For centuries, the Israelites have endured tremendous suffering and persecution, and even now, they're living under occupied rule. One glimmer of hope that they've held on to all this time has been the commitment they were told God made to them that they would be blessed abundantly by God for their continued faithfulness and endurance.

Remember that the people of Israel are principally a people of the old covenant with God: one based on adherence to God's law. This is hard to do, especially when there are 613 of these laws! It's made all the more difficult while in exile, being persecuted, being invaded, or any of the many other struggles they've had to deal with. But this covenant of blessing from God helps justify this faithfulness and desire to cling to the law in spite of the circumstances.

In short, it will all pay off some day.

Then along come some of their own people, telling them that there's a new deal, that the contract has been revised, at least as they understood it. It's not that God is abandoning God's covenant with them, but this new message is that it's based on God's grace, which no degree of legal adherence can earn them.

Umm, excuse me?

It stands to reason that the Israelites might be more than a little put off, likely wondering why they tried so hard to do this faith thing right in the first place. And on top of this radical reimagining of the covenant, it's also available to everyone else, even those who have been hell-bent on eliminating the Israelites from the face of the earth.

I'm pretty sure I would be annoyed, too, at the very least. So in the great tradition of taking your anger out on the messenger, the Israelites turn on the disciples. It's a kind of replay of what Sarah felt once she got what God promised her so long ago. It wasn't just that she wanted this child; she also would rather know that someone else (like Hagar) who didn't have this kind of agreement with God didn't get equal treatment.

The most curious part seems to be that God assents to this mistreatment of Hagar and Ishmael, just because Sarah asks for it. Most likely this was not something God wanted, but God realized it was inevitable that Sarah would find one way or another to get rid of her two perceived rivals, perhaps permanently, which God really did not want. So Hagar and Ishmael went into exile instead, and though it didn't come easy, the promise fulfilled to Sarah for a nation of descendants also came to Hagar.

How God's promises are fulfilled, and the timeline on which that happens, may well not line up with our wants or expectations. And if we try to put a fence around God's favor to hold close and control, we're sure to be disappointed. As the saying goes, though, the only reason we should be concerned with our neighbor's plate is to help ensure that they have enough.

Heads-Up

Connecting the text to our world

Not to brag (actually, it totally is to brag), but our daughter, Zoe, is brilliant. Yeah, I know that everyone thinks their kids are brilliant, but we're actually right. Aside from being a voracious reader and a natural at math and science, she's blessed with a gift her dad always lacked.

She's really good at taking tests.

She's gotten in with a pretty tight group of friends at her elementary school I like to call the "nerd herd." They're all top-notch students, and as often happens when you have a group of high performers, they tend to get a little competitive with each other. Sometimes, in fact, it can get a bit ugly.

Her class has these big assessments they do in schools now once each semester called "benchmarks" that are supposed to help determine both if each individual student is on track and, more broadly, if the school is doing its job in giving students the proper tools.

On the most recent reading benchmark, Zoe's friend (who we'll call Jessie) got a 97 out of 100. She was justifiably proud of her achievement and showed it to her nerd-herd friends, who all congratulated her for such amazing work. The teacher even called her out in class, noting how great she had done, eliciting "oohs" and "wows" from her peers.

Then the teacher gave Zoe her assessment; she got a 100.

Suddenly Jessie's face fell, and her shoulders slumped. She looked back to her own paper and soon was grumbling about how she didn't do such a good job after all, as if Zoe's score had any bearing on the remarkability of her own score.

The older we get, the easier it becomes to congratulate others on their windfalls or achievements, even if we still feel more or less like Jessie inside. Summoning authentically felt joy for another, especially when we feel like we deserved their fortune more than they did, is real heart work.

Soon enough, Jessie outscored Zoe on some new project and all was well. But the saddest part of the whole experience was that Zoe lost an opportunity to celebrate her own success in that moment, because she was too preoccupied with her friend's distress. She ended up feeling guilty and a little embarrassed instead of happy.

When envy creeps in, nobody wins. It's an all-too-human response, but no matter what, it ends up being a lose-lose proposition.

Prayer for the Week

Help me find the capacity to celebrate in others' blessing, whether or not I think they deserve it.

Popping Off

Art/music/video and other cool stuff that relate to the text

"John's Indecent Proposal" scene from *An Indecent Proposal* (movie, 2004)

The Sun Also Rises, by Ernest Hemingway (book, 1926)

Take
the Plate

Lectionary Texts For
June 28, 2020 (Fourth Sunday after Pentecost)

Texts in Brief
My dog ate my Bible!

First Reading
Genesis 22:1–14

God orders Abraham to take Isaac to a sacred spot to sacrifice him. Abraham does as God tells him, and just before he kills Isaac, God stops him. God praises Abraham's faithfulness and obedience, and then Abraham notices a nearby ram, which he takes and sacrifices instead.

Psalm/Prophet
Jeremiah 28:5–9

To put Jeremiah's message in plain modern English, he's saying, "Look, there are prophets and then there are *prophets*." Jeremiah comes from a long line of prophetic voices before him who offer portents of terrible, even gruesome consequences for choices made without the heart of God being considered first. But the one who divests themselves of this for the sake of embracing peace above all else is the one they've all been waiting for.

SECOND READING
Romans 6:12–23

The author of Romans wants us to stop thinking about each other and ourselves as inherently evil and instead believe we are made in and for goodness and love by God. There's a reiteration this week that we shouldn't take advantage of the fact that grace is inexhaustible and use it as an excuse to do whatever we want. Rather, we need to work that much harder to honor the way in which we are made. But by submitting like a slave to God's will for us, we are liberated from the shackles of a life of sin.

GOSPEL
Matthew 10:40–42

The disciples should notice those who honor the spirit of hospitality by opening themselves and their homes up not just to those of high stature or power but also to the nobodies in their midst. By honoring those from whom we have nothing to gain, we honor God.

Bible, Decoded
Breaking down Scripture in plain language

Hananiah—Jeremiah condemns Hananiah as a false prophet who preaches for rebellion against the God of Israel in his teaching. Because of this, Jeremiah says Hananiah will die, which he does.

Sanctification—This is a way in which something or someone is considered to be made holy, generally by being purified of evil or sin. Through sanctification, the person or object then is fit to be used as an instrument of God.

Points to Ponder
First Thoughts

This Romans text is far from the only text where Paul refers to our devotion as slave-like. It's a curious choice of words, especially considering that a lot of the people drawn to these early church communities were house slaves. The idea of going from one kind of bondage to another is probably not very appealing, but Paul's intent in describing our level of commitment to God this way is to illustrate how deep the relationship goes.

Social status often was determined from birth, so for someone born a slave, being entirely free was a foreign concept. They likely came from generations of enslaved family members, so their aspiration was likely not to be on their own (there would be nothing for them in this culture, which assigned their role at birth) but rather to end up with a good master. In that light, serving a master who is abundantly merciful, just, and compassionate would be as much as anyone could have probably imagined.

Digging Deeper

Mining for what really matters . . . and gold

When it comes to our midrashic approach to the texts, the first thing that jumps out in the Genesis text (aside from it being generally icky and creepy) is God's response after sparing Isaac. The degree of love God was seeking from Abraham ("I know that you fear God, since you have not withheld your son, your only son") is mirrored in the story of Jesus and how God's love is expressed similarly by God giving over God's only son to the world.

In a culture in which sacrificial atonement was the status quo, this was the religious currency of the time. A lot of the ways we express love today, or even faith-fulness, wouldn't have translated to the audiences back then. But just because that was the value set that was considered normal back then doesn't mean we have to try to fit everything into that same cultural and reli-gious framework today.

I recognize that this is a sensitive thing for a lot of Christians to even consider, since the emphasis on Jesus dying for us and the justification of our sin is so deeply embedded in our religious identity. But I think we need to ask ourselves why we believe what we believe sometimes, as well as whether the rest of Scripture supports this.

The idea that we are inborn with sin as a universal burden because sin started with Adam and Eve and never left us is known as *original sin*. And while we can look back to Genesis to try to make sense of this, the Christian concept of original sin didn't emerge until five centuries after Jesus's death, when Augustine of Hippo put it forward. Further, the idea of substitutionary atonement (Jesus dying for our sins) came even later than that. Subsequently, these ways of thinking then impacted all subsequent English translations of the Bible.

So while we take these beliefs, which we definitely can find a basis for in Scripture, as a given in our faith, it wasn't always that way.

It's easy to forget that the way people spoke and thought at the time of Jesus's life and ministry had no basis in empiricism or this notion of a single, absolute, and inviolate truth (generally argued to be based these days in observable fact). Most of the material world, inscrutable as it was, remained mired in mystery, from why we sneezed to why disasters happened. If something happened, it must be God's will, went the thinking of the status quo.

Back to the story about Abraham and Isaac. Remember that Abraham at this point is more than a hundred years old. He's just traveled far enough that the trip took preparation and even two assistants, then he finishes it up with a hike up a mountain. After all of that, he is able to hold his much younger son down and tie him to a rock. Either that or Isaac put his finger on the knots while his dad cinched up the rope!

The point is that while we spend time arguing about whether this is historic fact or metaphor, nobody would have pressed the issue by saying, "Wait, did that really happen?" They would have known well enough when a story was told for the message's sake and when something was a literal accounting of bona fide events. And the message was that true faithfulness is being willing to give up everything, even what is most precious to us. Abraham did it, and so did God.

Whether God required Jesus's sacrifice for the atonement of our collective sin isn't the heart of what the story is trying to tell us. It's the depth of sacrificial love that we are to aspire to. And in submitting ourselves to such a radically vulnerable degree of trust, we can also rest assured that God doesn't wish violence for us. Any of us.

Faith isn't expressed through killing or violence; it's expressed in being truly willing to give up everything else for God's sake.

Heads-Up

Connecting the text to our world

The images of flames shooting out from the ancient windows and swallowing up the historic church spire seemed too dramatic to be real at first. But it was true; Notre Dame Cathedral was on fire.

In a matter of hours, centuries of history and countless lives' worth of craftsmanship and artistry were lost. Fortunately, because of the quick response and remarkable bravery of the firefighters on sight, the blaze was contained before the iconic towers and much of the façade were destroyed forever.

In the days since the fire, there have been dozens of reports about the damage, the impact on the people of France and Christians worldwide, and plans already underway to restore Notre Dame to its previous place as an architectural marvel. Some political figures such as French president Emmanuel Macron put forward moon-shot claims that the restoration would be completed within as little as five years.

More remarkable than that to me, though, were the stories of the cathedral's original construction. Hundreds of people at a time worked over the span of more than a century to erect the original structure, with renovation and preservation projects underway even before the church itself was entirely completed. A Jesuit priest who was an expert on French religious architecture was interviewed about the history of Notre Dame, and he was the one who drove the notion home of how collectively selfless the act of creation really was.

Most of the people who ever worked on the original Notre Dame, he said, committed their lives to this work, knowing they would never see the vision of this monument fully realized. They did it in order to be a part of something great, something that transcended human ambition and ingenuity in isolation. It was a testament to the human species as a whole and our ability, despite our inherent self-centeredness, to get outside ourselves and find meaning in participating in beauty, even if we don't ever get to fully appreciate it ourselves.

The people who did this work, explained the priest, did it not so much for themselves but to honor God and to give a gift to people who would come after them. While I don't think God "needs" to be honored by monuments, the notion of committing so much to people I will never know is a humbling concept. On the surface it feels like a tremendous sacrifice, but one has to wonder if any of them regretted investing themselves in something so historically and religiously significant.

Prayer for the Week

I want to be able to give sacrificially but help me see when something being offered to me is about something more profound and important than the thing being offered.

Popping Off

Art/music/video and other cool stuff that relate to the text

The Shack, by Wm. Paul Young (book, 2011)

Fear and Trembling, by Søren Kierkegaard (book, 1843, 2009)

Leaving It All

Lectionary Texts For
July 5, 2020 (Fifth Sunday after Pentecost)

Texts in Brief
My dog ate my Bible!

First Reading
Genesis 24:34–38, 42–49, 58–67

This is an account of how Isaac comes to marry his wife, Rebekah. Abraham's slave goes out among the Israelites and waits by a well for God to show him who he should take back to Isaac to marry. Rebekah fulfills the sign the slave has asked God for. He takes her back to Isaac, who brings Rebekah to his mother, Sarah. Sarah blesses their marriage, and Abraham is relieved that his family line will continue.

Psalm

Psalm 45:10–17

A call to a woman who is to be married to a king to walk away from her family of origin and from any old ways and customs. From here forward, she is going to serve her new master. For this, she will be blessed with honor and many children, and people will revere her.

Second Reading

Romans 7:15–25a

Paul is struggling with a moral quandary of some kind, and maybe even the stinging reality of hypocrisy. He condemns things but still does them himself. He notes that the evil nature of physical desire and human impulse drive him to such acts and that he has to replace this with an equally powerful longing for the spirit. It's almost like he is at war with himself.

Gospel

Matthew 11:16–19, 25–30

The Gospel equivalent of a "kids these days" parent rant. Because Jesus is different in his demeanor and message, people judge and reject him rather than pay attention to the point at the heart of his ministry. No one will truly "get it" either without seeing more deeply with the eyes and heart of Jesus; only then will God's true nature come to light. The passage ends with an invitation to those feeling weighed down by sin or temptation to come to embrace this new "gospel way" and find relief.

Bible, Decoded
Breaking down Scripture in plain language

Nose Ring—The jewelry given to Rebekah is a gift of sorts, but along with the bracelets it is a sign of social status, representing that she is marrying someone important. Unlike some claims that the Bible speaks against body piercing, it was fashionable in the ancient Near East much as it is now. However, it would have only been decorative for women, because the only men whose noses were pierced were slaves.

Virgins—While we associate the word with sex nearly exclusively today, being a virgin had different meanings at the time of the Bible. The most literal interpretation is in reference to a woman "living separate," specifically not with another man other than her father. So it was another way to say "single," which could have also implied she hadn't had sex but wasn't that pointed. It could also just be a reference to any young woman.

Points to Ponder
First Thoughts

It's interesting to see how the custom of finding a wife was handled in this culture. Note that there is no personal encounter between Isaac and Rebekah before she is presented to him to marry. Instead of romance or a personal courtship, the importance is placed on allowing God to choose who Isaac should marry. This marriage is more of a contract than it is an emotional act of free will. Rather than falling in love and then marrying, the marriage comes first, with the hope that the couple will grow into love over time.

Many Christians take this Psalms text as a fore-shadowing of how we are supposed to act when we become "married to Christ." They interpret this as a call to pagans to renounce their old practices of idolatry, embracing this new faith with the devotion and fervor that would be asked of a wife to her husband.

The Romans text is one of the most scintillating and debated passages in the Epistles. We don't know what Paul is referring to that he does even though he hates doing it. It could be addiction, sexual tempta-tion, or simply just residual guilt from his past ways. It could also be as simple as his resentment of still being tempted, though he seeks to transcend it.

Digging Deeper

Mining for what really matters . . . and gold

I've heard so many theories on what this Romans text is alluding to that I can't even remember them all. Some say he's gay; others say he's married or just longs for a woman he can't have. Not surprising, given our puri-tanical roots, most of them have to do with sex and/or sexuality.

But if we get too hung up on the thing Paul is talk-ing about, we miss the broader connotations of the passage. To begin with, we have to remember that this comes just on the heels of Paul taking some of his col-leagues to task for taking fairly liberal license with the idea that after being baptized, they can do anything they want since they're justified by grace. No dice, he reminds them, since this is dishonoring the very gift extended to them by God in the first place. And while God will not turn from them because if this, it's a breaking of their part of the covenant they made in getting baptized in the first place.

It might be more helpful to think of whatever Paul is writing about less as a reference to one specific event or sinful tendency, and more collectively as human sinful inclinations in general. While we are to "despise" sin (it's common in the Bible to lean on hyperbole to add emphasis), we still don't seem to be able to shake it. This is why Paul refers to us elsewhere in his letters as both sinner and saint, comingled at the same time.

Expanding the thinking about his word choice further, it's helpful to think of his use of *I* as a sort of hypothetical device in reference to both him and his fellow Christians. We do this all the time, like when I say to my kids "I don't think I'd do that." I don't just mean me in this context; it's another way of saying "we don't do that."

If we think this way about it, this is the hug after the spanking, to think in parental terms some more. He just smacked his fellow Jesus-followers for taking advantage of God's grace, but he follows it up here with a bit of compassion, and even empathy, for the struggle to escape sinfulness.

It's an understandable quandary. We can't entirely escape sin, no matter how hard we try. So why try so hard, especially if we're loved and embraced by God anyway? Because, as Jesus notes in the Gospel text, our burden is actually made lighter in trying. It may seem like an impossible, futile exercise to keep turning to God for forgiveness and strength, but Jesus reminds us that just by doing this, the struggle is made at least a little bit easier.

The yoke isn't entirely lifted, but at least we have help as we carry it.

Heads-Up

Connecting the text to our world

I lived the first twenty-seven years of my life within a single forty-square-mile area. Though my family moved around, and I switched schools several times, they were all within the greater Dallas area. I even went to college in Denton, only about twenty-five miles north of Dallas. My first job after that was right back in the heart of the city. It was home; I knew it as well as I knew anything.

Then I got my first "real" job, teaching kids with special needs in a clinical environment. It was the first time I felt like I was really making a difference with the work I was doing. I had enjoyed a few gigs in the music business and had met some exciting people before then, but ultimately it was all about selling CDs, or "moving product" as they indelicately put it.

A few months into my new job, they asked me if I'd consider traveling as part of my work. Though the idea of being away from home for long stretches of time, especially alone in unfamiliar places, was intimidating. But I also knew that this was an opportunity I would forever regret if I passed it up because of my fear of the unknown.

I packed everything I owned except for two suitcases of clothes and loaded it into my mom's garage, and I was on the road within two weeks. I spent the next two-plus years going from Denver to Atlanta and from

Chicago to Seattle, with plenty of stops in between. I saw places and did things I had never considered before. My world exploded in size in a matter of months, and the more I traveled, the more I wanted to see.

More important, I felt like what I did really mattered. That's why I was able to let go and take the risk. I wanted assurance of change without loss, which I learned wasn't possible. Of course, I lost plenty when I went on the road. What I came to accept was that all I had to gain made the loss worth it. It made my burden of choice a hell of a lot lighter.

Prayer for the Week

I don't expect to be perfect any more than I expect to be off the hook for not being perfect. I just need patience and sometimes a little help.

Popping Off

Art/music/video and other cool stuff that relate to the text

Into the Wild (movie, 2007)

Harry Potter and the Sorcerer's Stone, by J. K. Rowling (book, 1998)

My Kingdom for a Horse

Lectionary Texts For

July 12, 2020 (Sixth Sunday after Pentecost)

Texts in Brief

My dog ate my Bible!

First Reading

Genesis 25:19–34

Rebekah, like Sarah, can't bear children until God blesses her with twins twenty years after she and Isaac marry. The twins fight in her womb, which God says is a precursor of their division into two tribes and conflict throughout life. Isaac favors the eldest, Esau, but Rebekah adores Jacob. When Esau is starving after a hunt, Jacob convinces him to exchange his inheritance for Jacob's food, which Esau later resents him for.

Psalm/Prophet
Psalm 119:105–12

David is constantly at war with enemies, but he remains faithful to God, even when his life is at risk. He asks for continued guidance and to be spared from his enemies, who wish him dead.

Second Reading
Romans 8:1–11

Remaining in a mindset of faithfulness to God and spiritual discipline takes focused effort, over and over again. Wherever we set our values or whatever we put our energy into—be it worldly priorities or spiritual growth—is where we will find our heart anchored. We get our mind properly conditioned and oriented through acting as we're called to act, which gets to the heart of what religious law had as its fundamental intent to begin with. All else leads to something that ultimately fades, crumbles, and dies. The only escape from that death cycle is an indwelling of the spirit.

Gospel
Matthew 13:1–9, 18–23

Jesus tells the parable of the sower, in which a farmer places seeds in various environments; some places are hostile to growth and others are fertile ground. Jesus goes on to explain that this refers to different human responses to the gospel. Short-lived faith tends to be based on a lack of understanding. Those whose faith is strictly impulsive and emotional will scatter at the first sign of hardship. Some will never yield anything if they can't first let go of earthly desire as foremost. But those who take the essence of gospel teaching in and allow themselves to be changed will see miraculous growth in their lives.

Bible, Decoded
Breaking down Scripture in plain language

Jacob—Jacob is considered one of the patriarchs of the nation of Israel. In fact, after wrestling with an angel all night and pressing God to bless him, he is renamed "Israel," which means "he who is strong against God." This is a foreshadowing, of course, of the hot-and-cold relationship the Israelites as a whole would have with God.

Heritage—The fact that David calls God's law his "heritage" is significant, since one's bloodline and birthright were everything back then. Conversely, this means that when Jacob robs Esau of his birthright, he's effectively robbing him of who he is in the culture. Esau becomes a person without identity and without roots.

Points to Ponder
First Thoughts

It's interesting to note which child Isaac and Rebekah love most. Though it's probably partly based on who they spend more time with (Isaac would have hunted more with Esau, and Rebekah would have been home more with Jacob), it also is reflective of the value we have in seeing ourselves reflected in our children. We're closer to those with whom we have more in common, and who do things more like we do.

The story of Jacob and Esau has some similarities to the one about Isaac and Ishmael. Though the latter brothers aren't as mired in conflict and deceit, this is all a means of giving us a familial background on the origins of all of the tribes descended from Abraham.

We should also notice that this Matthew text is one of the few times when Jesus explains the meaning behind his parable. Generally, rather than just using a parable as an illustration of a later-explicated point, Jesus leaves meaning more open-ended, depending on the audience to make conclusions. It could be that Jesus felt this was too important to leave to interpretation, or that those listening weren't getting it. More likely, though, is that this tells us more about the agenda of the author of Matthew, who is bent in many places in the Gospel on leaving little doubt about what's to be taken from the words.

Digging Deeper

Mining for what really matters . . . and gold

This Genesis text actually kicks off a longer collection of passages about Jacob known as the *toledot* of Jacob, which means *cycle* or *series*. It is also interpreted as the *descendants* or *generations* of Jacob, depending on how you view it. And really, this is the main attraction of the stories of the origins of the Israelites. As noted above, Jacob's name is changed by God to Israel after wrestling with the angel and demanding blessing, so the fact that the Israelites get their name from Jacob is why there's more time and attention spent on Jacob's story in particular.

In a broader context, though, the entirety of the stories of the descendants of Abraham, all of which precede the accounts of Israel as a nation or a people, speak broadly to who the people are as a community of shared history, bloodline, and culture. So in a sense, the story of Isaac is the story of "who we are" for the Israelites.

Given that, this tells us a lot about the cultural and historic DNA of the people. In some sense, the story of Isaac and his sons is the story of so many families, including deceit, conflict, tragedy, and unexpected miracles. We see the unfair allocation of good looks (and apparently brains) to the younger son, which results in the usurping of the eldest's inheritance.

If we consider this along with the pretty violent and forceful way Jacob pushes God to bless him, we see that the things that have come to him haven't come easily. This is the case, of course, with the people of Israel too. From one period of captivity to another, and even into the passage in Psalms where we see David's people under siege, we know the Israelites as a people of struggle.

Jumping to the Gospel text, we tend to think of the different types of soil as metaphors for different types of people, which is true at least in part. But consider them, instead, as states of being, receptivity, or readiness at different points in our lives. While we would love to think of ourselves as eternally rich, arable soil, sometimes our hearts grow rocky and hard, or the thorns of adversity and circumstance choke out the light that glimmers within us.

We're forever changing states of readiness to be in a good relationship with God. What doesn't change is God's readiness to be in relationship with us. The seed is forever the seed; it just waits for the right time, place, and environment in which to take root. Once that happens, the volatility of life's storms and states of inner being are less prone to wreak havoc. It just takes time and no small amount of nurturing to get there.

Heads-Up

Connecting the text to our world

"A horse, a horse . . . my kingdom for a horse!"

This is the infamous cry from the title character in Shakespeare's play *Richard III*. There's little to like about King Richard, from his hunched back to his sneering voice and his . . . let's say, lack of people skills.

Yes, we could think a little bit better of him because he needs the horse in order to remain in the battle at hand. But it also points to his volatility and tendency to be compelled more by whatever is right in front of him, rather than keeping a healthy perspective on the bigger picture. After all, he's on foot in the middle of a war, and what happens to his people if they lose their leader doesn't cross his mind in this scene.

In the Genesis text, Esau says he's starving, but do we really believe that? He just walked into the tent and smelled food, so he said what most of us would say:

I'm starving! I'd give anything for that yummy stew, bro.

Jacob sees an opportunity here and seizes it. That's not to say that it was a virtuous decision, but he has his eyes on the long game. He can always make more food, and he knows his brother is the type who is impulsive enough to give up too much for immediate gratification.

Esau is the hunter who knows the wild like the back of his hand, but which one do you think would actually last forty years in the desert? Esau would likely squander his resources as soon as he had them and die of thirst a week later. Jacob is, as Jesus calls us to be, wise as a serpent. His shortcoming is that he is driven by material desire, but given the two choices, who is more fit to be the patriarch of God's people?

Prayer for the Week

God, help me not crumble in the face of want; keep my eyes focused on the big picture.

Popping Off

Art/music/video and other cool stuff that relate to the text

Jacob I Have Loved, by Katherine Paterson (book, 1980)

Richard III, by William Shakespeare (play, 1592)

Wait for It

Lectionary Texts For

July 19, 2020 (Seventh Sunday after Pentecost)

Texts in Brief

My dog ate my Bible!

First Reading

Genesis 28:10–19a

Jacob has a dream along his journey in which he sees a ladder extending between heaven and earth. God tells him this will be his descendants' land someday and that his progeny will multiply and populate the region. In response, Jacob consecrates the place and declares it to be holy.

Psalm/Prophet

Isaiah 44:6–8

God declares, through the prophet Isaiah, to be the one and only God of all creation. God offers a sort of challenge to any deities who would challenge such a claim.

SECOND READING

Romans 8:12–25

Paul continues his theme of comparing a life led by spirit versus one led by "flesh." He claims we are invited into a relationship with God like that of an adopted child when we choose a spiritually informed way of living. And unlike the inheritance of those like Jacob and Esau, there's no limit to the bounty of love and peace afforded to God's children. There is no favorite, and we are even on par with Jesus in God's eyes. This is good news, despite present circumstance, which should offer us hope and endurance to deal with life's suffering and temptations. Having hope in such a promise is at the heart of faith.

GOSPEL

Matthew 13:24–30, 36–43

Jesus points out that despite the faithfulness of his disciples and those they teach, there is evil all around them. When the disciples ask if they should gather up the faithful and keep them safe from evil, Jesus tells them that good and evil should, and will, coexist in the world. Rather than them having to judge who is and isn't worthy, they should leave judgment to God.

Bible, Decoded

Breaking down Scripture in plain language

Luz/Bethel—The location for the story known as "Jacob's Ladder." Jacob is traveling north and has reached a point just northwest of the Dead Sea when he has this vision of becoming a forefather of the nation of Israel. Luz is the Canaanite name for the town nearby, but Jacob gives it the Hebrew name Bethel, which means "a holy place." Bethel later becomes a community just within the southern border of Israel.

Haran—This is a place with history for Jacob's family. Abraham's father (Jacob's great-grandfather) settled there for a period along the family's way to live in Canaan. This is a journey that Jacob and his family would have known well, so this probably made the sacred experience there particularly surprising in what had become mundane, familiar surroundings.

Points to Ponder

First Thoughts

Interesting that, in the Isaiah text, God uses both the first-person singular and plural in self-reference. Particularly interesting given the claim right at the beginning that God is "one." Examples like this (and even back to the first creation story in Genesis) lend credence to the concept of God being "many-in-one."

The Romans text begins to make more sense given the previous Epistle texts and our understanding now that many of these early Christians were house servants or slaves. And while Paul has compared our level of commitment to God to the fidelity a slave offered to a slaveowner, he notes that God looks on us not as property to be used but as a child to lovingly raise up and care for. This would be a refreshing perspective for someone who has never been seen as anything more than equal to livestock.

We could almost overlay the conversation Jesus has with his disciples over an imagined dialogue between Paul and the Christians he's writing to in Romans. It wouldn't be a stretch to imagine that what the slaves really wished for was for God to strike their owners dead or to allow the slaves to lead a successful rebellion, enslaving their owners in turn.

Instead, they're told like the disciples to wait. While it's not fulfilling in the moment, it's part of the "long game" we discussed in last week's study. Time and again, we find examples of how God's time and God's ways aren't necessarily the same as ours, were we left to our own devices.

Digging Deeper

Mining for what really matters . . . and gold

This is the second week in a row where Jesus explains his parable, which is unusual. But we have to notice that this part of the story happens in private, only with his disciples. For the public, he always leaves room for them to draw their own conclusions and to wrestle with meaning. For his disciples, who he is still training to teach, speak, and act as he does, this is a learning opportunity, not so much about what he is saying, but how he says it.

Here is where we realize how many layers of meaning there are in Jesus's stories, and conversely, how much we would miss if we didn't have all of the background information.

The word choice in the original Greek, which here is translated as *weeds* in English, is actually more specific than that. The reference is to a type of wild grass that was common at the time in that region and would spread throughout a field of grain. The tricky part is that the weed looked almost identical to the wheat stalk in its immature state. So if we go around yanking up anything we think shouldn't be there, we're likely to do more harm than good.

The only way we can really tell the difference is to wait until the wheat gets to its fruition stage and starts to yield grain. Only then is it evident what the true nature of the plant is.

In the story, the servants would have done harm to the harvest, though it would all have been done from a spirit of dutifulness. They were compelled by the evidence of the moment, unclear as it may have been, and felt the need to react. The difference between the master and the servant in this story, though, is patience and restraint.

If we step back from the literal scene being conveyed and apply the parable to us, it actually falls short on one level. In the story, a weed is a weed, is a weed—period. There's no chance of it changing its ways and, because it is in the company of wheat, longing to be something more than a destructive force. It has one sole purpose and one capacity, so it can't really help itself.

We're not let off so easily. We always have a choice, even if we've been told we're a weed (maybe even by family members or by a previous pastor). There's always opportunity to be the wheat. Jesus does have more patience and restraint than those in his company, who lack his scope of vision, but it also demonstrates a depth of hope that we should aspire to. It's so easy to label people we encounter as "good" or "bad"; Jesus, on the other hand, sees a field full of both wheat and what has yet to be realized.

Heads-Up
Connecting the text to our world

For anyone who has taught some kind of noninstitu-tional class like Sunday school, you know there are a few different types of participants you tend to get. There are the die-hard ones who never miss a week. You've also got what I call the "most-timers," who make a pretty regular practice of being there, but who have other conflicts from time to time. You have a couple folks who show up maybe once a month when they feel like there's nothing better going on, and finally you have the people who I call "the newbs."

Maybe it's just my . . . unconventional teaching style, but inevitably I'll have a few onlookers who come by any class once, or maybe twice, but never intend to hang around. I tend to teach in a way that doesn't required weekly attendance to follow along, partly because the definition of "regular attendee" in our culture today doesn't really lend itself to such a regi-mented schedule. Of the newbs, there are two subsets: those who want to meet the author of the book (a few on occasion), and those who know my work and have a grudge (all the rest).

It's pretty easy to tell who is who, just by their facial expressions and body language. And while the inter-ested newbs are usually pretty quiet, the grudge-holders definitely aren't. They usually come armed with a litany of challenging propositions they've thought through to try and shoot holes in what I'm teaching. By now, after about fifteen-plus years of doing this, I've heard nearly all of it.

Recently, I had a guy visit the class who clearly was a grudge newb. This dude was intense. He leaned forward in his chair and made no bones about dominating the time. While some of his questions were thoughtful and provocative, others felt hell-bent on forcing me into a binary proposition that I know better than to take.

By the time he left, I was sure I had him pegged. In fact, someone later confirmed that he did, indeed, teach his own class at another church in town that didn't exactly share our understanding of the texts. I filled in the rest of the story in my mind: I was the weed-tender to him, yanking up the good stuff and tossing it into the fire in order to sow my wicked theology. I know the type well, and he fit on every level.

A couple of days later I was talking to someone about the guy, feeling pretty good about how I handled the situation, when they painted in what I didn't realize was an incomplete picture of the man. Yes, he taught at a nearby church that didn't align with my work, but he was a different social and theological animal underneath. In fact, he had been working quietly behind the scenes in the same kinds of circles that I identified with. While he was fervently trying to remain faithful to the traditions of his upbringing, my friend said, he used every chance he could to expose himself to new ways of thinking and believing.

I felt like a tool, or should I say, a weed? Turns out I didn't know nearly as much as I thought I did. Good thing God is in charge of the wheat-weed-sorting and I'm not.

Prayer for the Week

Help me remember what my job is and isn't. And for the things above my pay grade, help me practice letting go.

Popping Off

Art/music/video and other cool stuff that relate to the text

Dallas Buyers Club (movie, 2013)

"Good News—Bad News: Lessons from a Zen Buddhist Fable," on *Medium* (blog post, January 27, 2017)

Connection, Not Coercion

Lectionary Texts For
July 26, 2020 (Eighth Sunday after Pentecost)

Texts in Brief
My dog ate my Bible!

First Reading
Genesis 29:15–28

Jacob works for Laban, and he really wants Laban's youngest daughter, Rachel. Laban makes him work seven years before sleeping with her, then tricks him into sleeping with Leah instead. A week later, right after his wedding celebration with Leah, Laban lets him sleep with Rachel, too, but requires him to work another seven years to pay this off.

Psalm/Prophet
1 Kings 3:5–12

God appears to Solomon, who has been made king as a young boy, replacing David as king of the Israelites.

God asks what he wants, and Solomon (who feels well out of his depth) asks for wisdom in leadership and discernment of both good and evil. God, happy Solomon didn't ask for material enrichment, grants his request, declaring that he will be a king of unparalleled greatness.

SECOND READING
Romans 8:26–39

Things are hard for the audience of this letter, but Paul tells them not to worry about how to bring their distress to God. Rather, all they have to do is to continue to love God and be open to the Spirit working through them for good. In doing so, they're afforded a place of honor in God's family as if they are all firstborn (the greatest status then for a child). Although the followers of Jesus are persecuted for their faith, God is still on their side, no matter what. We are right in what we are doing, as long as we follow God's call as revealed through Jesus's teaching and example.

GOSPEL
Matthew 13:31–33, 44–52

Jesus offers five short comparisons of the kingdom of God to things the disciples would understand. Each one reveals a different dimension of what God's nature is, no one greater or less important than the other. Finally, he reiterates that it isn't their job to judge or condemn; rather, they are called to teach and guide, leaving judgment to God.

Bible, Decoded

Breaking down Scripture in plain language

Complete the Week—The Hebrew wedding feast and celebration lasted seven days and was attended by those (generally men) who the father of the bride invited. Laban didn't want to disrupt the celebration, because it would raise suspicion that something was up, and his subterfuge of Jacob would have been exposed.

Go in to Her—This is about as direct as the Bible ever gets about sexy time. In this culture, a marriage wasn't official until the couple had slept together. Conversely, once they had slept together, there was no going back; they were married.

Points to Ponder

First Thoughts

There are three references in the Genesis text employing the number seven. First, Jacob works seven years to marry Rachel and is tricked into marrying her older sister, Leah, instead. Then he has to wait seven days to get to have Rachel. Finally, he has to work seven more years to pay back the debt for finally marrying Rachel, too. If we remember, this is a number that signifies divine perfection, which is curious in a story involving so much deceit, polygamy, and sex.

I know we don't talk about Eastern religious concepts like karma much in Christianity, but if it exists, I'd say Jacob gets a double dose in this Genesis story. He usurps his older brother's birthright by manipulating him, only to be tripped up on a technicality of birth order here by Laban. If we didn't know the story about him and Esau, it might be easy to feel sorry for him. But given the context, not so much.

The prayer Solomon offers in Kings is pretty remarkable, considering he identifies himself as a child who doesn't know up from down. It makes more sense, though, if we consider that this was likely written well after the fact by someone trying to explain where Solomon's tremendous leadership and wisdom came from. This practice is common throughout the Bible, helping free us from such a literal, real-time understanding of the stories.

Digging Deeper

Mining for what really matters . . . and gold

In Bible-nerd circles, we should call July "parable-palooza." Two weeks in a row with a Gospel parable are followed up by the blue-light special of Scriptures for parable fans. With five parables this week, we could dive into any or all of them and go along many a rabbit trail. Instead, let's consider why Jesus is dropping so many of these illustrations in a row.

Think of this as an invite-only intensive clinic on evangelism in the Jesus way. Here he has all of his freshly recruited disciples gathered together, learning not just about what Jesus stands for but also how he wants them to represent the movement to the rest of the world. He has fishermen, builders, tax collectors, and other salt-of-the-earth types along with him—not a scholar or priest in the entire lot.

He didn't recruit these people because of their theological training or family pedigree. They aren't particularly remarkable in the eyes of their communities, so they'll have to work at being taken seriously. They lack the fancy vestments or corner offices in the village high-rise to wow people into joining them. Chances are several of them can't even read, let alone sit down with the Torah and deliberate the finer points of the law.

That's not the job they're called to. What Jesus wants is for them to connect with people where they are, on a heart level. He specifically picked normal people because he wants his message to be by and for the regular folks. In order to get there, then, the disciples need to get this gospel stuff in clear, contextually relevant terms. In that sense, Jesus isn't just teaching them the content of what he's saying; he's modeling an example of how to teach it.

I imagine him looking around the room, one by one, and looking someone right in the eye when he offers up another parable. First, he connects, then he discerns, and finally he communicates. If he doesn't establish the first two steps, the final message won't ever land.

We get to the heart of this Scripture only by the end, when he says, "Therefore every scribe who has been trained for the kingdom of heaven is like the master of a household who brings out of his treasure what is new and what is old." I've never actually heard this part of the text preached on, likely because the parables lend themselves so easily to teaching. But for followers of Jesus who claim to have something to share with the world, this is our message.

We have discovered something we believe is so beautiful that we can't help but share it. Understanding how to do that, though, is where so many Christians fall short. We start talking in our own time and our own way, deaf to how receptive the person we're talking to really is, or what they're even able to hear. Further, we tend to jump into all the things we're excited to talk about without regard to whether our audience actually understands anything we're saying!

All the Jesus-speak and vernacular religious stuff might be familiar to us, but it's another language to others. Similarly, these ideas may have been part of our spiritual upbringing for decades, but that doesn't mean others share this experience.

What's old, sacred treasure to us is brand new to someone else. Don't assume anything, including whether the person we're talking to cares at all about what matters to us. Evangelism isn't the art of coercion; it's a practice of connection.

Heads-Up

Connecting the text to our world

Our son, Mattias, loves memes, which usually are single images or short video clips with some kind of clever caption or added effect to spoof them. While some of them can be worth a laugh, his depth of affection for the almighty meme well exceeds my ability to maintain interest.

Just this morning, I was talking my daughter through a relationship challenge she's having at church when Mattias stuck his phone in front of me. "Dad, check this out," he said, grinning widely. "It's an astronaut singing Rebecca Black's 'Friday.' Isn't that hilarious?" Bear in mind that he is on the high end of the autism spectrum, so we have to work more consciously than some on social context and cues, but this one triggered me. I told him to get the damn phone out of my face while I was talking about something more important.

Later, we processed the whole thing together. To Mattias, the meme was important, and the idea that it wouldn't be important to someone else simply hadn't occurred to him. He was actually trying to connect with me about something he hoped I would like, so my rejection in the moment felt personal. Conversely, his tone-deafness to what else was going on around him came off as insensitive and indifferent to his sister's feelings.

A daily practice of mindfulness in our family is learning the difference between talking with someone and talking at them. And while talking at people, regardless of receptivity or context, might sometimes get the results we want, in the end it ends up leaving more brokenness in its wake than connection.

The meme was kind funny, though, I'll admit.

Prayer for the Week

Help me practice connection over coercion.

Popping Off

Art/music/video and other cool stuff that relate to the text

The Poisonwood Bible, by Barbara Kingsolver (book, 2005)

The Very Worst Missionary, by Jamie Wright (book, 2018)

So Annoying!

Lectionary Texts For

August 2, 2020 (Ninth Sunday after Pentecost)

Texts in Brief

My dog ate my Bible!

FIRST READING

Genesis 32:22–31

Jacob is headed to see his brother, Esau, and is taking his wives, servants, and belongings with him. When they make camp by the Jabbok river for the night, Jacob encounters what the text describes as "a man," who he wrestles with and demands a blessing from. The man dislocates Jacob's hip during the wrestling match, but finally relents and offers him the blessing. The man renames Jacob "Israel," also revealing himself as God to Jacob.

Psalm/Prophet

Isaiah 55:1–5

Through the prophet, God calls the Israelites to come to God and have their fill of "the good stuff" of life. This bountiful offering is because of God's long-standing covenant with David. In the second part, God tells the Israelites that they will be examples to other nations, who will be drawn to them because of their faithfulness to the God of Israel.

Second Reading

Romans 9:1–5

Paul is very strong in his assertion about his own truth-telling and that these truths come from God. He also seems to be aggrieved about the fact that newcomers to the Christian faith may not be accepted as equals by their Israelite counterparts—namely because the Israelites lay claim to being the special, chosen people of God.

Gospel

Matthew 14:13–21

Jesus tries to get some alone time, but a crowd of needy people follows him, so he heals them. The disciples worry because now this crowd is away from home and it's getting dark. They suggest sending the people away to go find food, but Jesus orders the disciples to feed the people themselves. The disciples bring him what they have, and he blesses it, multiplying it into more than the crowd needs.

Bible, Decoded

Breaking down Scripture in plain language

Jabbok—The river where Jacob wrestled the angel. The name just means *luxuriant river*. It was along the journey to see Esau, who had left Haran (noted in Genesis 3). The rock (since named Peniel) and that spot on the river have since been consecrated as holy because of this story.

Peniel—Rock named by Jacob at the site where he wrestled the man. The name means *face of God* because Jacob claimed to have seen God face to face that night.

Points to Ponder

First Thoughts

Though a lot of the actual locations of these biblical stories are contested, depending on who you ask, I got to visit the spot where the citizens of Jordan say this encounter that Jacob had took place. As we tend to do with myths, I had imagined it as a vast, verdant area with a roaring river, but it was actually more of a modest creek, at least today.

Paul's letter of grievance to Rome precedes a trip he makes to Jerusalem, the epicenter of the Jewish community. It is likely that he is working out his stress about the upcoming trip because he is going to Jerusalem as an advocate of new, non-Jewish converts so that they will be accepted. He's so worried, in fact, that he is willing to sacrifice his own standing among his people in order to have the gentiles welcomed. Sounds a lot like church, doesn't it?

Note in the Gospel text that five pieces of bread plus two fish equals seven, our secret "holy number." Likely not an accident. This symbolizes that God's hand is involved in the situation. Also note how similar the blessing Jesus offers for the food here is to the last supper and now our own Communion rituals. Again, no accident.

Digging Deeper

Mining for what really matters . . . and gold

The word of the week is *persistence*. In Genesis, Jacob will not accept anything less than what he wants from the man he wrestles with all night. In fact, his apparent limp is even attributed to his persistent nature, having been a sort of war wound incurred in his conflict with this person who is revealed toward the end of the text to be God, or at least some supernatural or angelic being that embodies both God and humanity. Like his dark deal with Esau, Jacob is willing to accept some short-term discomfort for a longer-term payoff.

We have to also consider where he's headed in his trip. His brother, who is rightly pissed off at him, has gone a different way, far from his family of origin, after being tricked out of his inheritance. The ever-tenacious Jacob, though, won't accept this estrangement. He uproots his entire clan to venture out and reconnect with Esau.

In Romans, Paul clearly would rather not make his upcoming trip into Jerusalem, where he'll likely be condemned as a gentile-loving traitor. Remember that, in addition to evangelizing to these "others," he also spent a good portion of his career hunting his own people for the Roman Empire. Still, he is resolved to make the trip into the proverbial lion's den because he owes it to those he has brought into this new and growing Christian community.

In Matthew, we have two different miracles done by Jesus. First, he heals many in the crowd following him, and then he multiplies a handful of food into a feast for the big crowd. But none of this would have happened if the crowd hadn't persisted in tracking him down. Clearly, Jesus was ready to get out of there, but they weren't easily dissuaded. They knew what they wanted, and, by God, they were going to do what it took to get it. In fact, they left their homes so quickly that they didn't even have time to pack. Never mind that he was on a boat and they were walking, either! Talk about tenacity.

The lingering question is where the psalm fits in with all of this. God seems to be offering a clinic on making good financial choices, but if we consider it more broadly, it appears that it's a teaching moment about where we invest ourselves more generally. Don't spend your time, energy, and resources chasing after stuff that doesn't ultimately matter, says God. You have a big and important job to do! Don't be distracted, stay the course, and remember your mission.

Up to this point, Jacob hasn't likely won any awards for charm, and neither has Paul. And I'm guessing Jesus might have been a little bit annoyed that everybody followed him and asked even more of him after he was clearly worn out. But the results speak for themselves. When it comes to pursuing God's blessing, annoying persistence seems to get the job done.

To be clear, this doesn't mean that we can claim to be justified by God anytime we're being obnoxious. Sometimes, though, "no" simply isn't an acceptable answer, and just because something is hard doesn't mean it's not what we're meant to be doing. We keep at it because it's our calling, even if the rest of the world thinks we're kind of weird for it.

Hey, being weird for Jesus isn't the worst thing to be known for!

Heads-Up

Connecting the text to our world

I knew what Amy was going to say before I even asked. In fact it got to the point that I kind of dreaded asking her what she wanted for her birthday or other holidays because no matter what, the answer was always "a puppy."

Never mind that we already had a perfectly good dog, plus a couple of fairly decent children. How many living creatures does one house really need, anyway? I'd usually roll my eyes, and then ask, "Aside, from a puppy, what do you want?"

If she was feeling particularly persistent, her answer sometimes was "two puppies." I'm telling you that this woman never gives up.

One time she got me talking in hypotheticals. I must have been especially tired or in an unusually good mood or something, because I didn't even see the setup coming. "If we ever got another dog someday," she said, "what would you want to have?"

"I don't know," I sighed, "I've always loved mini Australian shepherds. They're so cute, it's about enough to make you explode." All she did was smile and nod. I knew that, one way or another, I was screwed.

Day after day, week after week, she started texting me pictures of mini Aussie puppies. Usually I didn't respond, until she sent me a photo of a baby girl who was rust and white, with the biggest, most pitiful eyes I had ever seen. She was sitting in her owner's grocery cart, looking up pitifully with her head cocked to the side.

Okay, I texted back, she's about the cutest thing ever. Amy didn't respond for a while, so I figured that was that. Then about forty-five minutes later she sent me a message.

> I got an appointment for us tomorrow at three
> to go meet her. We don't have to get her, but I
> want you to see her in person.

Long story short, Bella is my furry little baby girl. She's naughty, destructive, and affectionate. And yes, she's still about the cutest thing ever. "You know how to work me," I said to Amy, with Bella curled up, napping in my lap. "You always get what you want out of me, if you wait long enough."

"I know," Amy smiled. "I do."

Prayer for the Week

I know sometimes I put myself into things that don't give back the way they should to myself and others. Help me stay focused and give me the strength to be persistent in what matters.

Popping Off

Art/music/video and other cool stuff that relate to the text

Rocky (movie, 1976)

"Just Keep Swimming" scene from *Finding Nemo* (movie, 2003)

Fear Itself

Lectionary Texts For
August 9, 2020 (Tenth Sunday after Pentecost)

Texts in Brief
My dog ate my Bible!

First Reading
Genesis 37:1–4, 12–28

Joseph, Jacob's favorite son, gives a critical report about how two of his brothers watch after the family flock. In addition to being jealous of him, his brothers resent his criticism and decide to try to kill him when he comes to check on them again in Dothan. Another brother, Reuben, convinces them to just toss him in a pit instead. When a tribe of Ishmaelites came through, they sell him for silver. The Ishmaelites take Joseph to Egypt.

Psalm/Prophet

1 Kings 19:9–18

The Israelites have turned on Elijah for his critical prophecies, and they conspire to kill him. Elijah hides in a cave. A great wind comes by, followed by an earthquake and then fire, but God is in the silence after all of this, not the terrible signs. Elijah is to anoint Elisha as prophet in his place and two new kings to lead the Israelites and the Arameans, who will systematically slaughter most of the Israelites. No one will be left of the Israelites except seven thousand who are really faithful. Elisha will see to the death of any who escape from the two kings.

Second Reading

Romans 10:5–15

Paul reprimands those who are trying to decide who is and isn't worthy of heaven. He also asserts the importance of living out Jesus's new covenant from the inside out, rather than worrying foremost about the ancient laws. It's up to the people to share what they believe, so all have an opportunity to know the God of Israel. We have been given the gift of being the messengers of wonderful news.

Gospel

Matthew 14:22–33

Jesus sends the disciples across the Sea of Galilee while he goes away to pray. The boat is caught in a storm, and they're stranded until Jesus comes to them, walking on the water. They think he's a ghost until he tells them

who he is, but Peter asks him to prove it by command-
ing Peter to walk out to meet him. Jesus calls Peter, but
though it starts well, Peter starts to sink when he looks
down. Jesus saves him but laments Peter's anemic faith.

Bible, Decoded
Breaking down Scripture in plain language

Seven Thousand—Like the number seven, this represents godly perfection or completeness. So the idea is
that, after this bloody purge of the godless, the only
ones left are pure of heart and faithful to God.

Jehu and Hazael—Hazael is to be made king over
the region now called Syria, and Jehu (formerly com-
mander of the army of Ahab, who governed over the
northernmost region of Israel) is named the Israelite
king. The primary target of the Israelites' violence is
Ahab and his people, after Ahab has led them away
from God, worshipping Baal instead.

Points to Ponder
First Thoughts

Lots of death going on this week. Weeks like this help
us understand why some use the Bible to justify violence in the name of God. But it's important for us to
remember, as we've noted before, that many of these
stories are recorded well after the events themselves
have taken place. With this in mind, it makes sense that
someone would have wondered, how do God's own chosen people get so summarily slaughtered? Wouldn't
they have been protected by God? The response, as
we can glean it from this 1 Kings text at least, is that

the deaths happen because the Israelites have broken their covenant with God. And like the story of the great flood, God wipes the proverbial slate clean and starts again with a handful who seem to still believe.

By the time we get to the Romans passage, though, no one is beyond the potential reach of God's divine touch. In fact, it's made clear that it's our business only to bear God's likeness as revealed to us in Jesus's life, death, and resurrection to the rest of the world, not to be emissaries of justice on God's behalf. This is the byproduct of the new covenant.

Digging Deeper

Mining for what really matters . . . and gold

This 1 Kings text is hard on a couple of levels. Aside from what could be interpreted as divinely sanctioned genocide, we have a religious leader—Elijah—wading into politics. Talk about a hot-button issue in the United States!

There are those who argue that America was founded principally as a Christian nation and on biblically informed traditions and values that inform who we are as a country and people. Others tend to point toward founding father Thomas Jefferson and his vocal emphasis on the importance of the separation between church and state.

The fact is that if we're going to preach, teach, and deliberate about things that affect our daily lives within the context of our faith, we're going to be at least adjacently political. How, for example, can we not talk about how we care for—or don't care for—our poor when the gospel is very clear that this is central to our faith identity?

In this text, though, Elijah doesn't just touch on political matters; he is quite literally the kingmaker. In this case, though, all politics were religiously informed, and vice versa. There was no such thing to the people of Israel and surrounding territories as anything other than a theocracy. Even when the Roman Empire descended on the Middle East, they were governed by a Caesar who claimed to be the embodiment of the Divine on earth.

What rings true in a number of these texts, though, is that even when the stakes are high and our mission will win us no popularity contests, we're urged to follow God's call out of the safety of our caves, family compounds, or boats and respond without concern for the consequence. Joseph knows by now that his brothers hate him, so it's likely no surprise they attack him on his arrival. Peter probably isn't too shocked that physics takes over when he gets out away from the boat. And Elijah practically has WANTED posters in every saloon in Israel by this time.

Sometimes we have to do the hard things that some part of us fights against. Whether it's speaking out to an unforgiving audience or wading into choppy waters, God doesn't promise an easy ride. What we're promised, though, is that we're not alone in the deep water.

Franklin Delano Roosevelt famously said in one of his speeches that "the only thing we have to fear is fear itself." Maybe all Christians should have that tattooed on the backs of our hands for the next time we inevitably start worrying about whether we're alone in our struggle.

Heads-Up

Connecting the text to our world

I can just imagine the conversation while the boat tosses back and forth, Bartholomew leaning over the side, wishing he had brought along his Dramamine.

"I think we should fix up the outside of the boat," says James, "put a fresh coat of paint on the boat. Then maybe the right folks will wander by and come save us."

"I found some really original sign ideas in an email my cousin forwarded me," says Philip. "What if we hung something over the side that said something like 'God answers knee-mail,' or 'CH _ _ CH . . . what's missing? U R!' people will realize we're really clever and will come by to see what's going on in our boat. Then they can help us out."

"We just need to put up a screen at one end of the boat," says Thomas. "Andrew knows three chords on his guitar so maybe if he plays it, they will come."

"All we need is some candles and incense," says Matthew. "They'll know we are Christians by our chanting."

And it goes on and on, arguing about how to save the boat. Meanwhile there's Jesus, standing alongside the boat, listening to the whole thing.

"Peter," says Jesus. "Come here."

"Hey, Jesus!" Peter grins, throwing his legs over the side of the boat. He gets a few steps out in the water and pulls a Wile E. Coyote. He looks down and suddenly decides, despite the fact that Jesus is calling him out of the boat, he actually really kind of needed the boat more than he thought.

Then comes the Wile E. Coyote moment.

I wonder with this story if we get so hung up on the mystery of miracle that we miss the point entirely.

In an essay titled "Let Jesus Show" from his book *Secrets in the Dark*, Frederick Buechner says that "believing in Jesus is not the same as believing things about him such as that he was born of a virgin and raised Lazarus from the dead. Instead, it is a matter of giving our hearts to him, of come hell or high water putting our money on him, the way a child believes in a mother or a father, the way a mother or a father believes in a child."

He says, "If you tell me Christian commitment is a kind of thing that has happened to you once and for all like some kind of spiritual plastic surgery, I say you're either pulling the wool over your own eyes or trying to pull it over mine. Every morning you should wake up in your bed and ask yourself: 'Can I believe it all again today?' At least five times out of ten the answer should be No because the No is as important as the Yes, maybe more so. The No is what proves you're human in case you should ever doubt it."

Even the storms of life can be a means of blessing. When things are going badly, our hearts are more receptive to Jesus. A broken heart is often a door through which God can find entry. He still comes to us in the midst of our troubles, saying, "Take heart, it is I; do not be afraid."

Prayer for the Week

God, help me focus more on getting out of the boat than on taking care of it.

Popping Off

Art/music/video and other cool stuff that relate to the text

"The Only Thing We Have to Fear Is Fear Itself," by Franklin D. Roosevelt (speech, 1933)

"Wile E. Coyote vs. Gravity" (YouTube video): http:// tinyurl.com/y2ugchaq

When Rules Are Wrong

Lectionary Texts For

August 16, 2020 (Eleventh Sunday after Pentecost)

Texts in Brief

My dog ate my Bible!

First Reading

Genesis 45:1–15

Joseph reveals his identity to his brothers, who are at a loss of words out of shame for having sold him into slavery. He says that they shouldn't be afraid because God did amazing things even with such a terrible act. Because of this, Joseph feels like God meant for him to be in Egypt. He hugs his brothers and welcomes them until they aren't scared of him anymore.

Psalm/Prophet

Isaiah 56:1, 6–8

The prophet calls to his people to hold fast and stay faithful and righteous in their efforts, because God honors all who honor God. We never know when God will show up in our daily life, so we should live as if God is always there. Finally, God will bring people together who have been pulled apart, and they will be one under God again.

SECOND READING

Romans 11:1–2a, 29–32

Paul's colleagues are worried that because God also honors non-Jews, God has forgotten them. Just because mercy is an equal-opportunity gift doesn't make any of us less precious to God. Put another way: we don't have to be better than everyone else to be good enough.

GOSPEL

Matthew 15:(10–20), 21–28

Religious leaders are angry about Jesus's unorthodox interpretation of the law, but he says they're like the blind leading the blind. His point is that cleanliness laws with respect to the body are less important to God than is purity of the heart. We can keep all of the kosher laws but still act out of evil; this isn't what God wants. In the second half of the text, a foreign woman asks Jesus for healing for her child, but he calls her a dog. She persists in asking, so he agrees to heal the child because of the mother's persistent faith.

Bible, Decoded

Breaking down Scripture in plain language

Tyre and Sidon—Two cities in the region that is now modern-day Lebanon. Some translations say Jesus retreated there, so this might have been a place for him to get away and rest. But it may have also been for the express purpose of living out the theme in this week's texts, which is that no one, irrespective of where they come from or what they look like, is beyond the reach of God's grace, so they shouldn't be beyond ours either.

Dog—The Greek word found in the original text is *kunarion*, which is more directly translated as *little dog* or used in reference to a house pet. But unlike how we treat our pets today, people in Jesus's time didn't keep dogs around for affection and certainly didn't treat them like little people. They were useful in work and beneficial for protection. They got table scraps but definitely wouldn't have been allowed up on the couch to lick the plate clean on pizza night.

Points to Ponder

First Thoughts

I struggle with the way this Genesis text has been interpreted by some, though it's understandable. If we use our "everything happens for a reason" goggles, we could interpret this as letting the brothers off the hook because apparently God did this to Joseph for an only-now-known purpose. We have to keep in mind that this is how these texts were written, which was also how people thought about events at the time (and we still often do today). If something good comes to us, it must be a reward from God for living right. Conversely, if suffering or tragedy come along, it's because of something we did, too. That, or the suffering is part of God's plan, which will only make sense later.

I am of the mind that God never wants us to suffer, nor does God bring suffering on us, no matter how we act. We do just fine at heaping suffering on ourselves without God's help. What I do believe, though, is that God can make something beautiful and redeeming come out of even the direst circumstances.

So the next time something terrible happens, or even just something inconvenient, we should try not asking ourselves why God did that to us. Instead, ask, "what can God and I do together with this mess to make something beautiful?"

Digging Deeper
Mining for what really matters . . . and gold

There have been a lot of interpretations of this story in Matthew, many of which can feel less than satisfying.

In one interpretation, Jesus calls the woman a dog and declines her request for help because he is testing how resolved she is in her faith. But he has helped others without doing something like this, and it seems to stand in contrast with the "seek and you will find; knock and the door will be opened" concept of grace.

In another reading, Jesus did call her something akin to "dog," but some suggest it's more of a term of endearment, like "little pup." But there's really no cute way to call someone a dog that I'm aware of, and regardless, he still declines her request the first time.

A third perspective is that he's busy, maybe distracted by his work, and possibly tired after dealing with jerky priests earlier that day. Now he's having to explain his teaching, yet again, to these disciples who seem to need a lot of hand-holding in this discipleship process. It could have been that this was a moment in which Jesus was just being human, maybe even a bit of a jerk himself, but that the woman's faith finally turned his heart toward compassion. I've even preached this approach to it.

Or maybe the whole thing was a setup. Maybe the woman was in on the act the whole time. Imagine if Jesus figured his followers would need a "visual aid" to help them get over their fixation with adherence to the written law, which had been ingrained in them since birth. His point was that we can be law-abiding citizens and still not be right with God.

Because this woman was a Canaanite, Jesus was perfectly within his right to ignore her, call her a dog, or refuse anything she asked of him. By doing so, he hadn't broken any laws. No one would fault him for it—unless they had really been listening to what he just said.

Anyone who could look past the blindness of their own cultural norms would know that what he did was wrong. To treat anyone that way was completely contrary to the notion of the gospel teaching he had been emphasizing all along. As we know, though, hearing an idea in abstract doesn't necessarily have as profound an impact as seeing it lived out. By using this demonstration, Jesus is subversively exposing the absurdity and heartlessness of living only by human law.

Once again, Jesus reveals the brokenness of the human-made and human-enforced systems around him without bloodshed, conflict, or even a raised voice. And once something like that is seen, it's impossible to forget.

That's the radicality of the gospel!

Heads-Up
Connecting the text to our world

Teaching kids that there are times when breaking the rules is acceptable is never easy; teaching it to a kid on the autism spectrum is damn near impossible.

Our son, Mattias, is high-functioning on the spectrum, which means he kind of gets the best of all worlds. He's intensely smart, highly verbal, and talented in music beyond belief. He could tell us what note the frequency of the fan in the microwave made when he was three years old. In some ways, he's a genius.

And in others, he's kind of a ding-a-ling.

Telling the truth is an especially tricky one for spectrum kids, who tend to take things very literally and to latch onto rules and never let go. The idea of exceptions to said rules is foreign. So when we told him as a little guy to always tell the truth, and he then proceeded to explain to the old woman at church that he didn't want to sit with her because she smelled funny, he didn't get why we looked more than a little bit horrified.

"Well, she does stink," he said, looking dismayed.

"Maybe so," I said, "but just because something is true doesn't mean you always have to say it." He nodded, and we moved on.

The next day, my wallet was halfway buried in one of the houseplants. Pretty sure my wife, Amy, didn't do it, I turned to Mattias. "Did you do this?" I asked. He just stared at me blankly. After some back-and-forth, he finally confessed to it.

"But dad," he said, "you don't always have to tell the truth, even if it's true."

Remind me never to ask this boy if these jeans make me look fat.

It didn't occur to us how many layers of social norms were piled on top of what seemed to be a pretty universal rule: tell the truth. And while most of us understand that sometimes there are more important issues than stating the full, unadulterated truth, he didn't. He was just trying to do what the rule said, and people ended up getting hurt anyway.

If the Pharisees in Matthew were all on the spectrum, maybe they could be given a pass for idolizing the rules more than holding the rule of the primacy of love, compassion, and mercy above all others. Maybe I should send Mattias their way to explain it to them.

Prayer for the Week

God, help me see the potential and opportunity for beautiful change and redemption, especially in the hardest moments to find it.

Popping Off

Art/music/video and other cool stuff that relate to the text

Liar Liar (movie, 1997)

"I Think You're Fat," from *Esquire* (article, July 24, 2007)

Fall Apart Together

Lectionary Texts For

August 23, 2020 (Twelfth Sunday after Pentecost)

Texts in Brief

My dog ate my Bible!

First Reading

Exodus 1:8–2:10

A new Egyptian Pharaoh is wary of the Israelites' potential for revolt, so he submits them to brutal labor. They continue to grow in number, so he makes conditions even worse to try and break them. He tells Hebrew midwives to kill the newborn sons, but they are too scared to, so the Israelites' numbers grow even more. Pharaoh decides to have all of the sons drowned, but one family hides their son, finally sending him down the river, hoping he will be rescued. Pharaoh's daughter finds him, calls his mother to nurse him, and raises him as her own by the name Moses.

Psalm/Prophet

Isaiah 51:1–6

God entreats the Israelites not to lose faith amid lack, trial, and suffering because God will deliver them from it, both in this life and afterward, rescuing them from the hardship they endure on earth.

Second Reading

Romans 12:1–8

Instead of offering sacrifices of animals as in the past to God, we are supposed to give of our whole selves to God, sacrificially, to show God we are "all in." In living sacrificially, we have to also remember we're all instruments of God, used for different purposes, none more or less important than another. We can't let status, titles, wealth, or personal achievements convince us otherwise.

Gospel

Matthew 16:13–20

Jesus asks his disciples who people think he is. They say many people think he is a manifestation of one of the great prophets. He asks them who they think he is, and Peter responds that he is the Anointed One, sent by and descended from God. Because he sees Jesus clearly, Jesus tells him he will be a foundational part of the establishment of the future church to come after Jesus is gone.

Bible, Decoded

Breaking down Scripture in plain language

Moses—Translated, Scripture says this means "I drew him out of the water." However, the origins of his name etymologically may have been made up to make a point. Moses is drawn out many times in his life, including being drawn out to lead his people and drawn out of Egypt. Even at birth, he is pulled out of his culture and family of origin. So his entire life is informed by the experience of being pulled out of whatever context he is in.

Levite—Levites were descendants of Levi, a son of Jacob. They were considered the people from whom all priests among the Israelites came. So the fact that it's noted that Moses was born to Levites is intended to assert for us that he was ordained for a priestly call from birth.

Points to Ponder

First Thoughts

The story of Moses is the story of Israel in a sense. It's a pattern of being pulled apart and coming back together, as he is lost to Pharaoh's daughter and the river but then reunited with his mother. His life is a metaphor for the greater story of his people. This is part of what makes him a good leader.

Paul tells of something similar in describing the greater body of Christ that is to be represented by the church. Upon Jesus's death, the disciples first come together, then scatter out. Here, the early church in Rome is dealing with some internal politics that seem to threaten to splinter them. His effort in Romans is to remind them of their greater purpose, which can only be realized when they work in concert for the same purpose.

How do they do this? As Peter shows us, by seeing clearly who Jesus really is, regardless of our past, our problems, or what other people say. This clarity of vision and steadfast focus is what the greater community of Christians collectively is to be founded on.

Digging Deeper
Mining for what really matters ... and gold

Suffice it to say that happy endings don't seem to last long in the Bible, especially in the more ancient books. Just last week, we were celebrating the peaceful reunion of Joseph and his brothers, and within the first sentence of this week's Exodus passage, we can see the dark clouds already gathering. Joseph has died by the time this new king rises to power, leaving the Israelites without the familial sort of bond they had with the previous king because of his love for Joseph.

This is one of the problems when we lack shared history and shared story. Compassion and trust won out prior to this, despite the vast political and cultural chasms between Joseph and Pharaoh because they shared their lives with each other. So in spite of the struggle and inevitable friction that arose given the relationship of the Egyptians to the captive Hebrews, they stuck together; compassion and love won out.

Without that bond, though, trouble takes over. Fear becomes the dominant currency, which invokes violence and oppression as a possible antidote. Paul sees this potential already being sown in the young church in Rome, and he's trying to stave it off, reminding them that their bonds as fellow Christ-followers are far more important than the sum total of their differences. The problems, pressures, and threats aren't going to go away, so the only hope they have is to find something else to cling to through it all.

This entreaty from Isaiah says as much, too, if more implicitly. There's trouble in the community of the Israelites, so he's trying to hold them together. First, he wants them to stay focused on God and the covenant they have with God. This bond, he knows, is enough to sustain them through their suffering. But with that comes the inevitable shared story and shared lives of holding on together to the same rock. It's not that having someone along with us during hard times keeps it from hurting, but something about it helps make the potency of its sting a little bit more bearable.

There is plenty in our current climate that is intent on pulling us further apart, whether it's based on race, economics, country of origin, orientation/identity, or political affiliation. Those forces at play trying to rend the social fabric do so because it weakens us, revealing vulnerabilities that can more easily be exploited for personal gain.

Unity isn't just the right thing to do; it makes strategic sense. There's no promise anywhere in these passages that the struggles will stop forever. The call is to hold on, and to hold tight to each other as circumstances inevitably arise in waves of both dark and light. We're always stronger together than we ever will be apart. It's who we're made to be.

Heads-Up

Connecting the text to our world

We were late, once again, to pick up our daughter Zoe from her after-school practice. With two kids at schools across town from each other, both with different pick-up and drop-off times from day to day, sometimes it's hard to remember that I don't actually live behind the wheel of my car. It seems like if I'm not rushing to take them somewhere or pick them up, I'm frantically working on my "real job" to get caught up—which never happens—in the brief times in between.

Yesterday, Amy and I made the half-hour trek from the church up to Zoe's school and, as sometimes happens, we got caught in a traffic snarl. I could feel the tension in the car begin to rise quietly as we sat still on the road, time ticking away against us. When we finally pulled in the drive, it was clear that her teacher was less than enchanted with us. Amy went up to meet them and said the woman was shaking with anger, dressing her down for abandoning her parental responsibility, and threatening to kick Zoe out of her special program if it happened again.

That's what we get for being fifteen minutes late twice in three months, I guess.

It was clear by her face that Amy was rattled by the confrontation, and it wasn't long before we were at each other, transferring the energy the teacher dumped on her to each other. After several exchanges back and forth about whose fault it was and what we were going to do differently (not offered in the kindest of tones), I looked in the rearview mirror at Zoe's wide eyes, turned toward her lap.

"I'm really sorry guys," she said quietly, "I didn't mean to create any trouble."

"Oh no, honey," Amy said. "You did absolutely nothing wrong. Sometimes mom and dad have more going on than we can handle, and it kind of catches up to us in unexpected moments." Why we can talk to our kids this way but not to each other in those moments is a mystery worth considering, but her disposition in the back seat pulled us out of our defensive postures, reminding us that there was something way more important at stake.

"We love each other," I said, "very much. And just because we argue sometimes doesn't change that. And like your mom said, we want to do anything we can to allow you to have the opportunities you've earned." She smiled a little and the tension began to dissipate a little.

As we do every night, we sat down to dinner together and took turns sharing what we were thankful for. "I'm thankful for my family," said Zoe, grabbing her mom's hand next to her on the table.

So am I.

Prayer for the Week

I forget sometimes when stuff gets hard and chaotic that the "together" times are way more important than the challenges that come from being together. Help me remember that.

Popping Off

Art/music/video and other cool stuff that relate to the text
Gandhi (movie, 1982)

"One," by U2 (song, 1991)

Thinking like a Caterpillar

Lectionary Texts For

August 30, 2020 (Thirteenth Sunday after Pentecost)

Texts in Brief

My dog ate my Bible!

FIRST READING

Exodus 3:1–15

Moses, while taking care of his father-in-law's herds, comes upon a burning bush near the Mountain of God. God speaks to him from the bush, telling Moses that he will be the one to lead the Israelites out of Egypt. Moses feels unqualified, but God promises to be with him. When he asks God who to say sent him to lead the Israelites, God says to tell them that "I AM" sent him.

PSALM/PROPHET

Jeremiah 15:15–21

This text blends together both a personal and collective narrative, representing both the prophet's own voice, as well as the voice of the Israelites as a whole. The complaints and mourning of the faithful for suffering in spite of adhering to God's commands are met with a promise to both the one and the whole that deliverance and relief are theirs if they stay focused on God, even when things are hard.

SECOND READING
Romans 12:9–21

This letter to the church in Rome seems to be a response to divisions and resentment growing within the ranks. Paul urges them to live harmoniously and to serve as an example of who community should be to the world around them. He gets more specific toward the end, telling them that retribution is not their concern and that they should respond to all wrongdoing, evil, or harm with grace and kindness, leaving any consequences to God.

GOSPEL
Matthew 16:21–28

Jesus starts to explain the persecution awaiting him in Jerusalem, but Peter urges him to avoid it. Jesus, calling him an adversary of what needs to be done, tell him he's focused too much on self-preservation rather than matters of the spirit. You can't cling to the former too hard and expect to be able to embrace the latter.

Bible, Decoded
Breaking down Scripture in plain language

I AM—In the original Hebrew, the phrase is *ehyeh asher ehyeh*. The word *ehyeh* is a common verb of being, used to describe a state of being (I am tired), to precede an action verb (I am working), or before a title or identity of some kind (I am a carpenter). But in using it the way it is here, it's an establishment of ultimate sovereignty and self-sufficiency. All of the other "being" contexts above are either temporary, dependent on external circumstances, or both, whereas "I am that I am" is an assertion of existence that is not contingent or dependent on any other context or circumstance. It just is.

Mount Horeb—This is the same location where, by some accounts, Moses was given the Ten Commandments by God. Elsewhere, though, the commandments were said to have been given to Moses at Mount Sinai. Some historians suggest this is a discrepancy in accounts, but others believe they're names for the same place. Regardless, the point is the same, which is that location matters in Scripture, and this place is considered to be holy.

Points to Ponder

First Thoughts

On first blush, it seems like the theme this week could be "chin up, little fella." Sure, things suck right now, but if you keep dealing with it, it'll get better. But that feels sort of trite, not unlike the poster of the kitten clinging to the tree branch with the words "HANG IN THERE" underneath it.

If we look beyond this initial impression, though, we're faced with some of the most universally difficult questions about human existence. We wrestle with the nature of suffering, why we suffer (if there is a "why"), what can come from it, and how we respond to it. We can also look at the difference between suffering for the "right reasons" and simply suffering without any worthwhile reason.

Finally, it even raises some questions about the balance between free will and destiny, particularly in Jesus's case. Granted, the kitten poster might be easier to tack to a wall and forget, but much of this week's Scripture digs down to the root of the plight of the human condition.

Digging Deeper

Mining for what really matters . . . and gold

This week's Gospel message hardly sounds like good news to Jesus's disciples. Their own religious rulers are about to turn on their leader in a big way. Worse than that, there will be deceit even within their own ranks. And if we remember, it was just a couple of readings back when the disciples finally seemed to wake up to the true and full nature of who and what Jesus is.

As popular psychology often says, the first stage of grief is denial, which Peter embraces here in earnest. Then he moves quickly to the bargaining stage, skipping over anger to the so-called third grief step. What he is expressing is completely understandable. It's what any flesh-and-blood human being would be expected to do.

The thing is, Jesus expects something else from the disciples by now. If they truly do get what he's about, then they should be in a mindset to transcend typical human impulses, reaching for something beyond that.

Jesus doesn't literally think Peter has been possessed by dark, sinister forces or that he's been an undercover demon this whole time. He's pointing out in his typically hyperbolic way that Peter's human impulses and limitations are holding him back from what Jesus is inviting all of them into. If they really "got it," this wouldn't scare them. It's more like a stage of evolution, or what a caterpillar necessarily goes through in becoming a butterfly. Nobody sits around trying to talk the caterpillar into not weaving a home-made sarcophagus around itself because we know what is on the other side of it.

Peter is thinking like a caterpillar who lacks the understanding of its own potential for becoming something else. All he sees is the loss of what is known, surrendering it to the mystery of the possible, which seems like a fool's bargain to the caterpillar mind. Jesus, on the other hand, has a butterfly mind even though he's still a caterpillar on the outside.

Don't let what is be the enemy of what can be, Jesus is saying. Don't let our lack of vision or imagination be our own worst enemy. He's not saying that the journey will be fun, easy, or even something he'd just as soon avoid if he could. He's also not saying that he's having to do all of this against his will, and that God is making him go through with it.

What he's saying is that the price is worth the result.

Heads-Up

Connecting the text to our world

I was a championship-level worrier as a kid. Once, I practically ruined the last couple of weeks of summer break before my third-grade year because I was too freaked out to consider moving up to another grade level. After all, I didn't know how to be a third-grader!

When I reached my teen years, I was a devoted metal head. I had posters of my favorite bands lining every wall of my room and a drum kit in one corner, surrounded by big tower speakers. My jean jacket was covered in patches, and my hair was down past my shoulder blades. And despite what all of these sell-out adults around me tried to convince me of, I knew for a fact that I would never stop celebrating Metallica and Anthrax as the greatest bands of all time, maintaining a place in heavy rotation in my CD carousel until I was on my deathbed.

In my early twenties, the idea of ever getting married gave me a knot in my stomach. By the time I reached thirty (and was married), even talking about ever having kids made me break out in a cold sweat.

Just yesterday, I turned to Amy at one point and said, "If you had told me fifteen years ago that I would be producing podcasts for a living (which is the bulk of my livelihood today), I don't think I would have believed you." For starters, I'm not sure I had even heard of podcasts, if they existed back then, and though I had maintained a love for the recording studio and sound engineering since before my Metallica days, the equipment was so large and prohibitively expensive, that having my own production company was beyond my imagination's grasp.

And yet, despite all of those things having come to pass, among many others, I still find myself worrying about the possibility of present things passing away into something big, dark, and scary called "the unknown."

We are, all too often, our own stumbling blocks. We worship the gods of the present so fiercely that we crowd up all of our space where God might breathe. The chaperones at my old parochial school always told us to "leave enough room for the Holy Spirit" between us and our dance partners at social events. Maybe that advice doesn't just have to apply to hormonal, dancing teenagers.

Prayer for the Week

Help me loosen my grip on what is, making room for you to breathe.

Popping Off

Art/music/video and other cool stuff that relate to the text

The Very Hungry Caterpillar, by Eric Carle (book, 1969)

The Pianist (movie, 2002)

The Bitter Herb

Lectionary Texts For

September 6, 2020 (Fourteenth Sunday after Pentecost)

Texts in Brief

My dog ate my Bible!

First Reading

Exodus 12:1–14

The text is an account of the story that became the basis for the Jewish Passover celebration, including some elements of the Seder meal served during Passover. The Israelites are starting fresh, but before they do, they are to make a sacrifice of a lamb and mark their doors with its blood. God will pass throughout Egypt and those whose doors aren't marked will suffer the loss of their firstborn son. This fourteenth day of the first month of the Jewish year will be celebrated as Passover in recognition of God's presence passing over their homes and sparing their children.

Psalm/Prophet

Ezekiel 33:7–11

God orders Ezekiel to tell people what messages God gives him, including the unpleasant ones. If he doesn't it will cost him his life for disobeying God. God doesn't enjoy watching even those who turn from God suffer in their rebellion; rather, God longs for all—including all who have strayed among the Israelites—to return to God's merciful, life-giving fold.

Second Reading

Romans 13:8–14

Paul urges the Christians in Rome to be indebted to each other in nothing but their commitment to love one another. In living this thoroughly through, all other commands of God are realized. There's no time for self-indulgence, pettiness, and division, because God's presence with them is imminent.

Gospel

Matthew 18:15–20

Jesus offers some practical advice on church governance. If someone does you wrong, talk to them directly about it. If that doesn't work, bring someone else along the next time to try and help persuade them. If they remain toxic in their attitude and actions, confront them before the whole church. At that point if they continue, it's time to move on and not let their negativity pollute the waters of community, which is founded on something greater than personal squabbles. Jesus's spirit will be with them when anyone gathers in the spirit of unity.

Bible, Decoded

Breaking down Scripture in plain language

Bitter Herb—The Hebrew word for the bitter herb served at the Passover meal is *maror*. It is meant to symbolize the bitterness of the Israelites' time in slavery. But in a larger sense, it is a reminder that, even in the midst of plenty and celebration, there is a thread of suffering that weaves itself through human existence, lest we forget.

Firstborn Son—Ancient Egyptian culture practiced primogeniture, which means that the firstborn male in any family unit wielded unquestioned authority and control in a family. The Pharaoh himself was referred to as "the firstborn of the firstborn of the firstborn," which is why he ruled over the entire "family" of the Egyptian nation. So to kill all firstborn sons not only was a harsh consequence for participating in the enslavement of God's chosen people; it was a complete disruption of the way of life in Egypt. It directly repudiated their identity and values—the ultimate shaming insult.

Points to Ponder

First Thoughts

On first glance, it seems hard to reconcile the common currency of love described in Romans with the Gospel text about calling offenders out, sometimes in front of their peers. But this gets to the heart of what Paul later calls "speaking the truth in love." Yes, we can just as easily execute this Gospel mandate to the letter while missing the context necessarily married to it in Romans. If the confrontation is done in an effort to shame or to feel better about ourselves, then we've lost the point. We are to engage in such hard conversations with the earnest hope—even expectation—for redemption and reconciliation.

The second bit, which is especially hard for those of us who require closure in order to feel good about a situation, is knowing when to lovingly release someone. Putting healthy distance between ourselves and someone refusing to make peace, and doing it in nothing but love, may be harder than lovingly confronting them is. Though it may be tempting to have a sort of "peace out" mic-drop moment on the way out the door, we should actually grieve the loss to the greater whole, as we all are made better when together than we are alone.

Digging Deeper

Mining for what really matters . . . and gold

In three of our four passages this week, someone is having to deliver pretty bad, and in one case, both weird and bad, news to a likely unreceptive audience. Granted, in Exodus, the Israelites do learn that they will both walk free and that their firstborn sons will be spared, but what a violent, bloody way to get there! The lamb slaughtering was pretty routine in a predominantly sacrificial religious culture, but smearing the blood on their doorposts would raise some eyebrows, for sure.

And even as much as I'm sure they despise their captors on many levels, wishing someone's children would die is beyond the pale. Plus, someone is bound to notice that the only families with little male babies left are the ones with this blood on their doors. Guess who will get blamed for such heinous genocide?

Moses has the task of telling the Israelites they have to do this or lose their babies. He knows as well as they do that this will wreak havoc on the community, and lots of innocent little people will die. They'll be uprooted once again and will venture out—under fierce pursuit—into the wilderness. And for all of this, he tells them, they are to be thankful and celebrate.

Ezekiel is warned by God not just to convey the good news God offers for his people but also to share the so-called "bitter herbs" as described in Exodus. This won't win him any more popularity contests than it did Jeremiah, but it's his calling, like it or not.

Finally, in the Gospel (this is where we're supposed to find good news, right?), we're told we have to go back to people who have done wrong to us and confront them, face to face. Then if that goes to crap, we get to do it again, and even a third time, trying to set things right. Seems like the burden should be on the offender, Jesus. Since when did doing the hard stuff in the spirit of possible redemption and for the sake of community cohesion become my job?

Trust me, says God, I got this.

We see the ugliness right in front of us and the short-term trouble that will come with it, and our instinct is to turn the other way and bail. It's hard to imagine the better outcome on the other side of the trouble when we're face to face with something we'd just as soon avoid. We obsess on the negative, and it has a tendency to take over.

Heads-Up

Connecting the text to our world

"Hey bud," I said to my son, Mattias, who was four years old at the time, "it's time to head to the doctor." I had dreaded this day, because I knew how he would react when I told him why we were going there. And I knew he would ask, because he always asked.

"But why?" he said. "I'm not sick. I don't need a doctor."

"Not today," I said, "but he's gonna help you not get sick later."

"How?" he looked at me with suspicion. This is the part I dreaded. I sighed and put my hand on his shoulder.

"They have to give you some shots," I said. "They make your body so it can fight lots of bad stuff later that would make it sick." His eyes widened like saucers, and he started to turn red.

"No," he shook his head, "no, no. No shots. I'm not sick. I'm not going."

What followed was about as miserable as you might expect when you take a kid on the autism spectrum to "voluntarily" let someone stick multiple sharp objects into his body. There were screams, sweat, spit, and no small amount of tears. Oh, and Mattias cried too, as I recall.

Mattias is a really smart kid. If you explained to him in an abstract context that a few seconds of discomfort would spare you from potentially life-threatening disease, he would have agreed that it made sense. But in the moment, when the notion of salvation from some unknown, out-in-the-future threat was supplanted by the fear of needles, all bets were off. He wasn't having it.

It's easy to feel like a bad parent, dragging a reluctant little kid into an office where strangers are going to stab him repeatedly with syringes "for his own good." All you see in the moment is the misery and pain your kid is having to contend with. The parental urge is to protect them from it, but we don't because we see the big picture. We understand what they need more than they do in that moment and unfortunately what they have to go through to get there.

Hopefully as adults, we grow out of the kicking-and-screaming stage when it comes to taking the bitter herbs. It's not always the case, but that's what loving community is for, at least sometimes.

Prayer for the Week

I don't want to do the hard stuff, even when I know it's for the best. Help me trust, even when I resist it.

Popping Off

Art/music/video and other cool stuff that relate to the text

"There's Going to Be a Flood" scene from *Evan Almighty* (movie, 2007)

The Monster at the End of This Book, by Jon Stone (book, 1971)

This One Goes to Eleven

Lectionary Texts For

September 13, 2020 (Fifteenth Sunday after Pentecost)

Texts in Brief

My dog ate my Bible!

First Reading

Exodus 14:19–31

An angel protects the fleeing Israelites from the Egyptians pursuing them with a wall of smoke overnight. The next morning, Moses calls on God to part the sea's waters, and the Israelites cross. When the Egyptians follow, the seas converge on them and they drown. At this point, the Israelites believe without doubt that God has sent Moses to lead them.

Psalm/Prophet

Genesis 50:15–21

After Jacob's death, Joseph's brothers worry that in his grief, Joseph will decide to punish them harshly for selling him into slavery, so they tell him that Jacob's last wish was for him to forgive his brothers. Then they offer to try and make good by serving him like slaves. Joseph says he won't punish them, because he isn't God, who is the only one fit to judge. Instead he promises to provide for them and their families.

Second Reading
Romans 14:1–12

The audience is warned that it's not for them to judge people about which rules they follow in making their food choices, regardless of whether they follow kosher laws. Some honor the Sabbath while others don't, and it's not for us to feel better than those who believe or act differently. Instead, whatever we do should be done in a way that is honoring of God. In judging others, we're actually setting ourselves up for being judged by God for it.

Gospel
Matthew 18:21–35

Peter asks how many times he should forgive someone who does wrong to him, and Jesus's answer—through a parable, of course—is "as many times as God forgives you." In the story, a man begs for mercy on a debt he can't pay but then turns around and punishes one of his own debtors for his inability to pay a much smaller amount. In effect, not offering forgiveness without limit, while asking for it from God, is hypocrisy.

Bible, Decoded

Breaking down Scripture in plain language

Fear—When the Bible speaks about fearing God, it's not suggesting that we should actually be afraid. What it calls for is a high degree of reverence. But as we know, some prefer to present a God that quite literally scares the hell out of us. This is not what the word means in these contexts.

Talents/Denarii—Money at the time of the Gospels' writing was determined based on measures of weight of precious metal. One talent (*maneh*) of metal was equivalent at the time to one hundred denarii worth of the same metal.

Points to Ponder

First Thoughts

When I was a kid, I was a literal thinker, so when I read this week's Gospel text, I assumed we were supposed to forgive someone 490 times, and that's it. Depending on the relationship, that could last a good number of years, but after that, watch out.

It wasn't until later, when I learned the symbolic significance of the number seven that I started to understand the real point; forgive as much as the One who forgives completely, thoroughly, and without condition or account. That was a real relief, because I didn't have to keep that forgiveness notebook around anymore!

Digging Deeper

Mining for what really matters . . . and gold

There are several different depictions of this story in Exodus, one of which is in one of our alternate readings in Exodus 15:1–18. This one is more melodic or poetic, portraying God as the champion of the underdog, emphasizing God's care for the vulnerable rather than focusing on the mass violence done to the Egyptian army.

In this account, we see the archetypal parting of the Red Sea, which collapses down on the Israelites' pursuers, leading to their freedom. In another depiction, it's God who drives the Egyptian troops crazy, and they end up drowning themselves in the sea rather than getting swallowed up by it.

What gives with all of these apparently differing stories, especially with them stacked up basically right next to each other? Which one are we supposed to believe? Rather than surveying these all in some sort of critical comparison, let's consider the story of the Israelites more longitudinally. After all, the Pentateuch (the first five books of the Bible) are all about the story of the people of Israel.

In recent weeks, we've seen these same people really let God down. They've strayed from their biblical laws and seem to be getting distracted by the other pagan cultural ways and gods all around them. They're forgetting who they are, but maybe more important, they seem to be forgetting whose they are: the beloved children of the one and only God of Israel.

In our narrative, then, we see a people getting just the opposite of what they seem to deserve. They repudiate God with faithlessness, and they are met with grace, forgiveness, and salvation. And just in case we choose not to extrapolate this lesson and apply it to ourselves, it comes up again in Genesis, when Joseph does much the same thing for his brothers, who were all neck and neck for the "crap brother of the century" award.

Again in Matthew, Peter seems a little fuzzy on this "respond to wrongdoing with God-like grace" thing, and then the early church members seem to be suffering from a bit of collective amnesia about this, too, in Rome. If ever we need an example of God's timeless patient persistence and inexhaustible tenacity when it comes to us, these passages should do it. For that, we can be grateful.

Heads-Up

Connecting the text to our world

This week's theme reminds me of Nigel, played by Christopher Guest in the movie *This Is Spinal Tap*, when he's trying to explain to his interviewer why his amplifier goes to eleven. He explains, of course, that this is because most amps only go to ten, so this modification makes his "one louder."

"Why don't you just make ten louder instead of just adding a number?" asks the filmmaker.

"Because this one goes to eleven," Nigel repeats, incredulous.

Poor Nigel. Fancies himself an intellectual and bristles at even the faintest whiff of a suggestion that he's stupid. But as the old saying goes, if you throw a rock into a pack of dogs, the one that yelps is the one you hit.

This isn't to say that we humans are all painfully stupid, though I guess that compared to God, it's not a stretch. Heck, there are even texts that say as much, come to think of it! But the point here is that we're what might be called "slow learners."

Time after time, God explains in no uncertain terms that we are to forgive all others as generously and foolishly as God forgives us. And while we seem to accept this at least in principle, when it comes to putting it into practice, our mantra ends up being, What was the middle thing?

It's also not unlike my kids' propensity to "forget" to take out the trash or clean their rooms. Never mind that they have not once failed to remember on Sunday afternoon that it's allowance time. Remarkable how contextually convenient our memories are, isn't it?

Don't worry, though. If you forget (hint: you will), God will remind you, even if you ask about the middle thing.

Prayer for the Week

God, what was the middle thing?

Popping Off

Art/music/video and other cool stuff that relate to the text

"This One Goes to Eleven" scene from *This Is Spinal Tap* (movie, 1984)

"People with No Kids Don't Know" sketch in *Michael McIntyre's Comedy Roadshow* (standup special, August 10, 2013)

The Unknown
Unknowns

Lectionary Texts For

September 20, 2020 (Holy Cross Sunday—Alternate Texts)

Texts in Brief

My dog ate my Bible!

First Reading

Numbers 21:4b–9

The Israelites get impatient and complain about Moses dragging them out to the desert instead of leaving them in Egypt. God sends snakes to bite and kill some of them, which scares them back into line. God tells Moses to put a sculpture of a snake on a pole, and any of the Israelites who were bitten can look at it and survive.

Psalm/Prophet

Psalm 78:1–2, 34–38

The psalmist suggests that the contrition the Israelites showed in Numbers was effectively only lip service.

And even though God knew this, God still afforded grace to them, sparing them from the venom of the serpent's bite.

SECOND READING
1 Corinthians 1:18–24

While skeptics think the gospel message is absurd, those who embrace it "get it." Trying to rationalize or intellectualize faith is amusing to God, because we're trying to use our human skillset to discern something that is so beyond the human mind that it's silly to even try. Even the smartest among us is no match for God, the sum of all experience, knowledge, wisdom, and being. Better just to trust than it is to try and approach Christian belief reductively.

GOSPEL
John 3:13–17

Jesus is compared to the bronze serpent Moses fixed onto his staff. In this case, God is the one who lifts Jesus up as an invitation to all. It's up to us to turn toward the invitation.

Bible, Decoded
Breaking down Scripture in plain language

Bronze—Usually when bronze is employed in a story involving God in Scripture, it represents God's judgment. In the Numbers story, God first judges that dire consequences are necessary in response to anemic, arbitrary faith. But just as quickly, that same judgment bends toward mercy and protection.

Stumbling Block—There are four different versions of this term in Hebrew and two in Greek. In some cases, it's in reference to a rock or the like that gets in the way and causes us to trip. In the New Testament, though, sometimes it specifically refers to the trigger on a set trap, which is far more consciously insidious. So stumbling blocks both occur incidentally and are sometimes set with the express purpose of trapping someone.

Points to Ponder

First Thoughts

There's plenty to be confused about in the Numbers text. First, the Israelites complain they have no food, and right after that, they complain the food sucks. Given the fact that this is early in their trip (get ready, guys—this is a long one), they're probably working their way through the stores they brought with them. Either way, it demonstrates a lack of gratitude, a lack of faith, or some of both.

Then God sends this plague of poisonous snakes, only to turn around and offer the antidote. Instead of focusing on the theological implications of what this says about God, though, we should consider this metaphorically. The death is that of the bond between God and the people; by their own doing, that have effectively cut their spiritual lifeline.

Despite the reasonableness of the consequence (remember that faith and grace aren't always exactly reasonable), God extends the opportunity for reconciliation and redemption. It's not forced on the people, but it is certainly placed plainly before them to accept or reject.

The serpent and the cross, then, are practically interchangeable here. While some view the crucifixion as a necessary penance that God commanded, we (humanity) are the ones responsible for it. While it's meant as a rebuttal against Jesus's message, the ones we're actually punishing are ourselves. Leave it to God, then, to take the worst we can do to ourselves and turn it into the tool of our redemption.

Digging Deeper
Mining for what really matters . . . and gold

In the cycle of the church year, this Sunday is known as "Holy Cross Sunday" because it's a week when we are to pay particular attention to the divine mystery of what the cross represents. There's no better place to begin than with the original Greek from the first verse of the 1 Corinthians passage.

In some translations, the first phrase is *the word of the cross* while in others *word* is replaced with *message*. But even the original words themselves are enough to spark some argument about what the author really meant, depending on who was listening. And suffice it to say that, when it comes to the cross, not much has changed in that regard.

Specifically, in Paul's case, his use of the word *logos* is curious. In the Jewish culture, this was the word used to describe the written law, including both Moses's Ten Commandments and the more than six hundred laws that preceded them. But to Greeks, *logos* was a sort of universal truth or constant that held the cosmos together.

So is the symbolism of the cross an upending of the old law, establishing a new law, or a sort of cosmic truth that underlies everything that was, is, and will be? Good luck getting a straight answer about that!

That's our tendency though, parsing out meaning and significance, then sorting into neat, clean, discrete compartments where it will stay forever. Approaching this new reality, though, requires an entirely new frame of reference, says Paul. It defies categorization and refuses to be pinned to a handful of explicit religious doctrines (not for lack of trying on our part).

The cross is fundamentally scandalous because to try and understand it with a yes/no, either/or proposition is to fall short before we've even started. We're invited, instead, to set all of our assumptions, expectations, and body of prior knowledge aside and approach the cross with an open-ended willingness to be transformed by the experience.

If this week was called "Logical Cross Sunday," our traditional methods for making sense of things would be a great idea. Holiness, however, inherently embraces mystery. It's an opportunity, not a problem.

Heads-Up

Connecting the text to our world

While serving as part of the George W. Bush administration, Donald Rumsfeld made a statement in a Department of Defense briefing that drew no small amount of ridicule. But although his syntax was a little bit clumsy and his strategy was fundamentally being evasive, the sentiment of the words themselves actually was spot-on.

The question put to him was something like how he could know for sure that the Iraqi government was not stockpiling weapons of mass destruction.

"There are known knowns," said Rumsfeld, "there are things we know we know. We also know there are known unknowns; that is to say we know there are some things we do not know. But there are also unknown unknowns—the ones we don't know we don't know."

Put another way: we know what we know, and we are even aware of some of the stuff we don't know. But there's an entirely new level of ignorance when it comes to everything we not only don't know but didn't even know existed. We grow our body of collective human knowledge every hour of every day, and we can all benefit from that. On occasion, something like dark matter or the existence of some previously unknown species will pop up, which takes a big "ignorance stick" and muddies up all the waters we thought were just starting to clear for us.

We'll never completely think our way into a sense of peace and universal certainty. This isn't to say that we shouldn't continue to stretch our minds, experiences, and imaginations; it means that we should understand that no matter how many of us there are and how long we have, mystery will still be our silent partners.

Instead of fighting against mystery, paradox, and unanswerable questions, says Paul, why not surrender to their inevitability and even rejoice in the tension between the known and the unresolved? Ignorance, then, isn't so much a problem in itself as it is an inevitable dimension of being human.

My son, Mattias, figured he was done with music once he learned the twelve notes of our scale and could play them on his instrument. What more, after all, could there be? If he had drawn a circle around this concept called music and proscribed everything outside of it to be categorically not-music, then he'd be right. But that would be foolish, right?

The entirety of creation vibrates with music; he just grasped a few of the most basic tools that will help him unlock a door into universes he'll never reach the end of. That's what makes it beautiful.

Prayer for the Week

Help me recognize the music of creation as not just something to be understood and mastered but also as something to be appreciated and trusted.

Popping Off

Art/music/video and other cool stuff that relate to the text

"Turn Your Eyes upon Jesus," performed by Lauren Daigle (song, 2018)

The Universal Christ: How a Forgotten Reality Can Change Everything We See, Hope For, and Believe, by Richard Rohr (book, 2019)

What Were You Thinking?

Lectionary Texts For

September 27, 2020 (Seventeenth Sunday after Pentecost)

Texts in Brief

My dog ate my Bible!

First Reading

Exodus 17:1–7

Thirsty and exhausted, the Israelites criticize Moses for bringing them out into the desert without sustenance. Moses asks God what to do, and God directs him to a stone at Mount Horeb and tells him to hit it with the staff he used to part the sea. Water comes from it and the Israelites drink, but Moses names the place after their lack of confidence that God would take care of them.

Psalm/Prophet

Ezekiel 18:1–4, 25–32

Ezekiel shares a message from God, warning us about complaining that God's ways are unfair. If anything, says God, it's humanity that isn't dealing fairly in their relationship with God. Our suffering is brought upon us by our own transgressions, though God doesn't want to see us hurt, die, or struggle. We're invited, once again, to turn around from our current course and turn back toward God and God's desires for us.

Second Reading

Philippians 2:1–13

Our focus should be less on ourselves and our own welfare, and more on the well-being of our sisters and brothers. Jesus is the best example of this. If anyone had something to fear when it came to personal comfort and safety, it was him. But rather than focus on that, Jesus emptied himself out for everyone else's good around him, not giving with regard of what was in it for him. Likewise, we should be open, allowing God to use us as instruments for the greater God. By doing so, we find all we need and more.

Gospel

Matthew 21:23–32

Religious leaders try to set a trap for Jesus by asking him where he gets his authority, because if he says "from God," they can have him arrested for blasphemy. If he says his authority is from earthly sources, then it's like he is renouncing his place as Messiah. Instead, Jesus turns the question back on them, asking them as much about John the Baptist. When they realize they can't answer without fallout, he points out that he won't answer them for similar reasons. Through a parable, he compares them to someone who is honorable in their words but whose intent is empty.

Bible, Decoded
Breaking down Scripture in plain language

Wilderness of Sin—While it might seem poetically fitting that Exodus refers to God's people wandering in the "wilderness of Sin," that's actually a proper name for the area near Horeb where they were. *Sin* was the name of a pagan moon goddess commonly worshipped in the region, not to be confused with what we usually think of when we hear *sin* with a small *s.*

Massah and Meribah—Massah means *testing* more broadly, but here it is referring to the Israelites' testing of God to provide for them. Meribah means *struggle, quarrel,* or *conflict.* This is in reference to them fighting with Moses about taking them into the wild.

Points to Ponder
First Thoughts

Although both Massah and Meribah are mentioned elsewhere in the Bible, this is the only place where they are mentioned together. But anytime something takes place at one of these locations later in Scripture, we can assume that there is some sort of testing or conflict going on, or both.

Because the phrase in Ezekiel "The parents have eaten sour grapes, and the children's teeth are set on edge" is called a parable, we can assume this is a saying that was used colloquially pretty often. In fact, it pops up elsewhere throughout the Hebrew Bible. Basically it was an expression that was used to shirk responsibility for something that had happened. It's sort of like saying "Wasn't me," or even "Gah, kids these days!"

Oh, and as good as Jesus is at taking the religious scholars to task by using their own rhetorical traps against them, can you imagine how amazing he would have been in a rap battle?

Digging Deeper
Mining for what really matters . . . and gold

There are a lot of different reasons why we ask questions. Of course, most of the time (at least hopefully) it's because there's something we need to know that we're hoping to learn about, but that's not always the case.

In the case of the religious scholars in Matthew, they obviously have an agenda, and Jesus knows it. While they might try to sound sincere when they ask him about the source of his authority, they are actually looking for an excuse either to discredit him or have him arrested. They know they can't just beat the crap out of him or haul him away for no reason without causing a revolt.

In some cases, we ask questions in search of a loophole, like asking Jesus how much of our possessions we're supposed to give away or how many times we're supposed to forgive someone. If we're being honest with ourselves, we know the answer before we even ask it, but there's part of us that's hoping for a bare minimum that we can hang on to and still be okay.

Sometimes we ask questions to settle a fight, like who will have greater honor in the kingdom of heaven. We wouldn't ask such a question if we didn't already have in mind what the answer should be, and all we really want is confirmation.

Finally, there's the kind of question asked of Moses by the Israelites about why he led them out to this apparently godforsaken place. Of course they know why: to escape slavery. But the question is really just a veiled criticism of Moses's leadership and, indirectly, of God for telling Moses to take them there.

The times when Jesus most often answers a question correctly is when he recognizes that the spirit behind the words is earnest. This vulnerable openness is what Jesus is interested in, far more than the words that are said. He states as much in the parable he tells back to the crowd here. Talk is cheap, he says, without walking the walk to back it up. In fact, given a choice between someone who is oppositional to God in word or some other superficial way, but who is truly trying to pursue God's intent in their lives, Jesus will take this over a hypocrite any day.

Much of the time when Jesus asks a question, it is to reveal the true nature of someone's heart. It's not that he isn't already clear about our motives before asking the question, but it's a disarming, nonviolent way to expose truth, just in case our skills of self-deception are so adept that we believe our own disingenuousness. It's like the ultimate in verbal jujitsu!

Heads-Up

Connecting the text to our world

It took me a long time to understand as a parent that kids will say one thing and do another. Actually if I'm being honest, I'm still working on it. I'm a pretty literal thinker sometimes, especially when it comes to what people say. When I was young, the neighbor once told me that he would take me out for a ride on his Harley "someday." I asked my parents daily for what seemed like months when this magical motorcycle ride would happen. It never occurred to me that he was saying something to be nice or with the best of intentions, yet not backed up with any real follow-through.

It was beyond my comprehension, too, how when I would tell my kids to go get dressed, they would say "okay," yet when I came back later, they were still sitting there in their pajamas, blankly staring at me like a zombie.

"Do you remember what I asked you to do?" I'd say.

"Yes."

"Then why are you still sitting here?"

"I don't know," they'd shrug, at which point I'd feel my blood pressure start to rise.

It cuts the other way too sometimes, I've noticed. I'll tell them it's time to go, only to be met with howls of protest and some version of "over my dead body" being yelled at a fevered pitch. *This could be arranged*, I'd think to myself, biting nearly through my own lip in self-restraint.

What I learned over the years, though, is if I let them vent and protest without engaging them in conflict, they eventually calm down and, nine times out of ten, just go do what I asked them to do in the first place. And really, if I had to choose between a kid who argued but did what I asked, I'll take that over a kid who says they will and then sits there like a cadaver (again, could be arranged). I'd prefer that they just complied in both word and action the first time, but I'm also smart enough not to push my luck.

Prayer for the Week

I'm trying to make sure my words and promises aren't empty. Hold me to it.

Popping Off

Art/music/video and other cool stuff that relate to the text

Horton Hears a Who, by Dr. Seuss (book, 1954)

"Opposite Day," from *SpongeBob SquarePants*, season 1, episode 19 (TV series, 1999–)

You Really Love Me!

Lectionary Texts For

October 4, 2020 (Eighteenth Sunday after Pentecost)

Texts in Brief

My dog ate my Bible!

First Reading

Exodus 20:1–4, 7–9, 12–20

God gives the Ten Commandments to Moses to share with his people as their new digested version of the law. The Israelites witness a dramatic stirring around the event, which scares them. Moses tells them that they're not in danger; it's God making sure they get that this is important and needs to be followed.

Psalm/Prophet

Isaiah 5:1–7

God laments that despite having done all that could be done to provide generously for the Israelites, they still stand in defiance, straying from God. For this reason, God resolves, it's time to stop protecting them from all of the threats around them, as it seems they will have to learn to depend on God's protection and provision the hard way.

Second Reading
Philippians 3:4b–14

If anyone could trust in their social status to be their salvation, Paul says, it would have been him. He was raised from birth in the Jewish tradition, and he had even become a respected religious leader among his people. But now he sees these assets as having gotten in the way of his relationship with God as he was meant to be. And while he hasn't arrived entirely where God is calling him, he is eager to keep in pursuit of that call.

Gospel
Matthew 21:33–46

Jesus tells a story of people allowed to occupy land and use resources that aren't theirs; the longer they stay, the more they feel entitled to the land and resources. It gets to the point that when the landowner sends people to gather his crops, the occupiers kill them in order to keep the harvest for themselves. Jesus explains that no one is entitled to what is God's, but that it is up to God to afford grace as God will. To act out of such an entitlement is to second-guess God. Likewise, we alienate ourselves from God's party by taking advantage and not extending as much grace and hospitality to others.

Bible, Decoded

Breaking down Scripture in plain language

Vineyard—Wine was more than just a recreational drink for the people in biblical times, especially in the Middle East. With drinkable water in short supply, juice was purified in the fermentation process, allowing it to be drunk safely. This made it a staple at pretty much any table. So vineyards were everywhere, unlike today when wine magically comes from some valleys somewhere else. Drawing comparisons to vineyards would be like making comparisons to trees or someone's backyard today. Even the poorest among them would know exactly what he was talking about.

Covet—Another word for wanting something that isn't yours.

Bearing False Witness—A fancy way to say "lying."

Points to Ponder

First Thoughts

I can almost hear God saying throughout these passages what my third-grade teacher used to say:

> You're perfectly special, just like everybody else.

In Exodus, the Israelites are trying to figure out who they are apart from Egypt and the captivity they endured there for so long. In Isaiah, the idea of being beloved and chosen by God seems to ring hollow when things get hard. Paul urges his fellow Hebrews in Philippians not to mistake their legacy as God's people to mean that they are loved and no one else is worthy. And finally, Jesus offers a grave warning for those who rest too easily on our identities as Christians, Israelites, or anyone that feels like who they are has entitled them to anything from God.

Our call is to act as stewards of grace for all others, without exception. God offers as much to us and expects no less from us.

Digging Deeper

Mining for what really matters . . . and gold

When we talk about the Ten Commandments (the fancy Bible-nerd term for them is the *decalogue*), we usually consider what they mean. If we go a little deeper, we'll explore how they were imparted to Moses. But why here? Why now?

The Israelites have 613 laws already on the books, so why add ten more? Or are they a digested version of the prior ones, since they're on the move? Maybe the 613 laws were bulky and heavy, and God felt like this was more efficient.

We have to consider that the Israelites have just come out of captivity, where they were living under another culture's norms and rules. Their lives were pretty structured, if not by their own laws, then by the tasks and restrictions put on them by their captors. For the first time in many years, they're having to learn how to live together as free people.

Given the complaints of some who want to go back to Egypt, it's reasonable to believe there's some collective Stockholm syndrome at play here. It's not unlike retired military personnel who remark on how much they miss having someone tell them where to be when, and what to do. Such open-endedness can be more than a little bit disorienting.

The prior laws were very detailed and explicit, from what parts of meat could be eaten to when certain things were allowed. They were often about maintaining order, keeping people safe, and living with a degree of civility. They were also very clear about the consequences when these laws were violated. When it comes to the decalogue, however, there's no if/then dynamic at all.

They just say what to do, leaving off the "or else."

More important than the explicit guidelines for what to do, the new laws are a framework for how to be. They are intentionally broader, offering some sense of boundaries for identity and propriety, but what they actually mean could also be debated. For an example of this, we don't have to look any further than Exodus 20:13, which some interpret as "don't kill," while others specify that it's only in reference to an act of murder.

It's an evolution of sorts in the relationship between God and the Israelites. They're given a guide, but they're also entrusted to use their own judgment. It offers some communal connective tissue, while not proscribing each act and thought to the letter. It is, in a sense, its own invitation of liberation from strict legalism and cultural confinement.

Seeing laws as liberating can feel counterintuitive, but sometimes we venture further when we have something that permits us to stretch against it.

Heads-Up
Connecting the text to our world

When I was in grade school, I was a little bit of a control freak, especially when it came to relationships. To say I was an over-enthusiastic friend sometimes would be putting a kinder spin on it that it deserved. Another way to say it is that I was pretty suffocating.

It was beyond me to get that sometimes my best friend just didn't want to hang out. He might have had someone else over, or being the introvert that he was, sometimes he just wanted to be alone. All of that seemed so foreign to me that the only way I could process our differences was to take them personally.

He must be mad at me, I'd worry. Why is he ignoring me? So to assuage my anxiety, I'd push a little bit more for him to play, if for no other reason than to help validate in that much-needed moment that I was "friend material." The problem was that, the harder I pushed, the more he backed away. And the more he backed away, the more I worried. The more I worried, the harder I pushed . . .

You can see where this led, which is nowhere good.

While my insistence on being somehow deserving of his time and attention on my terms could be seen as entitlement, underneath that was a deep well of insecurity and a lingering sense of inadequacy. The problem was that no amount of face time or affirmation from him or anyone else was going to make that change.

Ironically, too, the harder I pushed for what I thought I needed, the further away from it I got. I was trying to control something (the relationship) and someone (my friend) that were not mine to control. In order to be the kind of friend I hoped I could be, I had to let go of it and allow the relationship to be whatever it ended up being. That release was one of the harder lessons in growing up that I had to get my head and heart around.

None of it is ours, and we don't deserve any of it, says God. And yet we are thoroughly blessed and completely loved beyond measure. Such a discipline of release is one of the tougher ones for us adults to internalize too.

Prayer for the Week

I have to remember that none of this is actually mine, and that I'm not entitled to anything in particular from you, God. No more and no less than everyone else.

Popping Off

Art/music/video and other cool stuff that relate to the text

"Four Yorkshiremen" sketch from *At Last the 1948 Show* (DVD, 1967)

Rainbow Fish, by Marcus Pfister (book, 1992)

Join the Party

Lectionary Texts For

October 11, 2020 (Nineteenth Sunday after Pentecost)

Texts in Brief

My dog ate my Bible!

First Reading

Exodus 32:1–14

While Moses is on Mount Sinai, the Israelites convince Aaron to melt their gold down into a new idol. God seethes at this and resolves to destroy them, but Moses urges restraint. He reminds God of promises made to Abraham's descendants, which ensure them they will multiply and inherit God's legacy on earth. God changes course, agreeing to show mercy instead.

Psalm/Prophet

Isaiah 25:1–9

The prophet offers praise to God, who has laid waste to a city full of people unfaithful to God and who were a threat to God's people. The prophet cries out that God is protector, provider, and source of all that transcends death.

Second Reading
Philippians 4:1–9
The letter to the church in Philippi notes that those who replace all worry for their futures and well-beings with dependence on God for everything will find the peace they are seeking. It ends with a list of virtues that should continue to guide their daily decisions, keeping them in proper relationship with God.

Gospel
Matthew 22:1–14
Jesus compares God's kingdom to a luxurious banquet thrown by a king where the VIPs don't show up. They either laugh it off as not worth their time or kill the king's messengers out of disdain. The king is furious, so he sends troops to slaughter the VIPs and burn their city down. Then he invites people from the street until the hall is full. When the king shows up at the party, he asks one guest why he isn't dressed properly. The man has nothing to say, so the king casts him into exile.

Bible, Decoded
Breaking down Scripture in plain language

Golden Calf—The golden calf is symbolic of the moon goddess, Sin, who we have seen the Israelites get lured by before.

Euodia/Syntyche—Two women who were members of the early church in Philippi. While we don't know what the fight was about, we can tell from Paul's words that they were in an argument about something. Ultimately, it doesn't matter what the conflict was about as much as the fact that it stood to threaten the cohesion of the new community. This was a frequent issue that Paul had to deal with, reminding each community in turn to stay focused on the big picture and the ways in which they had to treat each other if this "new thing" had any chance of surviving.

Points to Ponder

First Thoughts

While the Exodus text is yet another example of people not getting what they seem to rightly deserve, it's notable that this is one of a few cases when God has to be convinced to defer to mercy instead of destruction. We see something similar when Abraham pleads with God to make a deal with him on behalf of Sodom, though in that case, the conditions for salvation Abraham sets up as part of the deal aren't met, so the whole city is destroyed. In this Isaiah text, God destroys enemies of the Israelites out of compassion for them, as well as the price for blasphemy in the neighboring culture.

In the garden of Eden, though, there is no one to advocate for Adam and Eve, and yet God relents and saves them from their intended consequence. On the whole, these may tell us far more about ourselves, our relationship to God, and our own efforts to try to understand our environment than they do about the true nature of God.

Regardless, there is one prevailing theme that we can take away from each of these stories: God's mercy and forgiveness far exceed our capacity for obedience and faithfulness.

Digging Deeper
Mining for what really matters . . . and gold

There's a lot of historical context and rich symbolism in this Matthew parable that we have to understand if we're to make much sense of it. Otherwise, has anyone ever heard of such incredible violence surrounding a wedding before (other than the "Red Wedding" scene in *Game of Thrones*)? Invitees kill slaves, so the king burns a city down and engages in genocide. And as if that wasn't bad enough, he also exiles a poor guy for not being dressed correctly for the wedding, never mind that he was just walking down the street and got invited on the spot!

If this is really what the kingdom of God is, it's hard to get excited about being a part of that. Let's look at the symbolism, though, to try and un-muddy the waters.

The bride in this story is, collectively, the Israelites. This means that the groom is God, and the martial bond is the holy covenant that binds them together. What's a little bit confusing is that those invited to the wedding also are the Israelites, but there's a distinction between the individuals (the invited guests) and the bride (Israel as an entire people). So at this point, we see a repudiation of the invitation by God into this covenant, even though they are bound to God by their heritage.

The murder of the king's slaves refers to the rejection and killing of some of God's prophets, who brought the invitation to the people of Israel, many of whom rejected it. The subsequent destruction of the town refers to the destruction of Jerusalem. The weird part about this is that Jerusalem wasn't destroyed until 70 CE, which was a few decades after Jesus was killed. The Gospel of Matthew, though, wasn't written until ten or twenty years after Jerusalem was destroyed. This means that either Jesus was foretelling this coming destruction or the author of Matthew decided to insert this into Jesus's teaching after the city's ruin to help explain why it happened.

Next, we have the king (God) inviting everyone to the party, which seems like great news. The doors are flung wide open, and all are welcome. Except there's this one poor guy who is missing his wedding robe, for which he suffers for the rest of his life.

Talk about a wardrobe malfunction.

If this was a literal story, it would seem pretty absurd, but as it all represents some greater meaning, we have to dig further to understand. Back in these times, no one was supposed to come into the presence of a king or pharaoh without being properly dressed. To come without the right clothes was a grave insult to the kingdom itself, let alone to the king. We should also note that the ruler's responsibility was to provide these clothes for his guests. It wasn't like all of these new guests had to run down to the rental place and grab last-minute tuxedos. They would have been handed these robes when they entered the party.

For the one guest to be improperly dressed meant that he was not only insulting the king and those he represented but also was rejecting the gift offered by the king. In the parable, then, the wedding garment is the gift of Jesus and the divine grace and forgiveness God offered through him. It was available to everyone who came, but they had to accept it in order to join the party.

Some mistakenly take the final line, "Many are called, but few are chosen" to mean that God gathers us all together, then we draw straws to see who the lucky ones are. Everyone else is just screwed. That's not what the story tells us, though. God provides all who look for it with what they need to take part; whether we are chosen falls on us and our willingness to accept something, even if we think it's more than we can accept.

Heads-Up

Connecting the text to our world

My wife, Amy, was a preacher's kid before she was a preacher. In fact, she comes from a very long line of preachers, which means she has home visitations and potlucks running through her bloodstream. Like most kids, she also hated when her dad would drag her along after school on one of these visits with a church member.

That day, her dad said, they were going to see Betty, who had lived alone for years after her husband had died. She occupied much of her time by painting ceramics, he explained, which is why there would be pieces lining pretty much every wall of every room in the house. Amy rolled her eyes at the thought of the same stories she would hear her dad tell, just like at the last home visit, and the ancient, rock-hard gumdrops the lady would inevitably offer her.

"This is dumb," she said, her eyebrows knitting into a scowl. "Why do I have to go?" She went on to explain that she'd much rather be home playing with her friends.

"Because we were invited," said her dad, "and we're going to be gracious guests."

The house was as laden with ceramics as her dad had described, but they were much nicer than Amy had expected. This wasn't the errant scribbling of someone who was just passing time; she was really good. Amy sighed and sank into a chair in the corner, eyeing the work on the wall in front of her while her dad told the same old stories she'd heard a hundred times.

"Come on over, dear," said Betty, snapping Amy out of her semi-stupor, "I want to show you something." Amy looked at her dad, who nodded, so she followed. Betty took her to a back room that had been closed off, behind which she had her most elaborate, delicate pieces of work.

"Wow," Amy whispered, "they really are beautiful!" Betty smiled and walked her around the room as she looked each piece over.

"I want you to take one," said Betty. "Really," she nodded, noting Amy's hesitation, "anything you want." A few minutes later they came back to the living room to join her dad. Amy was empty-handed and looked embarrassed. Betty smiled and they said their good-byes, parting ways.

"What happened in there?" her dad asked. She looked into her empty lap.

"She told me to take one of her things," she said quietly, "but I felt bad because I didn't want to go in the first place. So I said no." Her dad sighed, shaking his head.

"If someone gives you a gift because they want to," he said "you take it because it's what they want. It's rude to turn it down, whether you think you deserved it or not." The ride home was quiet, but Amy has shared more than once about how that was the most important gift she never accepted.

Prayer for the Week

I don't know who should or shouldn't get what, God, including myself. I guess it's better if I leave that up to you.

Popping Off

Art/music/video and other cool stuff that relate to the text

About a Boy (movie, 2002)

The Unworthy Thor, by Jason Aaron (book, 2017)

My Looker
Is Broken

Lectionary Texts For
October 18, 2020 (Twentieth Sunday after Pentecost)

Texts in Brief
My dog ate my Bible!

First Reading
Exodus 33:12–23

Moses asks God for clarity about God's intentions, to which God says that Moses and the Israelites will find their destination and that God will be with them along the way. Moses asks not to even bother proceeding if this isn't the case. Moses wants to connect with God more personally, and though God assures him they will be well tended to, Moses can't see God's face without dying. God does propose allowing Moses to see God from behind instead.

PSALM/PROPHET
Isaiah 45:1–7
God claims through Isaiah to make the Israelites' way forward easier and to provide abundantly for them so they will know God does in fact care for them. There is a sense of longing for God's people to recognize God's presence in all things, all around them, yet there is a lack of recognition of this presence both within and around them.

SECOND READING
1 Thessalonians 1:1–10
In a letter to the church in Thessalonica, Paul and his fellow leaders tell the congregants that they pray daily for their church, and that they see the results of their spiritual gifts in the work the church is doing. They celebrate the church's persistence in the work of the gospel, despite the threats to them for doing so, assuring them that this persistence stands as an example to others. Word is spreading of their faith and community, and of their conversion; for this, Paul and his fellow leaders are grateful.

GOSPEL
Matthew 22:15–22
In a scheme to get Jesus to break the law, the church officials send spies into his circle to ask him whether he believes his followers should pay their taxes. He responds by asking them whose face is on the coins, to which they say that Caesar's face is on them. He says to give the government what is theirs (they made the money, after all), and to give to God all that God has made.

Bible, Decoded
Breaking down Scripture in plain language

Cyrus—Cyrus was the ruler of the Babylonians when they ended their occupation of the Israelites and of Jerusalem. The story goes that God told him to release the Israelites from captivity and to rebuild the temple in Jerusalem that had been destroyed during conflict. He did this and invited all Israelites to return to their land and live in peace.

Paul, Silvanus, and Timothy—While we know Paul and Timothy are early apostles of Jesus who helped establish the early church community, Silvanus is a pretty new name. But actually Silvanus is just another iteration of the name Silas, who also was an early apostle and church planter.

Points to Ponder
First Thoughts

That Moses's relationship with God is more than a little bit complicated and occasionally volatile is actually comforting to me. In some ways, it gives me permission not to feel entirely solid in my own faith and in whether I feel connected to the Divine. His faithfulness isn't expressed so much in a pearly white, permanent smile, no bad hair days, or a constant aura of happiness. His faith is measured in his tireless commitment to follow through on what he's called to by God. It doesn't mean it will be easy or that there won't be stumbles along the way; it just means he keeps going.

I can also relate to those days when we wake up and God seems to be nowhere to be found. It's an empty, vacuous sense of almost spiritual vertigo, like a boat unmoored from the harbor. Then other days, we wake up in the very same places, do and see the same things, and encounter the same people we did before, and yet something is different.

It's taken me years to come to terms with the idea that God was there the whole time; as my Nana would have said, it's my looker that's broken.

Digging Deeper
Mining for what really matters . . . and gold

There's an interesting tension throughout these texts between humanity longing for more evidence of God's presence, while God laments their fundamental lack of ability to see God in everything and everyone around them. And yet, in the first two cases, God relents and offers some evidence of God's presence among them anyway. The fact, though, that this happens more than once points to why God might hesitate in the first place to offer such evidence, since the attention and fidelity of people tends to be fleeting and fickle.

Even Moses asks for something more from God, maybe to help strengthen his own resolve or to have something to share with his people to help convince them that he is appointed by God for his role. And while the idea that God will let Moses see only the backside of God is a little bit of a weird visual, there's something important to this, which we'll consider in a minute.

In Thessalonians, there's a shift toward recognizing God in the spiritual gifts being used by the early Christians in Thessalonica. There's also a shift in how people around them perceive it, because when they explain to witnesses how they're able to do such miraculous things, people believe them and long to do likewise.

In the Gospel, Jesus already sees all of creation with God's eyes, which is why the Pharisees' efforts to trip him up fail, once again. What they fail to recognize is that each of their strategies to catch him in breaking the law are based on binary either/or premises, which Jesus sees through. In fact, he sees with a vision that transcends binary thinking all together, given that all is from and of God.

It's a micro-versus-macro perspective, and in a strategic sense, the longer, broader perspective inevitably wins out.

Back to the story about Moses wanting to see the face of God, we have to think about what the big deal is here. Is God insecure, or maybe going through puberty? Is hiding God's face necessary to continue to reinforce this idea of a transcendent, almighty creator who can't be approached? Or maybe it's something more like an episode of *American Idol*, where they're waiting for an opportune moment for the big reveal when Jesus becomes the so-called face of God among us.

But even when Jesus walks and talks like the rest of us and shares his wisdom in ways that are fairly simple and culturally relevant, we continue to fail to get it entirely. Sometimes the blindness is because we're more focused on the maintenance of the status quo because it suits us; in other cases, our fear can distort and cloud our vision. When it comes to Moses, though, these don't apply. The issue here isn't that God feels the need to withhold something from him either, but rather that Moses—as well as any other person—wouldn't be able to see the fullness of God, even if it were quite literally staring him in the face.

We're far better at embodying that fullness of the Divine than we are looking right at it. It's a strange phenomenon, but one that reinforces the idea that our relationship with God is more of an inside-out process instead of the other way around.

Heads-Up

Connecting the text to our world

Oliver Sacks was both a remarkable neurologist and a compelling writer, which made the books he wrote about neurological anomalies his patients experienced all the more fascinating. His book *Awakenings*, which tells of his efforts to use the compound L-DOPA to cure patients of their symptoms of Alzheimer's, was even made into a movie starring Robert De Niro and Robin Williams. But none of his stories captivated me quite like his short story "The Man Who Mistook His Wife for a Hat."

His patient had something called prosopagnosia, also known as face blindness, which made it nearly impossible to recognize faces. He could hone in on certain granular features on someone's face, like a mole or a crooked tooth, but he couldn't "see" their whole face. This is a hard concept for some people to absorb, since he would be looking right at them. His vision was perfectly functional too; the problem was that when his eyes scanned a person's face and sent the pieces that made up the face to his brain (something most of our brains just do without us even knowing it), his couldn't piece the puzzle back together.

It would be like someone had taken a five-hundred-piece puzzle and scattered the pieces across the floor, then asked you to identify what it was a picture of.

Because of this, he depended on unchangeable rituals in his daily schedule, as well as obvious visual cues from his friends and family so he would know who they were. If a room got rearranged or someone did as much as cut their hair or change the color of their lipstick, he might fall into a state of paralyzing disorientation.

It doesn't take much to put us in such a state spiritually sometimes either. If things don't go quite as expected, we can feel as if we're alone in the middle of a sea of chaos. The pieces are all still there; we just need some help putting them all back together.

Prayer for the Week

Sometimes I get so spiritually scattered that I can't make sense of much of anything, let alone my relationship with you, God. In those cases, help me put it back together.

Popping Off

Art/music/video and other cool stuff that relate to the text

The Man Who Mistook His Wife for a Hat and Other Clinical Tales, by Oliver Sacks (book, 1985)

The Man Who Mistook His Wife for a Hat (movie, 1987)

Holy Mic Drop

Lectionary Texts For

October 25, 2020 (Twenty-First Sunday after Pentecost)

Texts in Brief

My dog ate my Bible!

First Reading

Deuteronomy 34:1–12

God leads Moses to the top of Mount Nebo and shows him the territory that is to become the land in which the Israelites will establish their new nation. He tells Moses that though he can see the land, he isn't to enter it, so he stays in Moab until he dies and is buried in a secret place. He was the greatest among the Israelite prophets, and he had anointed Joshua to lead in his place after he was gone.

Psalm/Prophet

Leviticus 19:1–2

This is part of the original text from which Jesus's greatest commandment is derived. While the passage ends with the verse about loving one's neighbor as we love ourselves, the preceding verses all are fruits of this worldview and discipline: refrain from judgment, gossip, and putting others over personal gain and set aside all vengeance for wrongs done to us.

Second Reading

1 Thessalonians 2:1–8

The apostles are glad they persisted beyond the hostile reception they encountered in Philippi and went on to Thessalonica. As a sort of advance warning for when conflict inevitably comes, they note to the church in Thessalonica that their business is not about making everyone happy but rather to follow through in their calling. They recognize they ask a lot of the church there but assure them at the same time that they are so deeply loved that the apostles would give everything to support them.

Gospel

Matthew 22:34–46

The Pharisees test Jesus again, asking him to place a commandment above all others (which would be considered blasphemous). He responds that the two commandments about loving God, self, and others with all we have are equally paramount. He then asks them a question about who they believe the Messiah is that they can't answer. After that, they leave him alone.

Bible, Decoded
Breaking down Scripture in plain language

Mount Nebo—While there is a Mount Nebo today, some scholars dispute whether this is the same mountain described in Scripture. And although Christians tend to believe Moses was buried there, Muslims generally believe he was buried nearby in the wilderness. Nebo appears in the deuterocanonical text (Scripture considered to be holy but not canonized as part of the Bible) called Maccabees, which tells of Jeremiah hiding the ark of the covenant there to keep it from getting stolen by foreign insurgents.

Pisgah—Some linguists believe that this is just another name for Mount Nebo, but others suggest that it is just a name for the summit of the mountain. Regardless, it is often referred to as Mount Pisgah.

Points to Ponder
First Thoughts

When I visited Jordan, I went up to the top of Mount Nebo, which was a powerful experience. On the one hand, the history of that place with respect to my own faith background goes as far back as the land of Canaan. On the other, the political and religious tensions all around it were also palpable. From that point in Jordan, we could see much of the West Bank, Lebanon, and north into Syria. On clear days, you can see from there to Iraq, Egypt, and Saudi Arabia.

Knowing the amount of blood that has been spilled in that place filled me with a deep, lingering sadness. Just downhill to the north are the Golan Heights, which became a much-contested battleground, particularly when Israel claimed annexation rights over the land.

The spirit was heavy and somewhat ominous there, as if God's own tears had washed the blood from the soil. The only words I could muster in my own mind in that moment were *God, forgive us.*

Digging Deeper

Mining for what really matters . . . and gold

What we see in this week's Gospel is the verbal climax of a religion at war with itself.

On one side, we see a disruptive force, seeking to subvert the power structure of the status quo; on the other, we have one of the final efforts to crush that uprising before it grows beyond their control. And while we hear many sermons and lessons about the greatest commandment, sometimes we overlook the political implications of such an encounter.

It is a little bit surprising that Jesus answers the lawyer's question in the first place, as he is keenly aware of the unsavory agenda behind it. He knows that this man, who tries to flatter him with admiration, is a tool of the religious order against which he stands as a direct threat. But sometimes, the situation calls for us to take a stand and stake a claim.

Yes, Jesus knows he risks being arrested for holding any commandment above another, but he does it in a typically strategic way. In the very thing he does that some would claim was against Jewish law, he makes a claim that undercuts the very premise of its illegality. By placing the law of universal love above all others, and by asserting that all other laws and commands fall under the context of this tent, then making a claim emphasizing this law above others would not defy the prevailing principle of love in all things.

I know it's a bit of a mind-bender, but it's strategically brilliant while also demonstrating remarkable courage.

We should also note that in the preceding verses in Matthew, Jesus has driven moneychangers out of the temple, as well as calling out his fellow Jewish scholars for their lack of true understanding of the texts they studied so intently. Suffice it to say, then, that he's going full-tilt into no-more-mister-nice-Jesus mode. And as if he hasn't stirred things up enough, he actually goes on the attack, calling the Pharisees out in front of their own people.

In essence, he throws down the gauntlet by saying that they wouldn't recognize the Messiah if he was standing right in front of them. Oh, the beautiful irony of the scene! They're stumped because they can't tell him how they would know him for sure, especially since they haven't been convinced by his fulfillment of many of the prophetic identifiers laid out in their texts.

They came to discredit him, and they end up walking away with their tails between their legs. By now, they really have no options other than conceding he is who he says he is or ensuring that he and his ministry are eliminated before they grow roots and spread. What they don't realize, of course, is that the seeds have already been scattered and sown, and roots have already begun to form. By now they are already too late, and Jesus knows it.

From this, a revolution founded in radical love will be born.

Heads-Up

Connecting the text to our world

I grew up hearing every Sunday morning in our Baptist church services that I had better get myself right with God, because Jesus could very well come back that week. God forbid I might be caught face to face with Jesus with a sin that hadn't been addressed or less-than-sterling underwear. It was intense enough that I would wake up many mornings and wonder if I really needed to do my homework that day, especially if that was the day Jesus would return.

Heck, even if he came a week from now, it's not like my permanent record would keep me from going to college. Who needs college when I'm being raptured!?

Day after day it didn't happen, and after a while I got a little bit suspicious of these weekly warnings. I had heard the Chicken Little story, in case they were unaware; one's warnings of something world-changing will only be taken seriously for so long.

Then again, would I know Jesus if he walked right up to me? What if he didn't come surfing down from heaven on a wave of clouds, lightning bolts shooting from his fingertips? For that matter, if preachers didn't recognize him the first time, there was no guarantee they would the next time. Maybe my pastor had passed him on the way to church to preach another "Jesus is coming" sermon and didn't pay him a second glance.

Maybe he was a homeless man, an immigrant, a woman, or some other "unlikely" expression of God's kingdom he wasn't looking for or at least might refuse to recognize even if he saw it.

Or maybe Jesus is here; or maybe he never entirely left. Maybe I see him in my friends, my kids, my wife, the refugee on television, and even in the guy in riot gear hosing protesters back. Maybe he's looking right at me every time I look in the mirror.

I'm not saying I'm Jesus or that you are. I'm also not going so far as to suggest you're not. Seems like a safer bet to try and acknowledge the presence of Christ in everyone and everything—or at the very least the potential for it—and act as if we're face to face with him every day.

Prayer for the Week

God, help me recognize you in myself and everyone else, even when it seems hard to imagine.

Popping Off

Art/music/video and other cool stuff that relate to the text

"One of Us," by Joan Osborne (song, 1995)

Gethsemane, by Walter West (painting, 1954)

Empty It All Out

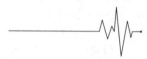

Lectionary Texts For

November 1, 2020 (Twenty-Second Sunday after Pentecost)

Texts in Brief

My dog ate my Bible!

First Reading

Joshua 3:7–17

God will make it clear to the Israelites that Joshua is now their new leader, as appointed by Moses and ordained by God. Joshua orders one man from each of the twelve tribes of Israel to carry the ark of the covenant into Canaan as a symbol that God has appointed this territory as their new home. When they reach the Jordan River, the water stops flowing until after they all cross. The men carrying the ark wait in the middle of the riverbed with the ark until everyone crosses over, and then follow them into Canaan.

Psalm/Prophet

Micah 3:5–12

Micah calls out other false prophets, warning that they will be humiliated and silenced by God. Micah, however, claims authority in speaking on God's behalf to call out hypocrites and unfaithful people of Israel on their misdeeds. Those who claim peace with their mouths but who resort to violence or injustice to fulfill their goals will find ruin when Jerusalem is laid to waste by God's wrath.

Second Reading

1 Thessalonians 2:9–13

The authors remind the church members in Thessalonica how Paul and his colleagues took them in and cared for them like they were family as they discipled with them. Paul celebrated, then, that he saw evidence of the fruits of that relationship and of them internalizing what the congregation was taught in all they did.

Gospel

Matthew 23:1–12

Jesus warns his followers to do as the church leaders say but not as they do. Just because they don't live according to their own teaching, he says, doesn't mean others have to do likewise. Then he criticizes their duplicity in expecting so much from those they teach, while doing little or nothing themselves. Although they love the adulation and titles that come with their positions, he says he is the one true example they need, just as they are to have only one God. It's more honorable to serve, he says, than to lead.

Bible, Decoded

Breaking down Scripture in plain language

Joshua—Though his birth name was Hosea, he became more commonly known as Joshua because it's what Moses called him. Born in Egypt before the exodus of the Israelites, Joshua served as an assistant to Moses until he was appointed by Moses before his death as Israel's new leader. He also played a fairly prominent role as a prophet and historical figure in Islam. The name Joshua is Hebrew for *God/Yahweh is salvation.*

Points to Ponder

First Thoughts

There's a lot this week on the difference between false and true prophets. In the earlier texts, the primary difference initially is dependent on who was anointed by God to hold such a role. Secondarily, those who preach one value system and live another are condemned as the reason God will bring judgment on the city of Jerusalem.

While Jesus does call similarly for the destruction of the temple (also foretelling his coming death), he doesn't do so in this text. He does, however, offer a solid basis for doing so, given that the soul of the religious teaching being offered is hollowed out by the disingenuousness and self-centeredness of those imparting it.

The most interesting difference here in Matthew is Jesus's distinction between the corruption of the messengers and the transcending value of the message. Just because a leader is corrupt, he says, doesn't mean value can't be gained from what they say and claim in word, if not in deed.

Digging Deeper

Mining for what really matters . . . and gold

It helps us understand Joshua's state of mind going into this scene if we've read the first two chapters of Joshua, and especially chapter 1. In that one section alone, God urges the fresh, new prophet to be strong and courageous. Now, I'm no psychologist, but if you're having to tell someone to be strong and courageous four times in a row like that, it probably means they're feeling neither strong nor courageous.

Who can blame him, really? He's gone through a lot with Moses and the Israelites to get here, and I'm sure he had assumed he would continue following in his mentor's footsteps right into the destination they had been waiting for these past four decades. All of a sudden, though, Moses drops dead and Joshua's in charge. No pressure!

I'm sure a million things were running through his mind. He was probably wishing he had paid better attention in that one freshman college class on leadership right about now, but God assures him he won't need that. All he needs (aside, obviously, from strength and courage) is to listen, wait, and serve God. If he learned anything from Moses's example, it's that he didn't feel adequately prepared either, and yet God worked through him and got them this far. Had Joshua wanted the role too much, or if he felt like he had it under control, that would have been his first, and gravest, mistake.

God doesn't call the already prepared; God calls the willing and faithful, equipping them with what they need, when they need it. The arrogance of the church leaders in Matthew emerge from their assumption that their appointment to the position entitles them to act as they wish and that because they know the law, they have it all sorted out. As Scripture says, though, the fools will be made wise (see: Joshua) and the wise will be made fools (see: Pharisees and scribes).

Sometimes the best preparation for God's work is more of an emptying out than it is a filling up.

Heads-Up

Connecting the text to our world

My son, Mattias, is a brilliant young musician. His tone on the saxophone is rich and warm, and he can hear anything once—from a pop song to a symphony—and replicate it from memory. He's been able to recognize and name any pitch or key he heard, from the revving of a car engine to the jingle on a commercial, since he was three years old.

Explaining to him that he's just scratching the surface is incredibly hard, though. How do you get through to someone with so much talent that knowledge and inherent skill are only pieces of a much larger puzzle when it comes to being a great artist?

One of his favorite styles of music is jazz, which works out well since it's also one of mine. I studied it in high school and college, and although I can't play a lick of it, I've come to recognize some common attributes in the players who rise to the level of music legends. So as he's gradually gotten older and more open, I've shared little bits along the way.

"So much of jazz," I said to him, "isn't about what you remember; it's about what you forget when you play."

"Huh" he looked at me like I was brain damaged.

"Yes," I went on, "knowing all of your scales, getting your technique down, learning to sight read, and practicing every day are important. But that's not all there is."

"Why not? Why am I learning all this stuff if it's not what I need?"

"Think of it like this," I said. "Your mind is a big container, and it will be shaped by the things you put in it. The more things like albums, practice, knowledge, and playing with other people you put in there, the more it shapes your container the way you want it."

"Okay," he nodded, "Then what?"

"Then, once you've filled it with all of these things for years and years," I said, "You turn the container over and pour it all out."

"Well that seems dumb," he scowled.

"I know," I smiled, "especially right now when you're still thinking about each note, each key change, tempo, and everything your hands are doing. But that's the thing; if you make yourself the right container, music isn't about thinking anymore. It becomes about opening up and letting it all flow through you. Then whatever you see, feel, hear, and experience can be shaped by that container of yours and expressed in music. You don't have to think about it anymore; it just flows."

"Hmm," he sighed, "maybe."

It's not something I figured he'd get the first time, or even the second. In fact there are technical masters who never transcend their basic skills because they can't let go to elevate to that place where they're more empty than full, acting more as a vessel than a source. But he heard me, and at least it's something else to add to his ever-growing, ever-changing container.

Prayer for the Week

God, help me always try to be a better vessel than a primary source.

Popping Off

Art/music/video and other cool stuff that relate to the text

Amadeus (movie, 1984)

Ray (movie, 2004)

Process
over Content

Lectionary Texts For

November 8, 2020 (Twenty-Third Sunday after Pentecost)

Texts in Brief

My dog ate my Bible!

First Reading

Joshua 24:1–3a, 14–25

Delegates from the Hebrew tribes meet in Shechem and are given a sort of ultimatum about who they will serve. They claim to serve the God of Israel, but their resolve is questioned. They reassert their fidelity, and Joshua declares on their behalf that they will now be accountable to each other to serve no other God from then on.

Psalm/Prophet

Amos 5:18–24

God is unsatisfied with the apparently empty rituals and offerings given by God's people. They are commanded to do away with such gestures and to be ready for God's justice to prevail over them.

Second Reading

1 Thessalonians 4:13–18

Words of consolation for mourners who grieve the loss of loved ones. They are not forever lost, but they are joined with Christ, as we will be either when we die or when Jesus returns.

Gospel

Matthew 25:1–13

The kingdom of God is compared to a wedding banquet where some who are invited aren't ready in time. They try to join late, but the doors are already closed. The lesson, Jesus says, is to always be prepared for God's coming, so that we are never caught by surprise.

Bible, Decoded

Breaking down Scripture in plain language

Shechem—Meaning *shoulder* in Hebrew, Shechem was located within the tribal territory of the Hebrew tribe of Manasseh. It was considered the first capital in Canaan for the newly established nation of Israel. Later, Jerusalem became the new capital.

Ordinances—While the Ten Commandments were given to Moses on Mount Sinai, the ordinances and statutes described in this Joshua passage were provided to the Israelites to help guide their self-governance while in the desert. Since Shechem represented their new geographic and spiritual home, all three were placed permanently here to stand as a reminder of the tribes' identity, laws, values, and history.

Points to Ponder

First Thoughts

This is a different side of God this week than we usually talk about. God rejects being worshipped, shuts people out of the kingdom for bad timing, and even is a little passive-aggressive when the Israelites promise to be faithful.

We're dealing with some history here, though, as we've seen over the last several weeks of making our way through the story of the exodus and wilderness period. The sort of worshipping that is being judged here is kind of like the way your kid comes over and gives you a big hug right before they ask you for something, or when they tell you how much they love you before they break it to you that they wrecked the car. This kind of flattery is insincere and self-serving, which is antithetical to the whole point of following God that culminates in the Gospels.

If we're coming to church to make sure we're paid up on fire insurance, we might as well not bother. If we only come to God in prayer when we want something, God prefers not to be treated like a celestial vending machine.

It's not that God is so insecure that we have to offer our constant reassurance as validation for God to be ok. Worship and prayer aren't so much self-interested quick fixes we do to get our needs met or to get out of trouble; they are spiritual disciplines of reorientation and focus, maintaining our perspective on what matters the most—our relationship with God.

Digging Deeper

Mining for what really matters . . . and gold

This is one of several passages quoting Jesus that are considered part of his eschatological sermons. Usually, when we hear the word *eschatology*, we immediately imagine the horsemen descending from the sky, dragons with multiple heads, and all of the fearsome (and honestly, weird) descriptions in Revelation about the end of the world. And while this isn't entirely wrong, it's not completely accurate either.

Eschatology includes any biblical texts dealing with the end of life, God's judgment and/or, the state of our souls after death. This is a big deal within the Jewish community, since the teaching offered by Jesus, Paul, and the other disciples and apostles departs pretty radically from traditional Jewish teaching. Traditionally, when a person of the Jewish faith dies, they stay dead until the second coming of the Messiah, at which time they'll be bodily resurrected to live again in the flesh.

In Paul's eschatological letter in Thessalonians, he focuses more on the immortality of the soul instead of the body. In fact, by his teaching, they are to believe that their deceased loved ones are already with God, and that this isn't something happening way off in the distant future. We will be rejoined with them, too, when we die.

In Matthew, we have one of several eschatological wedding-banquet parables, with this one offering a similar message as its parallel parable in Luke, the parable of the talents. In this version, we're not focused as much on not employing our spiritual gifts; instead the concern involves sleeping instead of staying vigilant. This is a recurring theme, from the prophets' "Sleeper, awake!" commands to the disciples who succumb to fatigue in the garden of Gethsemane.

The allegorical punch here has to do with falling victim to our physical weaknesses, impulses, or desires. Spiritual slumber can take many forms, from going through the motions in worship to using our prayer life as an obligatory check-in or personal request line. It's not meant to tell us to become insomniacs for Jesus; it's a call to full presence within our own lives and in our practices of connecting with God.

This is not about always having a backup pair of heavenly underwear handy in case something goes wrong or walking around in fear that we won't be right with God. It's about fully embracing a living, dynamic relationship with God as if every moment counts . . . because every moment does!

Heads-Up

Connecting the text to our world

"Process over content" is a way of thinking that is particularly hard to get younger people used to. When I used to work with students who had pretty profound learning differences, though, this was especially important to help them move past some barriers that kept them from realizing their full potential.

I had a high-school senior come to our clinic who was reading at a fourth-grade level. He was getting by most days, but he also knew that college would bury him with all of the material he was expected to read for each class. In order to give him what he needed, we had to go back to the very basic elements of reading, which was not easy to get him to buy into.

He had difficulty processing the fundamental sounds, or phonemes, that make up words. For a lot of us, our brains just connect the proper sounds to the letters, then compare this to a bank of memorized sight words we have learned and puts them together into phrases and sentences without us even thinking about it. And while he had memorized some words, his ability to absorb new ones was limited, plus he lacked what we called "phonemic awareness."

To help him develop phonemic awareness, we had to add a sense modality to help support his less agile auditory processing system. So we had to break down every single sound and help his brain learn how the sounds felt to make in his mouth. When the kinesthetic feedback combines with the auditory processing, a lot of people can start to jump the hurdles that have limited their reading ability.

Try explaining that to a senior who is making individual sounds, one at a time, into a mirror and describing how it feels. For him, it was more embarrassment on top of struggling with reading already, but once I got him to embrace the ideas behind it—that the exercises themselves weren't so much the point as the neurological retraining was—he started to get on board. Within a couple of weeks, he had it all down and was starting to apply it to words, then phrases, sentences, and paragraphs.

By the end of that summer, he had increased his reading level by six years. Beyond that, he now had the substrate skillset he needed to continue to hone his ability as he read more and more. And for the first time, he actually wanted to read because an entirely new world was open to him.

Some might think the first step was teaching him the content of the program, but that didn't matter. After I explained the purpose behind the process, his entire perspective changed. The component pieces of the program were just steps toward a larger journey, which had, for the very first time, come into focus for him.

Prayer for the Week

God, call me on it when I'm mailing it in. I know you expect more, and I want more from myself.

Popping Off

Art/music/video and other cool stuff that relate to the text

"Chuck Close—Painter, Educator," on Biography.com (article, April 2014)

My Left Foot (movie, 1989)

Spiritual Urgency

Lectionary Texts For

November 15, 2020 (Twenty-Fourth Sunday after Pentecost)

Texts in Brief

My dog ate my Bible!

First Reading

Judges 4:1–7

The Israelites upset God again, which is why God allows them to be overwhelmed by the Canaanites. Then when they call out for God to help them again, the prophet Deborah tells them to assemble ten thousand troops at Mount Tabor, where God tells her they will be able to prevail over their enemies.

Psalm/Prophet

Psalm 90:1–8, (9–11), 12

A proclamation of God as the source of all life and death and as the only one that is transcendent over all time. God's power and judgment are fearsome, says the psalm, and for this reason, we should use what little time we have in life to gain wisdom so that we might find God's favor.

Second Reading
1 Thessalonians 5:1–11

A warning not to lean too heavily on a sense of certainty or on any of the comforts and securities our physical life can afford us. We should, instead, stay clear-headed and vigilant in our purpose and know that we are always secure only in that we belong to God. Rather than depending on armor, weapons, and fortresses, which ultimately fail, we should put our confidence in the virtues of faith, love, and hope. These will not fail, and they endure well beyond all false constructs of human-made security.

Gospel
Matthew 25:14–30

Jesus offers a parable about the kingdom of God in which a landlord has his slaves take care of his valuables and returns later to see what they have done with the things they have been entrusted with. While the first two have put these things they were given to use and have multiplied the gifts, another stored his away out of fear of losing it. The ones who used the gifts are in the landlord's favor and the other finds only shame and alienation.

Bible, Decoded
Breaking down Scripture in plain language

Ehud—Whether Ehud was an actual person or an amalgam of folklore is debated, but his story reflects the circular sorts of storylines we find throughout the book: the Israelites stray from or offend God, and they are met with punishment or some consequence, at which point they call out to God, and God responds with rescue. The key narrative in the Ehud story is that he goes to visit the king of the Moabites, the people who occupy the Israelite tribes at this time. When he gets a private meeting with the king, Ehud kills him with a dagger he had hidden in his clothes. The story conveys that Ehud's ability to carry out the assassination is due to God's providence in response for Israel's repentance from sin.

Deborah—The only female prophetic judge listed in Scripture, Deborah is one of four judges who are seen as mouthpieces for justice and wisdom that comes directly from God. The role of these judges goes away once Israel establishes a system of governance ruled by a king.

Mount Tabor—Same mountain where the transfiguration took place. It was also a site from which, during the time of the second temple in Jerusalem, lights were offered to indicate holy days.

Points to Ponder

First Thoughts

This Matthew parable of the talents is a parallel narrative to the recent wedding-banquet parable. Only now that we know the wedding robes in that story are gifted to the guests by the host do the similarities become clear. The emphasis in both cases, then, is on putting all we are given to use, but not just that; we are to use them in the spirit of pleasing the One who has given them to us in the first place and in faith that in sharing them and spreading them around, they will only grow rather than run out.

In Judges, we see the effects of not embracing and utilizing the gifts of protection and of being God's beloved people have when these are rejected or even neglected or taken for granted. Like any true gift, they are not given with mandatory strings attached. However, there are consequences in not using them well.

It's kind of like when my parents gave me a coat because they had looked at the weather, but I left it on the back of the kitchen chair. The coat was there for me, and they had the foresight to know what I needed. The discomfort from the cold I experienced the rest of the day was because of my own shortfall.

Digging Deeper

Mining for what really matters . . . and gold

This Thessalonians text is filled with contrasting dualistic images. We are either drunk or sober, living in darkness or in light, awake or asleep. And although it's tempting to take these and fall into our common modernist, binary either/or thinking, we ought to consider the context in which this is being written.

The early Christians in Thessalonica are mired in a society all around them that maintains values and normalizes behaviors that are in stark contrast with what Paul is teaching. So although he is certainly hammering on these delineations, it's probably because he sees either the reality or the imminent risk of them slipping into being "of the culture" and not just in it.

This is not who we are, Paul is urging. He certainly gets this, having been a man of many identities. Not only was he a Jew; he was also a Pharisee. And aside from serving as an authority on the Jewish Scriptures and traditions, he was an assassin for the Roman authorities. If anyone knew the dark underside of succumbing to the norms and comforts of the surrounding culture, it was him. As any good parent or leader would, he wanted to spare his associates from such a moral slide.

How do we interpret the bits about pregnancy, seasons, and thieves at night? Let's consider these as possible contrasts, like the other images. Although we can largely plan for the cycles of the seasons, or for sunrise and nightfall, we can't (at least back in Paul's time) schedule exactly when a baby will be born. It happens when it happens. And while we might know there's a better chance of being robbed in the dark, we can't know most of the time when someone plans to break into our house.

That's why expectant families keep a hospital "birthing bag" ready by the door, and why people lock their doors and windows, not just when they get a weird feeling, but all the time. It's such vigilance that helps us be prepared when the unexpected happens.

This could make God sound sneaky, trying to catch us being bad. But the point here isn't about avoiding getting in trouble; it's about the peace we find in living in a regular state of spiritual wakefulness and moral vigilance. It's only in this way that it begins to inhabit us, both individually and as a community.

In other words, the urgency isn't so much about beating the clock as it is about the risk of losing our center and identity.

Heads-Up

Connecting the text to our world

When we were pregnant with our first baby (our son, Mattias, who is now fifteen), we didn't know enough to question medical professionals. So when Amy's obstetrician told us we should schedule an induction for delivery so that he would be in town, we trusted that this was what was best.

What we didn't know was that it was far more about convenience for him, as he didn't want to get a call on his trip, nor did he want to miss out on the money he'd make on the delivery. The problem was, Mattias wasn't ready to come yet. After a dozen or so hours of Amy pushing, and despite many efforts by the medical team to turn him the right way, he wasn't budging. We should have known at this point that we had a strong-willed boy on our hands!

What worried everyone, though, was that his heart rate and blood pressure dropped dramatically every time she pushed. It was only later that they discovered the umbilical cord was wrapped around his neck and was choking him when he entered the birth canal. Finally they had to resort to a C-section delivery when it was clear he wasn't coming otherwise on that day.

In the end, he was healthy and Mom was fine too. But after that, we were armed with a wisdom that empowered us during the next birth (our daughter, Zoe, who is now ten). Though doctors insisted on another C-section, we looked until we found a midwife willing to deliver naturally after a previous C-section. We also decided to refuse the drugs that force a woman into early labor.

While we were a little surprised the day Zoe decided to be born, as it wasn't quite the projected date, we were ready. Ninety minutes after reaching the hospital room, she was born with no complications. Every birth is different, and every family should make their own decisions. But if we were able to wind back the clock, we would have pushed harder against forcing the hand of nature that first time.

Prayer for the Week

God, help me live with a spiritual urgency rather than an urgency based on my schedule and to-do list.

Popping Off

Art/music/video and other cool stuff that relate to the text

October Sky (movie, 1999)

The Very Hungry Caterpillar, by Eric Carle (book, 1969)

Goat in Sheep's Clothing

Lectionary Texts For

November 22, 2020 (Twenty-Fifth Sunday after Pentecost)

Texts in Brief

My dog ate my Bible!

First Reading

Ezekiel 34:11–16, 20–24

The Israelites, who have been scattered to different regions due to conflict and occupation, are offered a promise from God that God will bring them all back together as one people. God will heal their wounds, provide for them, and put them back on firm ground, much like a parent would do for wayward children or a shepherd does for their sheep. God also ordains David to be the king over this newly reassembled Israel.

Psalm/Prophet

Psalm 95:1–7a

A prayer of praise and thanks to God as lord and creator of all things. It concludes with an image similar to the one in Ezekiel, with the people being God's (the Shepherd's) flock.

Second Reading

Ephesians 1:15–23

Paul is grateful for the faithfulness of his congregation in Ephesus. He prays on their behalf for wisdom and clarity in order for them to feel more deeply connected with God in all ways. Jesus is a testament to God's power, which is to prevail over all people in all times. This is the model of the church to come, with Jesus as head of it and the faithful as component members of the greater body.

Gospel

Matthew 25:31–46

Jesus speaks of separating those in God's favor (sheep) from those who aren't (goats). Those who are among the sheep will inherit all that is of God, and they will be known by the acts of mercy they have done for the weakest, most neglected, powerless, and marginalized among us. Whatever we do for them is like we are doing it to or for Jesus himself.

Bible, Decoded

Breaking down Scripture in plain language

Lean Sheep—Another word for the vulnerable or the victims of aggression, exploitation, and violence. In essence, God advocates for those who have limited or no agency to advocate for themselves.

David—While we might think from this that David was the first king of Israel, he was actually the second. His origin story, in which he kills the Philistine warrior Goliath with a rock and sling, is a relevant metaphor for the theme here that with God's power, the meek will inherit the earth and that God favors the little guy.

Points to Ponder

First Thoughts

We have lots of elevated images of God this week, with a strong emphasis of God as lord over all, having dominion over creation. And yet in the prophetic text, we have a portrayal of God as a manual laborer, a commoner just like King David was. So although God is seen as this overarching divine presence and source, God also is not beyond the seemingly mundane acts of connecting with and caring for the smallest of the small.

If you're like me, the Matthew text here may make you cringe a little bit. Though it's often used to preach about the importance of religious conversion (or else), the heart of the message is very different. Those who are considered goats are any of us who exploit, intimidate, bully, or otherwise take advantage of those who we find easy to use for our own means. In doing this, we are impugning the image of God in that person.

Ironically, this includes religious profiteers and bullies too.

Digging Deeper
Mining for what really matters . . . and gold

This passage in Matthew is the part of the final of five sets of teaching messages found in the book, also continuing the eschatological (God's coming kingdom) and apocalyptic (God's judgment) themes we have found in this most recent trip through the Gospel. There is a "great sorting out," which reverberates with the same themes found in the Ezekiel text last week. However, here, the sorting is based not on who we are by birth but rather on how we respond to all of God's children and in particular the vulnerable.

Sorting the good from the bad or the worthy from the unworthy is not a new theme here; it's been a drumbeat throughout Matthew's apocalyptic writing. One distinction here is that the goats don't seem to know they're goats any more than the sheep know they're sheep. Similarly, those listening to the parable have to ask for clarity, because they don't entirely get who falls into which camp.

If it was as simple as who was born of a particular tribe or practiced a certain religion, they would already know. The distinction, though, isn't as superficially evident as that. In Jesus's eyes, the goat-ness of each person resides in their hearts, or at least the capacity for goat-ness. Unlike the sorting of genetics, we're not born inherently good or bad; the identity is painted in by the life lived and the way we care for (or don't care for) others.

Note that in the list of merciful acts that qualifies one as a sheep, there's nothing along the lines of "I was a Muslim and you converted me," or "I asked for a dollar and you gave me a tract." The conversion that takes place that Jesus is concerned with here is personal and internal. It is well transcendent of any sacred rituals or religious or cultural labels.

Put another way, it can be considered a sort of road-map to finding God here among us. If we want to find God, go to the prisons, visit the sick, help the victimized, feed the poor. There's nothing in this text, or much of any other Gospel text for that matter, that tells us to go to church to find God. That's not to say that God isn't in church, but if that's the only place we look we may well wind up empty.

Instead of praying to God to make sure we're among the sheep, go out to the sheep and do what God would do. The examples are literally right there in front of us.

Heads-Up

Connecting the text to our world

The internet has provided opportunity for lots of amazing things. For one, I wouldn't be able to do the kind of work I do without it. When I was a kid someone tried to describe what this new thing called the World Wide Web was all about, and it made my brain kind of hurt. Now there is not a single day, and very few waking hours if I'm being honest, where something based on digital networking, social media, or mobile technology doesn't impact my life.

When something is that ubiquitous, it's easy to start taking it for granted. For example, I get annoyed when I'm trying to stream a web-based movie while my kids are playing online games and video chatting with friends and my home-based internet can't manage to keep up. When it works well, the internet and its component parts are practically invisible, with the devices and means by which we access information dissolved behind an immediate, on-demand experience of the media.

On the downside, it's easy to let the effects it has on how we see and experience the world go unnoticed too, including how we perceive and relate to other people. Depth of relationship has sometimes been replaced with a superficial skimming of a far broader network of acquaintances with whom we have very little personal investment. Because of the seamless ways in which ideas are shared and people are connected together, we tend to do what we've always done in nature—cluster together into groups of people who tend to look, think, and act more like we do—only exponentially more efficiently.

As any cohort of like-minded people tend to do, there's an echo-chamber effect within which the feedback loop of self-affirming bias builds on itself over time until even the bias itself is practically invisible. From there, tribal identities settle in and common ground gives fruit to more absolute, rigid ideology. By that point, there's an unspoken rule within the tribal group that maintenance of group identity and values is a prime directive. Any contaminant in the form of difference of identity, ideas, or norms is suspect at best and, at worst, is seen as a threat.

Once a tribal group has gotten to this place, there are two common options when dealing with such threats: assimilate or exterminate. The offender needs to adapt to the tribal status quo, or it has to be removed (see: prime directive). It's not usually in our nature, though, to engage in such aggressive or even violent behavior toward another person—unless they're not seen as entirely human. If, as Napoleon the Pig from the novel *Animal Farm* infamously said, "all animals are equal, but some animals are more equal than others," the lesser-than have to go.

This is how any average person finds themselves in goat-territory. From "All [fill in the blank] supporters are idiots," it's not too many steps into the dark waters of dehumanizing attitudes and actions. As long as the group's ideology is seen as more important than the personhood of the outsider, the consequences to them are little more than collateral damage.

The best opportunity for our inner goats to emerge are to try and deny they exist. If you're convinced you're 100-percent sheep, that's where the trouble can start. The good news is that none of us is completely a goat either, and God sees the sheepness in all of us. To look with God's eyes on others is to disarm the prime directive of group identity and sovereignty over individual humanity. It presents a world with far more complexity, nuance, unpredictability, and friction, but it's the only real way we have any hope of getting over the goat-sheep battle lines we've drawn all around ourselves.

Prayer for the Week

God, help me see the sheep, or at least the potential for it, within everyone. Including myself.

Popping Off

Art/music/video and other cool stuff that relate to the text

Animal Farm, by George Orwell (book, 1945)

"A New Report Offers Insights into Tribalism in the Age of Trump," in *The New Yorker* (article, October 12, 2018)